常用汉语同义词汉英双解手册

Handbook of the Chinese Synonyms with Bilingual Explanations

郑秀芝　王春光　编著

今日中国出版社

Handbook of the

Synonyms with Bilingual Explanations

China Today Publishers

(24 Baiwanzhuang Road, Beijing—100037, China)

Distributed by China International Book Trading

Corporation (Guoji Shudian)

(21 Chegongzhuang Xilu, Beijing, China)

P.O.Box 399 Beijing, China

First edition 1991

ISBN 7-5072-0068-X / H · 1

00800

9-CE-2325P

说　明

汉语中有大量的同义词，这使得我们的语言丰富多彩，能准确地反映事物间的细微差别，正确地表达人们的思想感情。但是由于同义词往往大同小异，它们之间的细微差别不易辨析，这也给学习汉语的人带来一定的困难，尤其是不以汉语为母语的人就更不易分辨。编写这本手册的目的，是为帮助外国学生和学习英语的中国学生、知识青年在理解和使用这两种语言（汉语和英语）时起辅导作用，并可作为对外汉语教学时的参考。

本手册从实用出发，尽量精选日常用语和阅读中碰到的同义词。共选同义词 343 组，754 个词条。如"二"和"两"，在有些场合可以通用，我们可以说"二百"或"两百"。但在有些场合却不行，我们说"两个人"，却不说"二个人"。"二"和"两"译成英语都是"two"。这对中国人不成问题，但对不以汉语为母语的外国初学者来说，何时需用"二"，何时需用"两"，何时可以通用，就不那么容易了。本手册除可供初学汉语的外国学生使用外，对已学过一些汉语的外国学生也有帮助。如"朴实"和"朴素"，都是形容词，都表示"不加修饰"的意思。译成英语，都有"simple、plain"的意思。但我们说"朴素的生活"，却不说"朴实的生活"。正确地理解和区分这些同义词，有利于外国学生提高汉语口语的表达能力和阅读、写作能力。

另外，对学习英语的中国学生和知识青年也有参考价值。如"平常"和"平凡"，译成英语时，都有"ordinary, common"的意思。但由于汉、英两种语言完全属于两种不同的语系，在使用时就不同。这本手册通过解释"平常"和"平凡"在汉语中的不同和相同点，并用英语翻译出来，可以使学生在翻译使用这两个词时做参考。

　　本手册在解释每组同义词时，根据这样两条原则：1.解释每组词的相同点和不同点时，重点放在不同点上，以便区别；2.解释力求简单明了。

　　本手册编写过程中，得到了戴尔清，于炳照，李祥仲，李连庆等同志的大力支持和帮助，并得到了出版社支鄂湘、阎凤兰同志的通力合作。定稿后，当代语言学家张寿康教授又在百忙中热情地为它撰写序文，才使得这本手册得以和读者见面，在此一并表示感谢。

　　由于水平有限，错误和不当之处在所难免，切望读者批评指正。

郑秀芝

王春光

Introduction

Chinese abounds in synonyms, which help to give the language its richness and variety. They enable us to convey fine distinctions precisely and to express our thoughts and feelings effectively. However, the task of differentiating their subtle shades of meaning can be daunting, especially for people whose mother tongue is not Chinese.

The objective in compiling this handbook is to afford assistance to foreign students of Chinese and Chinese students of English, and to supply teachers of Chinese as a foreign or second language with a much-needed work of reference.

The handbook, which is based strictly on the criterion of practical usefulness, is a select compendium of those synonyms which are most likely to be encountered in everyday conversation and in modern Chinese prose. It comprises 343 groups of synonyms, with a total of 754 entries. Special attention has been paid to phenomena which, while presenting no difficulty to native speakers, can prove serious stumbling blocks for non-native beginning learners. For example, the words 两 liǎng and 二 èr, both of which correspond to the number 2, are, in some cases, interchangeable. Thus, we can express "two hundred" either as 二百 èrbǎi or as 两百 liǎngbǎi. However, this is not always so. We say 两个人 liǎng ge rén — two persons, but never 二个人 èr ge rén.

Apart from its practical value at beginners' and elementary level, the handbook will be of use to foreign students who already have some command of modern Chinese. For instance, the two adjectives 朴实 pǔshí and 朴素 pǔsù both carry the meaning of unadornment 不加修饰, and are rendered in English as simple, plain. Nevertheless, we can say 朴素的生活 pǔsù de shēnghuó — a simple life, but not 朴实的生活 pǔshíde shēnghuó. By mastering these distinctions, foreign learners can enhance their powers of oral and written expression, and come to appreciate the nuances in what they hear and read.

The handbook will assist Chinese-speaking students of English in developing their awareness of the difference between the two languages. For example, the Chinese words 平常 píngcháng and 平凡 píngfán both become ordinary, common in English translation; but since the Chinese and English terms belong to two discrete linguistic systems, their usage differs. Because of its comparative strategy — the example and explanations are all accompanied by idiomatic English versions — the handbook will constitute a valuable work of reference for students engaged in translation work.

In interpreting the synonyms within each group, the compilers have followed two guidelines: 1. When explaining similarities and differences emphasis should be placed on the difference. 2. The definitions and examples must aim, above all at clarity, simplicity and straight-forwardness.

We offer our sincerest thanks to Yu Bingzhao, Li Xiangzhong, Li Lianqing, Dai Erqing and the many other friends who gave us their unstinting support and assistance; to Zhi Exiang and Yan Fenglan of *China Today*, for their efficient and wholehearted collaboration; and finally to the distinguished scholar of modern Chinese, Professor Zhang Shoukang, who so generously found time, amid his many commitments, to write the foreword to this book. Without them the handbook would never have seen the light of day.

Zheng Xiuzhi

Wang Chunguang

序　言

学习一种语言，语音是语言的读音；语汇是语言的材料、内容，学习语汇就必然要学读音，两者是统一的；语法是连缀词语的形式。这三者比较起来，学习语汇最为重要。学习母语和学习外语都是如此。

汉语是以语汇丰富著称的。学习语汇要丰富同义词语。"丰富"有两个意义：一是汉语的词汇系统中，同义词语是丰富的；二是学习者应当丰富、积累自己的同义词语，充实语言的建筑材料，便于在表达思想、事物和感情时，能够意到笔到，得心应手。

学习母语要注意分辨同义词语。古人已懂得同义词语的收集和分辨。《尔雅》可以说是分辨同义词语的最早的书，是第一部"同义词典"。比如："初、哉、首、基、肇、祖、元、胎、俶、落、权舆，始也。"始是以上名词的共同意义，也就是说，"初、哉"等是同义词。《尔雅》的用意还是在分辨。比如"初者裁衣之始，哉者草木之始，基者筑墙之始，肇者开户之始，祖者人之始，胎者生之始"，等等（见郝兰皋《尔雅义疏》）。可以见出《尔雅》的编者是意在分辨的。现代汉语的同义词语，比古代汉语丰富得多，学习母语更要加以分辨。

分辨同义词语有很多用处。一则分辨同义词语要在运用词语的语境中分辨其同，更要分辨其异。这样就可以提高人们的求同、求异的思维能力。二则分辨同义词语的异同，才能更适合情境地运用词语。比如该用"郊野"的地方就不能用"原野"，因为"原野"的意义范围比"郊野"大。该用"操持"的地方就不能用"把持"，因为"把持"有贬斥的色彩。三则有了这种认识，可以说，在说写中就具有了选择、推敲词语的功力。作家、文章家都十分注意同义词语的选择和推敲。如：

1.他是最使我感激，给我奖励的一个。（鲁迅《藤野先生》原稿）

这一则，鲁迅先生在定稿的时候，把"奖励"改为"鼓励"，这属于同义词的选择。这一修改是确当的。"奖励"侧重物质上的奖赏，而"鼓励"则重在精神上的勉励。因为"鼓励"就更符合鲁迅先生与藤野先生关系的实际情况。

2.另一位先生听得厌烦，把嘴里香烟屁股掷到街心。（叶圣陶《多收了三五斗》原稿）

这一则中的"掷"，作者修改稿改为"扔"。"扔"和"掷"是同义词。"掷"有文言意味，用"掷"则语体不协调。改为"扔"就口语化了。

以上的例子，说明分辨同义词语很重要。

分辨同义词语，不仅学习母语重要，而且对说汉语的人学英语，说英语的人学汉语，也就是说，对内、对外的汉语教学都要十分重视这一点。

1984年6月1日，王力先生在参加《语言教学与研究》创刊五周年的纪念会上说："欧美人不懂我们中国话'穿'和'戴'的区别。他们说汉语常把'戴'说成'穿'。我就听见一位美国朋友说过'我今天没穿眼镜','我今天没穿帽子'之类的话。为什么会出现这种情况呢？很明显，在英语里'穿'和'戴'是用一个词来表示的。"（见1984年第3期《语言教学与研究》第6页）王力先生的话揭示了认识汉语和英语之间同义表达的相同点和不同点十分必要。那个纪念会，我也参加了。王力先生的话，我当时听了，便深表赞同。

要认识、分辨汉语、英语同义词在表达上的异同点，就要有一本工具书。郑秀芝同志和王春光同志编著的《常用汉语同义词汉英双解手册》（以下简称《手册》便是这样的工具书。

这本《手册》是很有特点的。第一，注意应用。从选词来看，它选编了汉语同义词343组，含词目754条，而且这些都是从日常使用的口头语和书面语言中精选出来的，从应用出发，一些生僻的词没有入选。第二，辨异简明。从释义来看，它用汉语和英语讲清各组同义词在含义，用语、语法特点、感情色彩等方面的异同，并把着重点放在"异"的方面，简明扼要，重在分辨。第三，对译双解。从举例来看，各组同义词中每个词条都有适当的例句来显示意义和用法。每个例句都分别用汉语和英语对译，以便比照分辨，它称为"汉英双解"是十分确当的。总括以上各点，形成了这本《手册》的一大特色：不仅具有汉英同义词比较研究的价值，而且具有指导语言实践的实用品格。

郑秀芝同志近三十年来一直从事外语院校的汉语研究和教学工作。1986 年秋曾应聘赴美讲学。在对外汉语教学方面积累了丰富的经验和资料。由她和王春光同志合著的这本《手册》，就体现了他们的教学经验和研究成果。在改革开放的今天，国际交往日益频繁，友谊交流方兴未艾，编写这本《手册》是很有现实意义的。《手册》是应运而生的，相信它会受到广大读者的欢迎，取得很大的社会效益。是为序。

张寿康

Preface

To learn a language we must study both phonetics and vocabulary, for phonetics gives pronunciation, while vocabulary is the content of a language. Grammar links vocabulary. Of the three, vocabulary is the most important, whether one is learning one's mother tongue or a foreign language.

The Chinese language has a rich vocabulary. To learn vocabulary, we must enrich our synonyms, first by learning them systematically, then by accumulating our own supply to express our thoughts and feelings in either verbal or written form.

To learn the Chinese language, we must be able to discriminate synonyms. The ancient Chinese knew how to accumulate and discriminate synonyms. *Erya* can be regarded as the first synonym dictionary in China. For example it says that "chū (begin), zāi (start), shǒu (head), jī (foundation), zhào (commence), zǔ (ancestor), yuán (first), tāi (foetus), chù (begin), luò (fall), and quán yǔ (start) all mean shi (beginning)." That is, these words are synonyms. *Erya* then makes discriminations. For example, "Chū is the beginning of tailoring, zāi is the beginning of growing grass and trees, jī is the beginning of building walls, zhào is the beginning of setting up a household, zǔ is the beginning of man, tāi is the beginning of life," etc. (See Hao Langao's *Erya Yishu, Detailed Notes of Erya*.) So it can be seen that the editors of *Erya* noted the minor differences among synonyms. Modern Chinese has far more synonyms than the ancient language, so to learn it well we must discriminate among them.

Discriminating synonyms has three main benefits. First, in noting the similarities and differences of synonyms, we promote our thinking and discriminating abilities. Second, we can use the appropriate word for the contest. For example, jiaoye (wild land in the outskirts) can't be replaced by yuanye (open country), since yuanye is larger than jiaoye in its connotation. Similarly, caochi (handle) can't be replaced by bachi (dominate), since bachi is derogatory. Third, we can sharpen our ability to choose the right and appropriate word. Writers pay much attention to the right choice of word. For example:

1. He's the one who made me feel most grateful and gave me reward (jiǎngli). (Lu Xun's original manuscript for *Teacher Fuj ino*)

In his last version Lu Xun changed "reward" to "encouragement" (gǔli). This change was very appropriate, since reward has a material aspect,

11

whereas encouragement has a spiritual aspect. "Encouragement" was more appropriate for the actual relationship between Lu Xun and Teacher Fujino.

2. Another gentleman, tired of listening, cast (zhi) his cigarette butt to the middle of the street. (Ye Shengtao's master copy of *Taking in Three to Five More Dou of Grain*)

Here "cast" (zhi) is replaced by "throw" (rēng), since "zhì" is classical writing style, thus inappropriate in the context. "Rēng" is more colloquial.

The above examples show the significance of discriminating synonyms.

Knowing the differences and similarities of synonyms is important to people learning Chinese either as their mother tongue or a foreign language.

On June 1, 1984, while attending the celebration of the fifth anniversary of *Language Teaching and Study* magazine, Wang Li said, "Europeans and Americans can't tell the difference between chuan and dai (both mean 'wear'). They often confuse the proper usage of these two words. I heard an American friend say, 'Today I am not wearing (chuan instead of dai) glasses,' and 'Today I am not wearing (chuan instead of dai) a hat.' Why does such a problem exist? Obviously because chuan and dai are both expressed by 'wear' in

English." (See *Language Teaching and Study*, No. 3, 1984, P.6.) In this way Mr. Wang demonstrated the necessity to know the differences and similarities of synonyms in both Chinese and English. I also attended the celebration and quite agree with him.

To properly discriminate Chinese and English synonyms we need a dictionary. The Handbook of Chinese Synonyms with Bilingual Explanations, compiled by Zheng Xiuzhi and Wang Chunguang, exactly meets our requirements.

This handbook has three advantages. First, it's practical. The compilers have selected 343 groups of Chinese synonyms, altogether 754 entries, from common oral and written expressions. Rarely used words are not included. Second, the handbook offers concise discriminations in both Chinese and English for each group of synonyms as to meaning, usage, grammatical characteristics and emotional overtones. Third, every entry is used in a sample sentence in both Chinese and English to show its meaning and usage. This arrangement is also convenient for comparison. The handbook thus not only contributes to comparison and research of Chinese and English synonyms, but guides language learning.

Zheng Xiuzhi has been engaged in teaching

and researching Chinese in a foreign languages in-stitute for nearly 30 years. In 1986 she was invited to lecture in the US. Thus she has accumulated rich experience and background in teaching Chinese as a foreign language. This handbook that she and Wang Chunguang compiled reflects their teaching experience and research results. The compilation of this handbook during China's period of reform and intensified international exchange is significant. I believe it will be welcomed by many and prove to be of considerable practical use.

Zhang Shoukang

凡　例

1.本手册在编写时，同组词按音序编排，领先的是首词。

2.每组词都用汉语拼音字母注音，并标明调号；轻声字，不标调号。

3.每个词都注有相应的英文词语。

4.每组同义词都用汉语和英语说明它们的相同点和不同点。

5.每个词都有例句。例句也都用汉语和英语写出。

6.在英文解释中，有些词采用缩写。

如: sb. —— somebody

　　 sth. —— something

　　 syn. —— synonym

　　 etc. —— et cetera

　　 v. —— verb

　　 adj. —— adjective

　　 adv. —— adverb

　　 n. —— noun

7.本手册的辨析方法：每组同义词都先分别阐述各个词之间的细微差别并举例说明，然后讲解这组同义词在词义、词性、色彩或手法等方面的共同之处。

To the Users

1. The entries in this handbook are arranged in alphabetical order, according to the *hanyu pinyin* transliteration of the head word in each group of synonyms.

2. All entries are transliterated according to the *hanyu pinyin* system, and provided with tone markings. Toneless and unstressed syllables are indicated, and special attention is paid to tone variations which affect sense.

3. Each entry and sense is supplied with a number of English equivalents chosen to convey its full spectrum of meaning.

4. The definitions, which are given in both Chinese and English, are designed to bring out the similarities and differences between the synonyms in each entry group.

5. Each entry is followed by examples of usage, with idiomatic English equivalents.

6. The English explanations employ commonly used abbreviations, such as sb. — somebody; sth. — something; syn. — synonym; etc. — et cetera; v. — verb; adj. — adjective; adv. — adverb; n. — noun.

7. Method of differentiation: Each synonym in

the group is explained individually, with the aid of copious examples, and with comparisons and cross–references where appropriate, so as to clarify subtle differences in meaning and usage. The entry group concludes with a brief review of the area of synonyms. Regard is had to syntactical function, tone, register, etc.

目 录

A

1	ai	爱戴
		爱抚
		爱护 …（1）
2		爱好
		嗜好 …（2）
3		爱惜
		珍惜 …（3）
4	an	安定
		安全
		平安 …（4）
5		安顿
		安放 …（5）
6		安静
		平静 …（5）
7		安居
		安身 …（6）
8		安排
		安置 …（7）
9		安适
		安闲
		安逸 …（7）

10		安慰
		宽慰 …（8）
11		安详
		慈祥 …（9）
12		安心
		放心 …（9）
13		安葬
		埋葬 …（10）
14		暗暗
		偷偷 …（11）
15		暗害
		暗算 …（11）
16		暗含
		暗示 …（12）
17		按照
		遵照 …（13）
18	ao	懊悔
		懊恼 …（13）
19		奥秘
		奥妙 …（14）

B

20	ba	把持

		把握		31		抱怨
		掌握 …(16)				埋怨 …(26)
21	ban	颁布		32	bei	背叛
		发布				叛变
		公布 …(17)				违背 …(27)
22		办法		33	ben	奔驰
		措施 …(18)				奔跑
23	bang	帮助				奔腾 …(28)
		援助		34		本来
		赞助 …(19)				原来 …(29)
24	bao	包含		35		本领
		包括 …(20)				本事 …(30)
25		保护		36		本质
		庇护				实质 …(31)
		掩护 …(21)		37	bi	比赛
26		饱满				竞赛 …(32)
		丰满 …(22)		38		鄙视
27		保卫				轻视 …(33)
		捍卫 …(22)		39		必定
28		保持				必然
		坚持				一定 …(34)
		维持 …(24)		40		毕竟
29		宝贵				究竟 …(35)
		贵重		41		必须
		珍贵 …(24)				必需 …(36)
30		暴露		42	bian	鞭策
		揭露 …(25)				督促 …(36)

2

43		边疆			**C**
		边境 … (37)			
44		辩白	55	cai	猜测
		辩护			探测
		辩解 … (38)			推测 … (48)
45		辨别	56		才干
		辨认			才华
		鉴别 … (39)			才能
46		变革			才智 … (50)
		变化 … (40)	57		材料
47	biao	标明			资料 … (51)
		表明 … (41)	58		采纳
48		表达			采取
		表示 … (41)			采用 … (52)
49		表现	59	can	参加
		体现 … (42)			参与
50		表扬			加入 … (54)
		赞扬 … (43)	60	cang	仓促
51	bu	哺育			匆匆
		抚育 … (43)			匆忙 … (55)
52		不单	61	ceng	曾经
		不但 … (44)			已经 … (56)
53		不管	62	chan	产生
		不论			发生 … (57)
		无论 … (45)	63	chang	场所
54		不免			场合 … (57)
		难免 … (46)			

64	chen	陈列
		陈设 … (58)
65		沉寂
		沉默 … (59)
66		陈旧
		破旧 … (60)
67		沉思
		深思
		寻思 … (61)
68		沉着
		冷静 … (61)
69	cheng	成果
		结果
		效果 … (63)
70		成绩
		成就
		成效 … (64)
71	chi	持续
		继续 … (65)
72	chong	充分
		充足 … (66)
73		重复
.		反复 … (67)
74		充满
		弥漫 … (68)
75	chu	出生
		诞生 … (69)

76	chuan	传授
		教授 … (70)
77	chui	垂死
		垂危 … (70)
78	cuo	错误
		过失 … (71)

D

79	da	答应
		允许
		准许 … (72)
80		达到
		到达 … (73)
81		打量
		端详 … (74)
82		打算
		盘算 … (75)
83		大胆
		勇敢 … (75)
84	dai	带
		戴 … (76)
85	dan	耽搁
		耽误 … (77)
86		担任
		担当 … (78)
87		担心

4

		担忧 … (78)			**E**
88		诞辰			
		生日 … (79)	99	e	恶果
89		但是			后果 … (89)
		可是	100		遏止
		然而 … (80)			遏制
90	dao	道歉			制止 … (90)
		抱歉 … (81)	101	er	二
91	di	抵偿			两 …… (91)
		赔偿			
		补偿 … (82)			**F**
92		抵挡			
		阻挡 … (82)	102	fa	发表
93		抵制			宣告
		抵抗 … (83)			宣布 … (93)
94	dong	动员	103		发达
		发动 … (84)			发展 … (94)
95	du	度过	104		发觉
		渡过 … (84)			发现 … (95)
96	dun	顿时	105		发明
		立刻 … (85)			创造 … (96)
97	duo	多少	106	fan	烦躁
		几 … (86)			急躁 … (97)
98		夺取	107	fang	妨碍
		掠夺 … (87)			妨害 … (97)
			108	fen	分辨
					区别 … (98)

5

109		分别			搞
		分离			做 … (110)
		离别 … (100)	119 gao		高兴
110		分派			喜悦
		分配 … (101)			愉快 … (111)
111		愤慨	120 ge		歌唱
		愤怒			歌颂 … (112)
		气愤 … (102)	121 gen		根据
112 feng		风景			依据 … (113)
		景色	122 gong		功夫
		景物 … (103)			时间 … (114)
113		风气	123		功绩
		风尚			功劳
		风俗 … (104)			功勋 … (115)
114 fu		肤浅	124		公平
		浮浅			公正 … (116)
		浅薄 … (106)	125		公约
					契约
G					条约 … (117)
			126 gu		鼓励
115 gai		改变			怂恿 … (118)
		转变 … (107)	127 guan		关切
116 gan		干净			关注 … (118)
		清洁 … (108)	128 gui		规矩
117		感激			规则 … (119)
		感谢 … (108)	129 guo		果断
118		干			武断 … (120)

6

130	果然	
	居然	
	竟然 … (122)	
131	过程	
	历程 … (123)	

H

132 hai	害怕	
	惧怕 … (124)	
133 han	含糊	
	模糊 … (125)	
134 hao	好像	
	似乎 … (126)	
135 he	和蔼	
	和气 … (127)	
136	合作	
	协作 … (128)	
137 hong	宏大	
	庞大 … (129)	
138 hou	后悔	
	忏悔 … (129)	
139 hu	忽略	
	疏忽 … (130)	
140 hua	滑稽	
	诙谐	
	幽默 … (131)	

141	华丽	
	壮丽 … (132)	
142	化装	
	化妆 … (133)	
143 huai	怀念	
	想念 … (134)	
144 huan	豢养	
	饲养	
	喂养 … (134)	
145 hui	回顾	
	回忆 … (135)	
146	会见	
	接见 … (136)	
147 huo	活动	
	运动 … (137)	
148	活泼	
	活跃 … (138)	

J

149 ji	基本	
	根本 … (139)	
150	激动	
	感动 … (141)	
151	讥讽	
	讽刺 … (141)	
152	几乎	

	简直 … (142)	165	教导
153	讥笑		指导
	嘲笑		辅导 … (154)
	嗤笑 … (143)	166	教室
154	急忙		课堂 … (154)
	连忙 … (144)	167 jie	解除
155	计划		废除
	规划 … (144)		破除 … (155)
156 jia	家乡	168	界限
	故乡 … (145)		界线 … (156)
157	家属	169 jin	进步
	家族 … (146)		先进 … (157)
158 jian	坚定	170	进攻
	坚决 … (147)		进击
159	检查		进犯 … (158)
	检验 … (148)	171 jing	精力
160	简单		精神 … (159)
	简略 … (149)	172 jiu	纠正
161	俭朴		更正 … (160)
	俭省 … (150)	173 jue	决
162 jiao	骄傲		绝 … (161)
	自豪		
	傲慢 … (151)		**K**
163	交换		
	交流 … (152)	174 kan	看
164	矫正		瞧
	改正 … (153)		望 … (162)

8

175	看法 观点 见解	… (163)
176 kao	考查 考察	… (164)
177	考虑 斟酌	… (165)
178 ke	渴望 盼望	… (166)
179	克制 抑制	… (167)
180 kong	空洞 空虚	… (167)
181 kua	夸奖 夸耀	… (168)

L

182 la	拉拢 笼络	… (169)
183 lao	牢固 稳固 坚固 巩固	… (170)
184 li	黎明 凌晨 拂晓	… (171)

185	礼拜 星期	… (172)
186	历来 向来 从来	… (173)
187	力量 力气	… (174)
188 lin	临时 暂时	… (175)
189 ling	灵活 灵巧	… (176)
190	伶俐 聪明	… (176)
191 liu	流畅 流利	… (177)
192	流浪 流落	… (178)
193	流亡 逃亡	… (179)
194 lü	屡次 一再	… (179)

M

195 mao	毛病 缺点 缺陷	… (181)

9

196 mei	美丽		206 ou	偶尔	
	漂亮 … (182)			偶然 … (194)	
197	美满				
	圆满 … (183)		**P**		
198 mi	秘密				
	神秘		207 pang	胖	
	机密 … (184)			肥 … (195)	
199	密切		208 ping	平常	
	亲密 … (185)			平凡 … (195)	
200 ming	明白		209 pu	普遍	
	清楚 … (186)			广泛 … (196)	
201	名誉		210	朴实	
	荣誉 … (187)			朴素 … (197)	
202 mo	陌生				
	生疏 … (188)		**Q**		

N

203 ni	溺爱		211 qi	欺负	
	宠爱 … (190)			欺侮	
204 ning	凝视			欺压 … (199)	
	注视 … (191)		212	期间	
205 nong	浓厚			时代 … (200)	
	深厚 … (192)		213	奇怪	
				古怪 … (200)	
			214	其他	
				其余 … (202)	
			215	奇特	

O

独特 … (202)

216　启程
　　　出发 … (203)

217　启发
　　　启示 … (204)

218　企图
　　　妄想 … (205)

219　气概
　　　气魄 … (205)

220　气候
　　　天气 … (206)

221　气派
　　　气势 … (207)

222 qia　恰当
　　　适当 … (207)

223　恰好
　　　恰巧
　　　正好 … (208)

224 qian　签订
　　　缔结 … (209)

225　前后
　　　左右 … (210)

226 qiang　抢救
　　　挽救 … (211)

227　强迫
　　　强制 … (212)

228 qin　勤劳

勤勉 … (212)

229 qing　轻易
　　　容易 … (213)

230　轻便
　　　简便 … (214)

231　情况
　　　情形 … (215)

232　情绪
　　　心情 … (216)

233　庆祝
　　　祝贺 … (216)

234 qu　屈服
　　　降服 … (217)

235　取消
　　　撤消 … (218)

236　去世
　　　逝世
　　　死 …… (219)

237　趣味
　　　兴趣 … (220)

238 quan　全部
　　　整个 … (220)

239　权力
　　　权利 … (221)

240 que　确定
　　　决定 … (221)

241　确实

11

切实 … (222)

R

242 re	热情	
	热心 … (223)	
243 ren	人民	
	公民 … (224)	
244	认识	
	知道 … (225)	
245	认为	
	以为 … (226)	
246 rong	荣幸	
	幸运 … (226)	
247 ruan	软弱	
	懦弱 … (227)	

S

248 sao	扫除	
	排除	
	消除 … (229)	
249 shan	煽动	
	鼓动 … (230)	
250 shang	商量	
	讨论 … (230)	
251 shen	申明	

	声明 … (231)	
252	慎重	
	郑重 … (232)	
253 sheng	生命	
	性命 … (232)	
254	生活	
	生计 … (233)	
255 shi	失望	
	绝望 … (234)	
256	施行	
	实行 … (235)	
257	时常	
	经常	
	往往 … (236)	
258	食品	
	食物 … (237)	
259	使命	
	任务 … (238)	
260	适合	
	符合 … (238)	
261	事情	
	事件	
	事故 … (239)	
262 shou	收获	
	收成 … (240)	
263	手法	
	把戏 … (241)	

264		首要		275 ting	调节 … (252)
		重要			停留
		主要 … (241)			停止 … (252)
265 shu		舒服		276 tong	同意
		舒适 … (242)			赞成 … (253)
266		熟识		277 tou	投降
		熟悉 … (243)			投诚 … (254)
267 sun		损害		278 tui	推辞
		伤害 … (244)			推托
268 suo		所有			推卸 … (255)
		一切 … (245)		279 tuo	唾弃
					抛弃 … (256)

T

W

269 tan	谈判		
	协商 … (247)	280 wan	完备
270 te	特别		完美
	特殊 … (248)		完善 … (257)
271	特点	281	顽强
	特色		顽固 … (258)
	特性	282 wang	忘怀
	特征 … (249)		忘记 … (259)
272 teng	疼	283 wei	伟大
	痛 … (250)		巨大 … (260)
273 ti	体会	284 wen	温和
	体验 … (251)		温柔
274 tiao	调整		温顺 … (261)

13

285	稳重		297	消息
	庄重 … (262)			新闻 … (272)
286	问		298 xin	辛苦
	打听 … (262)			辛劳 … (273)
			299	新奇

X

				新鲜 … (274)
			300	欣赏
287 xi	稀罕			观赏 … (275)
	稀奇 … (264)		301 xing	醒目
288	吸取			夺目 … (276)
	吸收 … (265)		302 xiu	修理
289	希望			修缮 … (276)
	期望 … (265)		303 xu	虚假
290	习惯			虚伪 … (277)
	习气 … (266)		304	须要
291	细致			需要 … (278)
	仔细 … (268)		305 xun	寻求
292 xiang	相信			追求 … (279)
	信任 … (269)		306	询问
293	详尽			盘问 … (279)
	详细 … (269)		307	迅速
294	向导			急速 … (280)
	引导 … (270)			
295	向			**Y**
	朝 … (271)			
296 xiao	消灭		308 ya	压抑
	幻灭 … (272)			压制 … (281)

14

309 yan　严格
　　　　严厉 … (282)
310　　　严密
　　　　精密 … (282)
311　　　严肃
　　　　认真 … (283)
312 yao　要求
　　　　请求 … (284)
313　　　要紧
　　　　紧急 … (285)
314 yi　　一概
　　　　一律 … (286)
315　　　一齐
　　　　一起 … (287)
316　　　一瞬间
　　　　一刹那 … (288)
317　　　一向
　　　　一直 … (288)
318　　　一致
　　　　共同 … (289)
319　　　屹立
　　　　矗立
　　　　耸立 … (290)
320　　　义务
　　　　责任 … (291)
321 ying　应付
　　　　敷衍 … (292)

322 you　犹豫
　　　　踌躇 … (293)
323　　　友情
　　　　友谊 … (293)
324 yu　　预备
　　　　准备 … (294)
325 yuan　渊博
　　　　广博 … (295)

Z

326 zao　遭受
　　　　遭遇 … (297)
327 ze　　责问
　　　　质问 … (298)
328 zhan　瞻仰
　　　　敬仰 … (299)
329 zhao　招呼
　　　　召唤 … (300)
330　　　召集
　　　　召开 … (300)
331　　　照顾
　　　　照料
　　　　照应 … (301)
332 zhen　镇定
　　　　镇静 … (302)
333 zheng　正规

15

	正轨 … (303)	339 zhou	周密
334	证明		周详 … (308)
	证实 … (304)	340 zhu	主意
335	正直		主张 … (308)
	正派 … (304)	341	注重
336 zhi	指摘		着重 … (309)
	斥责 … (305)	342 zi	自尊
337 zhong	忠诚		自负 … (310)
	忠实 … (306)	343 zun	尊敬
338	重		尊重 … (311)
	沉 … (307)		

16

A

爱戴 àidài　爱抚 àifǔ　爱护 àihù

爱戴 (love and esteem)　表示敬爱和拥护的意思。一般用于领袖、师长或有声望的人。to love, respect and support; often used in reference to leaders, teachers, parents, and prestigious people: 周总理受到人民的爱戴。Premier Zhou was much loved and esteemed by the Chinese people.

爱抚 (show tender care for)　着重抚慰，表示对人的疼爱。使用范围小，只对人不对物。一般不带宾语。to take tender care of sb., to show love and tenderness; used with reference to people, never to things. It has a limited range of usage, and does not generally take an object: 她爱抚地摸着孩子的头。She caressed the child's head tenderly.

爱护 (take good care of; cherish; treasure)　表示喜爱和保护的意思，使用范围较大，既可指人也可指事物（不管是具体的还是抽象的）。to love and protect sb. or sth.; has a wide range of usage, and may refer to people or things (either concrete or abstract): 她爱护儿童。

1

She takes great care of children. ／大家要爱护公共财物。Everyone should take good care of public property.

〔相同点〕：都是动词，含有褒义，表示喜爱的意思。对象常是人。Syn. v. approbatory terms, used to express fondness and love, especially towards people.

爱好 àihào 嗜好 shìhào

爱好 (love for; be fond of; be keen on) 着重于喜爱，常用于好的方面，是动词。v. emphasizes liking, enjoyment; often used in reference to things which are considered good：他爱好京剧。He is keen on Peking opera.

嗜好 (hobby; addiction; habit) 常指特殊的习惯，多用于不好的方面，是名词。n. generally indicates a strong or unusual predilection; often used in reference to sth. considered bad：他的嗜好是抽烟。Smoking is his addiction. ／他三年前就戒掉了酗酒的嗜好。He stopped the habit of excessive drinking three years ago.

〔相同点〕：都表示对某事物或某活动有浓厚的兴趣。Syn. used to indicate keen interest in some matter or activity.

爱惜 àixī 珍惜 zhēnxī

爱惜 (cherish; treasure; use sparingly) 着重在
"爱"，不随便丢弃。emphasizes one's feeling
of love for sb. or sth. which one would not
abandon lightheartedly: 我们应当爱惜人力物
力。We must use manpower and material sparingly.

珍惜 (treasure, value; cherish) 着重在"珍"，指对
人或事物十分看重。对象常是珍贵或难得的
事物。stresses the value placed on sb. or sth.;
to accord high regard to a person or attach
great importance to sth., often used in
reference to sth. that is treasured or rare: 我
们应该珍惜时间。We should all value our time.

〔相同点〕：都是动词，表示对人或事物珍惜，不使
受损失的意思，都是褒义词。Syn. v. to cher-
ish sb. or sth., allowing no one else to hurt or
damage the cherished object, approbatory
terms.

安定 āndìng　安全 ānquán　平安 píng'an

安定 (stable; calm; settled) 是稳定的意思，指在生
活、形势等方面平静、正常。emphasizes
stability, indicates that life, situation, etc. is

stable and normal: 解放以后，他生活安定了。After liberation, he led a stable life.

安全 (safe; secure) 着重表示有保障，没有危险，可用于国家、生产、交通、人身等方面。emphasizes safety, used to indicate a situation free from danger for a person, a country, production or traffic: 我们要保证安全生产。We must ensure safety in production.

平安 (safe and sound; without mishap) 着重表示没有危险，没有事故，多用于人身。used to describe the absence of danger and mishap, particularly in reference to people: 一路平安。Have a pleasant journey. / 他平安到达目的地。He arrived at his destination without mishap.

〔相同点〕：都是形容词。都含没有事故或没有危险的意思。Syn. adj. indicating the absence of mishap or danger.

安顿 āndùn　安放 ānfàng

安顿 (find a place for; settle down; arrange for) 着重表示安排妥当。可用于人，也可用于物。emphasizes proper arrangement, used in connection with people or things: 家里都安顿好了吗? Have you arranged everything in the flat yet? / 先把学生安顿好。First, let's get the students settled in.

安放 (lay; place; put in a certain place) 着重在 "放"，使物体处在一定位置的意思。emphasizes the action of putting sth. in a certain place: 把仪器安放好。Put the apparatuses in their proper places.

〔相同点〕：都是动词。都表示使物体有一定的位置。Syn. v. to place sth. in a certain position.

安静 anjing 平静 píngjìng

安静 (quiet; peaceful) 着重指没有声音、安稳。常形容环境、心情、事物或人的状态。emphasizes soundlessness, smoothness and steadiness, pertaining to environment or state of mind: 病人需要安静。The patient needs peace and quiet. / 保持安静! Keep quiet!

平静 (calm; quiet; tranquil) 着重指平稳、没有动荡。常形容心情、表情。emphasizes calmness of freedom from disturbance, often used to describe feelings and facial expressions: 他很激动，心情久久不能平静。He was very excited and it was long before he calmed down.

〔相同点〕：都是形容词。都表示没有声音，安定不动的意思，可以形容环境、心情。Syn. adj. indicating soundlessness, stability or motionlessness, used to describe peaceful environment or state of mind.

5

安居 anjū　安身 anshen

安居 (dwell in peace) 表示安定地居住、生活的意思。to enjoy peaceful and stable living conditions: 安居乐业 Live and work in peace and contentment

安身 (make one's home; take shelter) 表示在某地生活和居住，大多是在贫困的环境下。to live in a certain place; particularly in reference to a poor or makeshift dwelling: 他无处安身。He has nowhere to make his home. / 他们只能在破庙里安身。They had to take shelter in a dilapidated temple.

〔相同点〕：都是不及物动词。表示在某处居住和生活的意思。常不带宾语。Syn. v. indicating that sb. lives in a certain place. Usually there is no object.

安排 anpái　安置 anzhì

安排 (arrange; plan; fix up) 着重在"排"，表示有条理分先后主次地处理事情。多指工作上的处理。emphasizes arrangement, mostly referring to the orderly arrangement of work or to the addressing of problems according to order of importance: 我们为外宾安排参观游

览。We arrange visits and sightseeing for foreign guests.

安置 (find a place for; settle down; arrange for） 指使人或事物有着落。多指处理人事工作的活动。indicates that a proper place is found for people or things, often used in connection with the placement of personnel: 复员军人得到了适当的安置。Proper arrangements have been made for the placement of demobilized soldiers.

〔相同点〕：都是动词。都含有合适地处理，使有着落的意思。Syn. v. to make proper arrangements or find a suitable place for sth. or sb.

安适 anshi 安闲 anxián 安逸 anyì

安适 (quiet and comfortable） 着重指安静而舒适。stresses quiet and comfort: 安适宁静的生活对一个年老的专家来说也是需要的。An elderly expert also needs a quiet, comfortable and peaceful life.

安闲 (peaceful and carefree; leisurely） 着重指安静、清闲的意思。emphasizes calm and leisure: 他很安闲自在。He is very carefree. / 安闲的心情 a relaxed mood

安逸 (easy and comfortable） 着重指生活舒适、安闲的意思。有时含有贬义。refers to a comfortable, peaceful and carefree life, sometimes pejorative: 他贪图安逸的生活。He seeks an easy life.

〔相同点〕: 都是形容词。表示 (心情、生活) 安定的意思。Syn. adj. indicating that one feels comfortable and at peace.

安慰 ānwèi   宽慰 kuānwèi

安慰 (comfort; console) 着重在"安", 表示心情安适、平静。emphasizes that someone is restored to a quiet, comfortable and calm frame of mind: 同志们的关怀给了我很大的安慰。The comrades' solicitude was a great comfort to me.

宽慰 (comfort; console) 着重在"宽", 表示宽心, 解除烦恼。emphasizes relief from a vexation: 这样一想, 我心里才宽慰了一些。This thought brought me a little comfort. / 我因情况没有变得更坏而宽慰自己。I console myself with the thought that it might have been worse.

〔相同点〕: 都是动词。都有使人心情安适的意思。Syn. v. to restore someone to a cheerful frame of mind.

安详 anxiáng　慈祥 cíxiáng

安详 (serene; composed; unruffled) 表示稳重、从容不迫。indicates steadiness and calm: 他举止安详。He behaves with composure.

慈祥 (kindly) 多用在双亲或领导或长者身上。多指老年人的态度、神色和蔼。often used to describe leaders, parents or elderly people, indicates a benign, kindly attitude or expression: 慈祥的面容 a benign face / 他非常慈祥。He is very kind.

〔相同点〕: 都是形容词。表示态度和蔼的意思。Syn. adj. describing kindness and pleasantness.

安心 ānxīn　放心 fàngxīn

安心 (feel at ease; be relieved; set one's mind at rest) 着重表示由于感到安全而使人心情安定。indicates serenity occasioned by a feeling of safety or security: 听到这个消息，她就安心了。She was relieved at the news. / 春播不完成，大家都不安心。None of us can feel at ease until the spring sowing is finished.

放心 (set one's mind at rest; be at ease; rest assured; feel relieved) 强调的是没有忧虑和牵挂，心

情安定。indicates serenity, because there is no cause for worry：你放心，一切都会安排好的。You can rest assured that everything will be all right. ／我对他不大放心。I have no trust in him.

〔相同点〕：表示心情安定的意思。多用来形容心情。都是形容词。Syn. adj. often used to describe a tranquil frame of mind.

安葬 anzang　埋葬 maizang

安葬 (bury — the dead) 举行一定的仪式掩埋死者。用在比较郑重的场合。to bury the dead with ceremony (used on solemn occasions)：人民用最隆重的礼节安葬烈士。The martyr was interred with solemn obsequies.

埋葬 (bury) 掩埋死者的遗体。有时可用比喻义，指把某种腐朽、反动或其他的东西消灭、除掉。to bury the body of a dead person without ceremony, sometimes used figuratively, meaning to get rid of sth. bad, reactionary, etc：我们埋葬旧世界，建设新世界。We bury the old world and build a new one.

〔相同点〕：都是动词。表示把死者埋在地下的意思。Syn. v. to bury the dead.

暗暗 ànàn　偷偷 tōutōu

暗暗 (secretly; inwardly; to oneself) 表示在暗中，不显露出来的意思。indicates that sth. does not appear outwardly: 暗暗地跟踪 follow someone secretly / 他暗暗发誓要为牺牲的同志报仇。He vowed to himself to avenge his comrades who had laid down their lives for the country.

偷偷 (stealthily; secretly; covertly; on the sly) 形容行动不使人觉察。indicates that an action is so performed as to avoid detection: 偷偷地瞧了他一眼 stole a glance at him / 偷偷地告诉他 tell him on the quiet

〔相同点〕: 都是副词。表示在黑暗处或私下里的意思。Syn. adj. covert.

暗害 ànhài　暗算 ànsuàn

暗害 (kill secretly; stab in the back) 表示暗中杀伤或陷害人的意思。to kill or frame sb. secretly: 他被坏人暗害了。He was killed secretly by an evil-doer.

暗算 (plot against) 着重在"算"，表示在暗中图谋伤害或陷害别人。The key element is 算 (calculate): to make a secret plan to hurt or

11

frame sb.: 他遭人暗算了。He fell prey to a plot.
〔相同点〕: 都是动词。表示暗中陷害别人的意思。都是贬义词。Syn. v. to frame sb. secretly, pejorative.

暗含 ànhán 暗示 ànshì

暗含 (imply) 表示做事说话包含某种意思，而不明白显示出来。indicates that what is done or said implies a certain meaning, although it is not declared openly: 他的回答暗含着对我们工作的批评。His reply implied a criticism of our work.

暗示 (drop a hint; hint; suggest) 有不直接表示，而是用含蓄的言语或动作使人领会的意思，可用作名词。n. to refrain from communicating one's ideas in a straightforward manner, but to drop hints by word or gesture: 他暗示要我走开。He hinted that he wanted me to leave. / 她没有懂我的暗示。She didn't take my hint.

〔相同点〕: 都是动词。有明白地表示的意思。Syn. v. to refrain from expressing one's ideas overtly.

按照 ànzhào 遵照 zūnzhào

按照 (according to; in accordance with; in the light

of; on the basis of) 可用于各种语体，不带尊敬色彩。used in any kind of context, does not imply respect: 计划已按照老师的意见修改了。The plan has been revised in accordance with the opinions of the teacher. / 我们按照实际情况决定工作方针。We decide our working policies in the light of actual conditions.

遵照 **(obey; conform to; comply with; action in accordance with)** 表示遵从照办。多用于书面语体，带尊敬色彩。to obey or act accordingly, often used in written language with a connotation of respect: 我们遵照上级的命令办事。We act in accordance with orders from above.

〔相同点〕：都是介词。介绍出行为的根据。Syn. prep. indicating the basis of an action.

懊悔 àohuǐ　懊恼 àonǎo

懊悔 **(feel remorse; repent; regret)** 是动词。着重在"悔"，指心里恨自己不该做错了事或说错了话。后悔以前没有做好的意思。v. The key element is 悔 (regret); to feel remorse for errors of word or deed, or regret for not having done better: 我懊悔不该错怪了她。I regretted having blamed her unjustly.

懊恼 **(annoyed; vexed; upset)** 着重在"恼"，指心里

13

不痛快，别扭，对别人或自己的言行感到烦恼的意思。The key element is 恼 (angry): to feel chagrined for one's own or other's words or deeds: 他工作没做好，心里很懊恼。He was quite upset at not having done his work well.

〔相同点〕: 都是指心理活动，都含有后悔，恼恨的意思。Syn. v. describing activities of the mind, and carrying the meaning of regret or resentment.

奥秘 aomi　奥妙 aomiao

奥秘 (profound; mystery) 重点在"秘"，指还没有被了解或被认识的内容和道理。The key element is 秘 (secret): this indicates that a certain matter or truth is as yet unknown or uncomprehended: 我们探索宇宙的奥秘。We probe the mysteries of the universe.

奥妙 (profound; subtle; secret) 重点在"妙"，指内容和道理的深奥微妙。The crucial element is 妙 (subtle): this refers to a matter or truth which is difficult to comprehend because of its profundity and subtlety: 不难明白其中的奥妙。It is not difficult to see what is behind it. / 这件事其中定有奥妙。There must be more to this matter than meets the eye. / 奥妙无穷 extremely subtle

14

〔相同点〕：都是形容词。都有深奥的意思。Syn.
adj. containing the meaning of profundity.

（用同意）：猶指省等 同事等或或能爲。Syn.
adj: containing the meaning of profundity

B

把持 bǎchí　把握 bǎwò　掌握 zhǎngwò

把持 (control; dominate; monopolize) 贬义词。指独占位置或权利，不让别人参与。a pejorative term, to take exclusive possession of position or power: 他把持一切权力。He monopolizes power.

把握 (hold, grasp) 1.有抓住某人某物的意思。to take hold of sb. or sth.: 透过现象，把握本质。See through the phenomena to grasp the essence. 2.还有表示成功的可靠性的意思，多用于"有"和"没"的后边。indicates certainty of success, usually placed after 有 or 没: 他很有把握地回答了所有的问题。He answered all the questions with assurance.

掌握 (grasp; master; know well) 1.了解事物，因而能充分支配或运用。to have knowledge of a matter which enables one to control or make good use of it: 他掌握一门外语。He has a good command of a foreign language. 我们要掌握现代化生产技能和科学知识。We must master modern techniques of production and scientific knowledge. 2.还有主持、控制的意思。to direct or control: 我们掌握工作进程。We have the work under control. / 每个人要掌握自己的命运。Everyone must be in command of his or her own destiny.

〔相同点〕：都是动词。表示用一切力量把某种事物抓住。对象可以是具体的或抽象的事物。Syn. v. to hold and control sth. with total power; The object may be either concrete or abstract.

颁布 bānbù　发布 fābù　公布 gōngbù

颁布 (issue; promulgate; publish)　着重指向下颁发。颁布者一般是高级领导机关或其成员，意思比"公布"郑重。emphasizes that sth. is issued to those of lower standing by higher leading bodies or their members. 颁布 (issue) is more formal in register than 公布 (publish): 我们的政府颁布了一项新法令。Our government has promulgated a new decree.

发布 (issue; release)　着重指宣布的意思，对象常是新闻、命令、指示等。refers mainly to the release of news, orders, directives, etc.: 发布命令 issue an order / 发布新闻 release news

公布 (promulgate; announce; publish; make public)　是指公开通告，使大家知道。公布者除了高级领导机关，还可以是一般机关。公布的内

17

容除法令外，还可以是成绩、帐目等。indicates that sth. is announced or made known to the public by high leading organs or other bodies. The announcement may pertain to laws, decrees, achievements, accounts, etc.: 我们公布了参加会议人员的名单。We have published a name—list of those attending the meeting. / 汉语拼音方案公布了。The pinyin romanization system has been published.

〔相同点〕: 都是动词。公开发表的意思。对象多是法令、命令等。Syn. v. to make laws, decrees, orders, etc. known to the public.

办法 bànfǎ　措施 cuòshī

办法 (way; means; measure) 口语和书面语都常用，既可用于大事也可用于小事。used in reference to important as well as trivial matters, in both spoken and written language: 我们应该找出克服困难的办法。We must find a way to overcome difficulties. / 照你的办法去做吧。Do it your own way.

措施 (measure; step) 一般用于较重要、较严肃的事情上。多用于书面语，特别是公文、政治语体。emphasizes the measures taken to address important and serious problems; often used in written language, especially in official

18

documents and essays of a political nature: 采取重大的措施 adopt an important measure

〔相同点〕：都是名词。表示处理事情的方法、方式和步骤。Syn. n. the ways, means and procedures for handling matters.

帮助 bangzhù　援助 yuánzhù　赞助 zànzhù

帮助 **(help; assist)** 指替人出主意或给予物质上、精神上的支援。to make suggestions or give material or spiritual support to sb.: 她帮助我学习外语。She helped me learn a foreign language. / 我帮助他搬行李。I help him with the luggage.

援助 **(help; support; aid)** 指用人力、物力支援别人。to support with manpower or material resources: 我们尽一切可能援助他。We have done everything we can to help him. / 技术援助 technical assistance

赞助 **(support; assist)** 指表示赞成并给予支援。to confer approval and support: 这个展览得到他们的赞助。This exhibition was sponsored by them.

〔相同点〕：都可作动词和名词。表示给予支持的意思。常用作褒义词。Syn. v. n. to give support to sb.; often used as terms of approbation.

包含 bāohán 包括 bāokuò

包含 (contain; embody; include) 是内里含着的意思，着眼于事物内在关系。to imply, with the emphasis on the internal elements of abstract things: 他的建议包含着不少合理的因素。His proposal contains many reasonable elements.

包括 (include; cover; consist of; comprise; incorporate) 着重指总括。对象不限于抽象的事物。The central meaning is of summation; the object may be either abstract or concrete: 房租每月七元，水电费包括在内。The rent is seven yuan a month, including water and electricity. / 我们的设计已经包括了你们的意见。Our design incorporates your suggestions.

〔相同点〕: 都是动词。表示总括在一起的意思。Syn. v. to sum up.

保护 bǎohù 庇护 bìhù 掩护 yǎnhù

保护 (protect; safeguard) 是保养维护，使事物不受到损害的意思。是中性词 a neutral term, to maintain sth. in perfect condition and protect it from damage: 保护环境，防止污染。protect the environment against pollution / 保护

20

人民的利益 safeguard the people's interests ／
运动员都学会了互相保护和自我保护。The
sportsmen have all learned to protect each other
and themselves against injuries.

庇护 (shelter; shield; put under one's protection; take under one's wing) 指包庇、祖护的意思。主要用于贬义。只适用于对人或与人有关的事物，如缺点、错误等。mostly a pejorative term, applied to people or matters related to people, such as mistakes or errors: 我们绝不能庇护任何坏人。We should never shelter any evil-doers from punishment.

掩护 (screen; shield; cover) 指采取遮掩的方式予以保护。是中性词。多用在军事上，一般适用于人，用于事物较少。neutral in tone, a military term seldom used in non-martial contexts: 军队掩护村里的人转移。The army covered the villagers' evacuation.

〔相同点〕：都是动词。都有保卫人或事物使之不受损害的意思。Syn. v. to protect people or things from harm.

饱满 bǎomǎn　丰满 fēngmǎn

饱满 (full; plump) 常用于形容人的精神、精力、情绪充足。有时形容事物。often used to describe people who are full of vigor and en-

21

ergy and in exuberant spirits, and sometimes also to describe things: 他的精神饱满。 He is full of vigor. ／这是颗粒饱满的小麦。 This is plump-eared wheat.

丰满 (plentiful; full-fledged) 除了充足的意思之外，还常形容人体胖得匀称、好看。有时形容鸟的羽毛齐全好看。 to be ample; often used to describe a plump person or a bird with full, beautiful plumage: 我有好几年没看见她了，如今长得越发丰满了。 I haven't seen her for several years. Her figure is fuller than ever. ／这只鸟的羽毛很丰满。 It is a full-fledged bird. ／粮仓丰满。 The granaries are full.

〔相同点〕：都是形容词。都有充足、足够的意思。 Syn. adj. to be adequate.

保卫 bǎowèi　捍卫 hànwèi

保卫 (defend; safeguard) 表示保护，使不受侵犯的意思，使用范围较广。 to protect sb. or sth. from encroachment; has a wide range of applications: 保卫祖国是公民的责任。 It is the duty of all citizens to defend their country. ／我们应该保卫国家主权和领土完整。 We must safeguard national sovereignty and territorial integrity.

捍卫 (defend; guard; protect) 表示抵御外来势力、

确保安全的意思，宾语多是抽象事物，也可以是领空、领海等。to resist external invading forces and ensure safety. Its objects are often abstractions such as territorial sky, territorial sea, etc.: 捍卫国家主权 defend national sovereignty ／捍卫民族经济权益 protect the economic rights and interests of the nation

〔相同点〕：都是动词。都表示抵抗外来势力，使不受侵犯的意思。Syn. v. to resist external invading forces, and prevent encroachment.

保持 bǎochí 坚持 jianchí 维持 wéichí

保持 (keep; maintain; retain) 着重在表示使原样不变，时间延续较长。stresses the maintenance of sth. in its original state over a long period of time: 我们应该与公司保持密切联系。We should maintain close contact with the company. ／他与他的老朋友保持通信。He keeps up a correspondence with his old friends.

坚持 (persist in; adhere to; uphold; insist on) 表示打定主意，坚定不移地继续干下去。to make up one's mind to do sth. steadfastly: 坚持真理 adhere to the truth ／我们应该坚持上次会议上提出的条件。We must insist on the terms put forward at the previous session. ／他坚持学习马列主义。He studies Marxism-Leninism with

23

persistence.

维持 (keep; maintain; preserve) 表示要作出努力，使事物继续存在下去，是暂时的，或有一定限度的。to exert efforts to enable sth. to continue its existence, temporarily or within certain limitations: 我们应该维持好会场的秩序。We should keep the meeting in good order.

〔相同点〕：都是动词。表示保持原来的东西继续存在下去。Syn. v. to maintain the continuing existence of sth.

宝贵 bǎoguì　贵重 guìzhòng　珍贵 zhēnguì

宝贵 (valuable; precious) 指极有价值，非常难得。适用的范围较大。denotes sth. of great value or rarity, has a wide range of applications: 世间一切事物中，人是第一个可宝贵的。Of all the things in the world, people are the most precious.

贵重 (valuable; costly; expensive) 表示价值高，值得重视。用于具体事物。of great monetary value and deserving care and attention; used of concrete objects: 这种药品很贵重。This medicine is costly.

珍贵 (valuable; precious; rare) 指事物价值很高，意义深刻而又稀少。适用范围较小，只用于物。refers to sth. of great value, significance

24

and rarity, only applied to things: 这是珍贵的
历史文物。This is a rare historical relic. / 这是他
给我的珍贵的纪念品。This is the precious sou-
venir he gave me.

〔相同点〕：都是形容词。都表示极有价值的意思。
Syn. adj. referring to sth. of great value.

暴露 bàolù　揭露 jiēlù

暴露 (reveal; lay bare) 指有意和无意地让隐藏的
东西显露出来。常与目标、原形、嘴脸等搭
配使用。to disclose one's secrets, intentionally or otherwise; especially, to reveal one's
aim, original identity or true features: 他暴露
了身份。He revealed his identity. / 矛盾还没有
充分暴露。The contradictions have not yet fully
come to light.

揭露 (expose; unmask;) 指有目的地公开隐藏的事
情。特别是阴谋和罪行。一般不用于自身。
denotes the deliberate revelation of things
hidden, particularly conspiracy or crime. As a
rule the term is not used to refer to the revelation of one's own secrets: 揭露敌人的阴谋
expose the enemy's plot / 我们一定要毫无保留
地揭露他的错误。We must expose this mistakes without any reticence.

〔相同点〕：都是动词。都有把隐藏的事物公开出来

25

的意思。Syn. v. to make publicly known things hidden or kept in the dark.

抱怨 bàoyuàn　埋怨 mányuàn

抱怨 (complain; grumble) 责怪程度较重，表示心中不满，数说别人不对的意思。to vent one's discontentment or enumerate mistakes made by sb.; has a strong note of censure; usually applied to persons：她抱怨他工作不细心。 She complained of his carelessness in his work.

埋怨 (blame; complain; grumble) 责怪程度轻，表示因为不如意，而对某人或某事表示不满的意思。to express one's disgruntlement with sb. or sth. The blame is milder. The term can be applied to either persons or things：他的话里有埋怨的情绪。 Here was a note of complaint in what he said. / 他老爱埋怨。 He is always grumbling. / 这场球打输了，大家找原因，不要互相埋怨。 Let's try and find out what went wrong instead of blaming one another for losing the game.

〔相同点〕：都是动词。表示因不满意而责怪别人。Syn. v. to blame sb. for sth. one considers dissatisfactory.

26

背叛 bèipàn　叛变 pànbiàn　违背 wéibèi

背叛 (betray) 程度较重。指投到敌对方面，改变立场，抛弃本方利益，多用于重大事件。to abandon one's position, the interests of one's party, or work for the enemy; often used in connection with important issues. The tone of this expression is strong: 他完全背叛了他的国家。He has completely betrayed his country.

叛变 (betray one's country; turn traitor) 指不仅背叛了原来的立场，而且变成了敌对方面，词义更重一些。to go over to the opposite side or even to that of the enemy. The implication is even more serious: 他叛变投敌了。He turned traitor and went over to the enemy.

违背 (violate; go against; run counter to) 程度较轻。指违反、不遵守、不依从，不一定用于重大事件。to fail to obey or observe certain rules or to comply with someone's wishes; not necessarily used only for major events. The tone is less severe: 违背法律 violate the law / 我们不能违背人民的意志。We can't go against the will of the people.

〔相同点〕：都是动词。有向着相反方向行动的意思。Syn. v. involving the idea of running counter to a given direction or acting contrary to sth.

奔驰 bēnchí   奔跑 bēnpǎo   奔腾 bēnténg

奔驰 (**run quickly; speed**) 着重于"驰"，很快地飞跑，用于一般交通工具，人、动物或其他物体。denotes the action of running or moving forward very fast, used of vehicles, animals, people, etc.: 火车向前奔驰。The train sped on. ／骏马在草原上奔驰。Sturdy steeds gallop on the grasslands.

奔跑 (**run**) 表示很快地跑、奔走的意思。to run fast: 他拼命地奔跑。He ran for all he was worth.

奔腾 (**gallop; surge forward; roll on in waves**) 着重于"腾"，形容马跳跃似地跑。还常比喻某些液体的流动，如大海、江河、山洪、热血、铁水以及感情。originally refers to galloping horses, now also used to describe the rapid flow of water or other liquids, such as the sea, rivers, floods, blood or molten iron, as well as the surge of human emotion: 浩浩长江奔腾不息。The mighty waters of the Changjiang (Yangtze) River roll on incessantly. ／山洪暴发，犹如万马奔腾。Torrents of water rushed down the mountain like ten thousand horses galloping onward.

28

〔相同点〕：都是动词。表示跑得很快的意思。Syn.
v. to run very fast.

本来 běnlái 原来 yuánlái

本来 (original; at first) 1.强调原先的情况，多用
于上半句，下半句有时用"但是""可是"等跟
它呼应，表示语气的转变。emphasizes the
original condition of sth., mostly used in the
first part of sentence, and followed by
adversative conjunctions such as 但是 or 可
是, indicating a change in tone: 会议本来定在
星期五举行，可是后来他们改时间了。The
meeting was originally scheduled for Friday, but
the time was subsequently changed. 2.表示理所
当然，应当这样。indicates sth. is so as a
matter of course, or that it should be so: 事情
本来就该这样办。Of course, that is the way it
should be dealt with. ／这样的事本来就不应该
发生。Such a thing should never have been allowed to happen in the first place.

原来 (original; former) 1.表示发现真实情况。它
时常是用真实情况对上半句加以说明或解
释。indicates that the true state of affairs has
become apparent; often used to give the au-
thentic explanation of circumstances previously mentioned: 原来这是一个骗局。It

turned out to be a fraud. 2.表示起初，没有经过改变的意思。used to express the idea that a circumstance remains unchanged: 他还住在原来地方。He still lives in the same place.

〔相同点〕：都是副词。都表示以前情况和现实情况比较，表示语气的前后转变。Syn. adv. used when comparing the present with the past, indicating a change in tone.

本领 běnlǐng　本事 běnshi

本领 (skill; ability; capability) 表示经过特别学习才能掌握的较复杂的技能。多用于书面语，具有庄重色彩。refers to a complex skill that can be mastered only after specialized study. The expression is rather formal in register, and most often used in written language: 他有组织生产的本领。He has the ability to organize production. / 我们应该掌握解决实际问题的本领。We should master the skills needed to solve practical problems.

本事 (skill; ability; capability) 常用于口头语体。指技能和能力。a certain skill or ability, often used in spoken language: 看你有没有本事爬上这棵树。Let's see if you are capable of climbing the tree. / 你有外科医生的本事吗？Do you have surgical skills?

30

〔相同点〕：都是名词。表示从事某种活动的能力或技术，经常换用。Syn. n. the ability or skill to do sth. The two words are usually interchangeable.

本质 běnzhì 实质 shízhì

本质 (essence; intrinsic quality; innate character) 着重指事物或人所固有的、根本的或本来的属性。指事物独有的深刻的特性。the innate and essential nature of people or things, or the special underlying characteristics of things: 这两件事本质上不同。These two things are different in essence. ／我们应该透过现象看本质。We should see the essence through the appearance.

实质 (substance; essence) 是一般用语。着重表示跟外部的表现形式不同。指事物的实在内容。不用于人。the actual content of sth.; a commonly used term, emphasizes the difference between the substance of sth. and its external manifestation. It is not used with reference to persons: 理想问题，实质上是一个人的世界观的问题。The kind of goal one cherishes in fact shows one's attitude towards the world.

〔相同点〕：都是名词。都有最主要的性质的意思。

Syn. n. the most important characteristics.

比赛 bǐsài　竞赛 jìngsài

比赛 **(match; competition)** 常用于体育、文娱活动等方面，可以带宾语。often used of sports and recreational activities, can be followed by an object：明天我们两个学校比赛篮球。Tomorrow there will be a basketball match between our two schools. ／今天我们有音乐比赛。Today we are holding a musical contest.

竞赛 **(contest; competition; emulation; race)** 着重指竞争，争取优胜。常用于生产、经济、建设、军事等方面。emphasizes competition in fields such as production, economy, construction and military affairs：工厂里开展劳动竞赛。A labor emulation drive has been launched in the factory. ／两国开展军事竞赛。The two countries started an arms race.

〔相同点〕：表示互相间争高低的活动。Syn. v. to contend with each other for victory or superiority.

鄙视 bǐshì　轻视 qīngshì

鄙视 **(despise; contemn)** 是鄙弃、低劣的意思。to regard a practice as contemptible or a person

32

as inferior to others: 说谎者被同事所鄙视。
Liars are despised by their workmates.

轻视 (look down on; underestimate; despise) 看不起的意思，与"重视"相对。语义较轻。This is the opposite of "重视" (to take sth. seriously). The tone is relatively light: 他对这次期中考试很轻视。He underestimates the significance of the mid-term examination. ／ 他从不轻视体力劳动。He never looks down on physical labor.

〔**相同点**〕：都是动词。都有看不起的意思。Syn. v. disdain sb. or sth.

必定 bìdìng 必然 bìrán 一定 yídìng

必定 (be bound to; be sure to) 表示根据情况判断，一定会是这样。一般不作形容词，也不作定语。indicates that things will turn out in a certain way, judging from the situation; not normally used as an adjective or attribute: 明天我们必定把图纸送到。We will be sure to send you the blueprints tomorrow.

必然 (inevitable; certain) 表示客观事物的发展必定如此，并非偶然。还可作形容词用，作形容词时常常充当定语，如"必然的联系"。indicates that objective matters will develop in their own way, and that the development is by no means accidental. When used as an ad-

33

jective, it most often functions as an attributive, as in the phrase 必然的联系 (inevitable connection): 这是必然结局。This is the inevitable outcome. / 他们必然要和我们作拼死的斗争。They are bound to struggle desperately against us.

一定 **(fixed; specified; definite; regular)** 表示坚决或确定。可作形容词。作形容词时可做定语。denotes resolution or definiteness. When used as an adjective, it functions as an attributive: 他一定是被什么要紧事拦住了。He must have been held up by urgent business. / 她一忙起来，吃饭、睡觉都没有一定的时间了。When she gets really busy, she doesn't keep regular hours for eating or sleeping. / 我们的目的一定能够达到。We are certain to attain our goal.

〔相同点〕：都是表示肯定的副词，都可以充当状语，都含有"非这样不可"的意思。Syn. adv. functioning as adverbial modifiers, indicating that sth. is necessarily so.

毕竟 bìjìng　究竟 jiūjìng

毕竟 **(after all; all in all; when all is said and done; in the final analysis)** 只用于非疑问句，表示终归、到底或追根究底所得的结论。means eventually, after all, when one gets to the root of the matter. It cannot be used in interrogative constructions: 她的缺点同她的成绩相比，毕竟是第二位的。Compared with her achievements, her shortcomings are, after all, secondary.

究竟 (outcome; what actually happened) 表示追究，既可用于非疑问句，也可用于疑问句。implies investigation, used both in statements and interrogative sentences: 大家都想知道个究竟。Everyone wants to know what actually happened. / 明天的会究竟谁去参加？ Who is actually going to the meeting tomorrow?

〔相同点〕：都是副词。说明事物的结果。Syn. adv. referring to the outcome of sth.

必须 bìxū　必需 bìxū

必须 (must; have to) 副词。是应该要的意思。它是助动词，常用在主要动词前面，共同作谓语，不能单独作谓语，也不能作定语。adv. ought to do sth., "should", an auxiliary verb, often used in front of the main verb to form the predicate. It may not be used either as predicate or as an attributive: 我们必须指出他的缺点。We must point out his shortcomings. / 你必须刻苦学习。You must study hard.

必需 (essential; indispensable) 动词。是一定要的意思。可以作谓语和定语。v. absolutely required, used both as predicate and attributive: 应该把学院的资金用在最必需的地方。The college should spend funds on what is most needed. ／这些是工业发展必需的原料。These are the raw materials essential for industrial development.

〔相同点〕: 都有一定要，必不可少的意思。Syn. referring to that which is indispensable or absolutely necessary.

鞭策 biāncè　督促 dūcù

鞭策 (spur on; urge on) 原意是用鞭和策赶马。现在经常用的是比喻义。有严格督促，使更进步的意思。多用于对自己或长辈对小辈。语义较重。originally to whip on a horse, now used in a figurative sense, meaning to supervise sb. and urge him or her on to make great progress. It is often used when one encourages oneself or when an older person encourages a younger one to do sth.: 我们要经常鞭策自己，努力学习。We should constantly urge ourselves to study hard. ／领导的表扬是对我们的鞭策。The leadership's praise spurs us on.

督促 (supervise and urge) 表示一般的监督，催

促，使之不断进步。对己对人都可以用。语义较轻。to supervise; urge; spur sb. on to make constant progress; used in reference to oneself or other people: 督促大家及时归还工具。Urge everybody to return the tools on time. / 已经布置了的工作，应当认真督促落实。We must supervise and speed up fulfilment of the assigned tasks. / 督促他按时完成作业。Keep an eye on him and push him to finish his homework on time.

〔相同点〕: 都是动词，又都可以作名词。都有使之前进的意思。Syn. v.; n. urge sb. forward.

边疆 biānjiāng   边境 biānjìng

边疆 (border area; borderland; frontier; frontier region) 指靠近国界的较大片领土。a large area of land near the national boundaries: 我们必须保卫边疆。We must guard the frontier. / 我们应该支援边疆建设。We should support the construction of the border areas.

边境 (border; frontier) 范围比边疆小。只指紧靠国界的长条领土。indicates a more limited area than 边疆; the long narrow tract of land along the border: 敌人封锁了边境。The enemy closed the frontiers. / 越过边境 cross the border / 边境线 border line / 边疆纠纷 border dispute

〔相同点〕: 都是名词。都有靠近国界的地方的意思。Syn. n. a tract of territory near the national boundaries.

辩白 biànbái　辩护 biànhù　辩解 biànjiě

辩白 (offer an explanation; plead innocence; try to defend oneself) 指把问题分辩清楚（一般指在被误解的情况下分辩，使事实得以澄清）。to offer a clear explanation; normally used in the sense of clarifying a misunderstanding of which one is the victim: 别人说他毁坏工具是有意的，而他却辩白说:"那完全是粗心大意。"Other people said that he had broken the tool on purpose, but he said that it was entirely due to carelessness. / 事实很清楚，他决定不再辩白了。The facts were clear, so he decided to stop explaining himself.

辩护 (speak in defence of; argue in favor of; defend) 为了保护别人或自己而进行分辩。to speak with the aim of defending oneself or others: 不要为他辩护了。Don't try to defend him. / 被告人有权获得辩护。The accused has the right to defend him or herself.

辩解 (provide an explanation; try to defend oneself) 指分辩、解释。to offer an explana-

38

tion to defend oneself or sb. else: 错了就错了，不要辩解了。A mistake is a mistake, don't try to explain it away. / 你不要总是辩解。You should not keep on trying to explain things away.

〔相同点〕: 都是动词。都有为达到预定的目的而进行解释，争论的意思。Syn. v. to explain or argue for a certain purpose.

辨别 biànbié 辨认 biànrèn 鉴别 jiànbié

辨别 (differentiate; distinguish; discriminate) 着重指分辨、区别。emphasizes differentiation: 晚上可以用北极星辨别方向。We can use the polestar to distinguish directions at night. / 我们要学会辨别是非。We should learn to distinguish what is right and what is wrong.

辨认 (identify; recognize) 着重根据人或事物的特点进行辨别，然后作出判断。to distinguish sb. or sth. according to his, her or its characteristics, and then draw a conclusion: 他的笔迹容易辨认。His handwriting is easy to identify. / 相片已经模糊，不能辨认。The photo is faded beyond recognition.

鉴别 (distinguish; differentiate; discriminate) 着重通过审查而确定事物的特征。lays stress on ascertaining the characteristics of things by means of examination: 有比较才能鉴别。On-

39

ly by comparing can one distinguish. / 鉴别文物
make an appraisal of a cultural relic

〔相同点〕：都是动词。都有认清和区别的意思。
Syn. v. to make a distinction between similar
things.

变革 biàngé　变化 biànhuà

变革 (transform; change) 表示变动、革新的意
思。使用范围较小，多用于"社会""自然"等
方面。usually refers to social and natural
changes; has a limited range of usage: 社会变
革 social change / 变革自然 transform nature

变化 (change; vary) 表示改变原来的样子的意
思，使用范围较大。to change the original
state or things, has a wide range of applications: 气温的变化 variations in temperature /
我的家乡有了很大变化。Great changes have
taken place in my home village.

〔相同点〕：都是动词，也都可以作名词。都表示改
变的意思。Syn. v.; n. change.

标明 biānmíng　表明 biǎomíng

标明 (mark; indicate) 指做出记号或写出文字使人
知道。常用于具体事物。to use writing or
other marks to aid identification or under-

standing; generally used in relation to concrete things: 货箱上标明"小心轻放"。The crate is marked "Handle with Care". / 在这幅地图上北京是用一颗红星标明的。Beijing is indicated with a red star on this map.

表明 (make known; make clear; state clearly) 指表示清楚。常用于抽象事物，把内在的思想、感情等显示出来。to show sth. clearly; often refers to abstract things such as thoughts or feelings: 有迹象表明会谈即将恢复。There are indications that the talks will be resumed soon.

〔相同点〕：都是动词。都有表示出来，使人清楚明白的意思。Syn. v. to show sth. clearly.

表达 biǎodá　表示 biǎoshì

表达 (express; convey; voice) 常用于说出自己的思想或感情。to express ideas and feelings: 激动的心情难于用语言表达。Words can hardly express my excitement.

表示 (show; express; indicate) 指用语言或行动显出某种思想感情的意思。to manifest one's thoughts and feelings through words or actions: 这是友好的表示。This is a manifestation of friendship. / 我向你表示衷心的祝贺。I wish to convey to you my hearty congratulations.

〔相同点〕：都是动词。都有把意思说出来的意思。

41

Syn. v. to express one's ideas.

表现 biǎoxiàn　体现 tǐxiàn

表现 (expression; manifestation; display; show; manifest; show off) 1.指表示出来。to display: 他在工作中表现很好。He is doing well in his work. ／他表现出极大的勇敢和智慧。He has displayed immense courage and wisdom. 2.故意显示自己的意思，含有贬义。to show off, sometimes pejorative: 他好表现自己。He likes to show off.

体现 (embody; incarnate; reflect; give expression to) 指具体地表示出来。专指用具体事物显现出概括的和原则的意义。to show sth. clearly in a specific way, for instance by using concrete examples to make clear one's principal ideas: 这个提案体现了发展中国家的利益和要求。This proposal reflects the interests and demands of the developing countries.

〔相同点〕：都是动词。都有把内在的事物显现出来的意思。Syn. v. to give expression or outward shape.

表扬 biǎoyáng　赞扬 zànyáng

表扬 (praise; commend) 指对好人好事公开赞美。

to praise publicly good people and good deeds: 教师表扬了十个勤奋的学生。 The teacher commended ten students for their diligence. / 工人们的工作得到了表扬。 These workers have been praised for their work.

赞扬 (speak highly of; praise; commend) 指称赞、表扬。speak highly of sb. for some quality or achievement: 他们的良好的体育作风博得广泛赞扬。 Their fine sportsmanship won widespread acclaim. / 这种一心为公的精神值得大加赞扬。 This spirit of selflessness deserves commendation.

〔相同点〕：都是动词。都有对好人好事称赞的意思。又都可以作名词。Syn. v.; n. to eulogize good people and good deeds.

哺育 bǔyù　抚育 fǔyù

哺育 (feed; nurture; foster) 着重表示喂养的意思。现在常用它的比喻义。stresses the idea of feeding or nurturing, nowadays often used in a metaphorical sense: 哺育雏鸟 feed little birds / 青年一代在新思想哺育下成长。 The younger generation is growing up nurtured by new thought.

抚育 (foster; nurture; tend) 是爱护、养育的意思。着重指"扶持""照料"。The emphasis is on cherishing, bringing up: 抚育子女 bring up children

〔相同点〕：都是动词。都有养育的意思。Syn. v. to nurture.

不单 bùdān　不但 bùdàn

不单 (not only; not merely; not simply) 多用于口语。"不单"还有一个意思，就是"不止"，而"不但"没有。used most often in spoken language, has the additional meaning "not merely", which is not shared by 不但：会说英语的不单是这些学生。They are not the only students who can speak English. ／他不单是老师也是大夫。He is not only a teacher, but a doctor as well.

不但 (not only) 用在书面语体和口语体。used both in spoken and written language: 我们的产品不但要求数量多而且要求质量好。Our products should not only be manufactured in large quantities but should also be of good quality.

〔相同点〕：都是连词。都有不光、不仅的意思。常用在句子前半部分，后一部分里通常有连词"而且""并且"，副词"也""还"或"连"等相呼应。Syn. conj. expressing the idea of "not only" used in the first part of a sentence, the second part of which often contains conjunctions such as 而且 or 并且 meaning 'but

44

also', or adverbs such as 也, 还 or 连 meaning 'too' or 'and'.

不管 bùguǎn　不论 bùlùn　无论 wúlùn

不管 (no matter — what, how, etc.; regardless of)
用于口头语体居多。最适宜与口语词搭配，后面不宜用"如何、何、是否、与否"等文言词。often used orally, and most suitable for use in spoken language. It cannot be followed by such classical Chinese expressions as 如何，何，是否 or 否：不管怎么样，我也要去。In any case, I'll go. ／不管工作多忙，我们都挤时间学习。No matter how busy we are, we always find time to study.

不论 (no matter — what, who, how, etc; whether ... or; regardless of) 口头语体和书面语体都常用。used in both spoken and written language: 全村不论男女老幼，都参加了抗旱斗争。All the villagers, men and women, old and young, took part in the battle against the drought.

无论 (no matter — what, how, etc.; regardless of)
多用于书面语体。常跟"如何"组成"无论如何"。often used in written language, frequently combined with 如何 (how) to form a phrase meaning "at any rate"：无论是谁都不能违反纪律。Nobody is allowed to violate disci-

45

pline, no matter who he or she is. ／无论发生什
么情况，你都要保持冷静。You must keep
calm, no matter what happens. ／无论如何，现
在已经来不及了。Anyhow, it's too late now.

〔相同点〕：都是连词。用于上一分句，表示任何条
件，下一分句常有"都、总、全、就、也"等
词跟它呼应，表示结果不变。Syn. conj. ex-
pressing the idea that something is so under
all conditions, used in the first part of a sentence, and followed by 都，总，全，就 or 也
in the second part to show that the outcome
remains unchanged.

不免 bùmiǎn　难免 nánmiǎn

不免 (unavoidable) 是副词，指免不了的意思。后
面只跟肯定形式。adv. inevitable;
unavoidable. It may be followed only by an
affirmative clause: 这段路太窄，交通不免有
时堵塞。This section of the road is so narrow that
traffic jams are unavoidable now and then.

难免 (hard to avoid) 指不容易避免，后面可以跟
否定词，意思不变。是形容词。adj. hard to
avoid. The meaning remains the same even
when it is followed by a negative: 人总难免不
犯错误。It is hard for people not to make mistakes. ／犯错误是难免的，你认真改了就好

了。It is hard not to make mistakes, but if you correct them conscientiously, everything will be all right. / 人们的看法有时难免带片面性。Sometimes people cannot help being one sided in their views.

〔相同点〕：由于某种原因而导致不如意的结果。常可换用。Syn. referring to unhappy results proceeding from certain causes. They are generally interchangeable.

C

猜测 cāicè　探测 tàncè　推测 tuīcè

猜测 (guess; conjecture; surmise) 是猜想、估计的意思。to guess or reckon: 据我猜测，他多少与这事有关。I surmise that he is more or less involved in the affair. ／考古新发现否定了过去对这个问题的猜测。The new archaeological finds have disproved previous conjectures on this subject.

探测 (survey; sound; probe) 是试探、测量的意思。to survey or sound: 他们去探测水深。They are going to take soundings. ／他们正计划探测这一悬崖的高度。They are planning to gauge the height of this bluff.

推测 (infer; conjecture; guess) 是推断、估量的意思。to infer or assess by a logical process. 根据科学家的推测，世界气候趋于变暖。Scientists have inferred the tendency of global warming. ／猿人化石可以帮助我们推测猿人的生活情况。The fossils of ape-men can help us infer how home erectus lived.

〔相同点〕：都是动词。都含有料想、估计的意思。Syn. v. to presume or reckon.

48

才干 cáigàn　才华 cáihuá
才能 cáinéng　才智 cáizhì

才干 (ability; competence) 着重指办事和实践活动
的能力，如领导、指挥、组织等的能力。
emphasizes the ability to do an efficient job,
practical competence, especially in such areas
as leadership, command and organization: 我
们在工作中增长才干。We improve our competence on the job.

才华 (literary or artistic talent) 着重指表现出的智
慧和能力。多用于科学、文化和艺术方面，
指某人在这些方面所表现出的能力和特长。
intelligence and ability displayed in science,
culture or the arts: 他是一位很有才华的作
家。He is a gifted writer.

才能 (ability; talent) 着重指知识和能力。除用于
比较重要的实践活动方面，还可用于思维活
动方面。说"某人有才能"，主要指某人不仅
有知识，而且有一定的能力。knowledge and
capability, used in relation to practical work
of a certain importance as well as intellectual
activity. If someone is said to have 才能，he
or she is not only knowledgeable but also capable: 他是一个很有才能的工会领导人。He
is a very able trade union leader.

49

才智 (ability and wisdom) 着重指智慧，多用于思维方面。sagacity, often used of intellectual activities：充分发挥年青人的聪明才智。give full play to the intelligence of young people

〔相同点〕：都是名词。都含有较高的思维能力或办事能力。Syn. n. outstanding intellectual or practical ability.

材料 cáiliào　资料 zīliào

材料 (material; data; makings; stuff) 1.着重指未经加工的素材。常说"写作材料""调查材料""汇报材料""档案材料"等。unprocessed raw materials, often used in reference to a writer's preliminary material, the raw data from a survey, data in reports and archives, etc.：关于这个刑事案件，我们已经收集了不少材料。We have collected sufficient data about this criminal case. ／根据现有的材料还不能得出肯定的结论。We cannot draw any definite conclusion from the available data. 2.还指造成物质成品的素材，如木料、水泥、钢材、砖瓦等称为建筑材料。而"资料"不能这样说。the materials that go to make finished products, or building materials such as wood, cement, steel and bricks. 资料 cannot be used in this sense：这些都是盖新房的材料。These are the materials for building the new houses. 3.还指人具备某种才能，因而能够从事某种工作，如"当厂长的材料"。people who have the potential to do a certain kind of work. For example, "He has the makings of a factory director.": 她不是当演员的材料。She does not have the makings of an actress.

资料 (means; data) 1.着重指用作依据的加了工的材料。常说"统计资料""图书资料""历史资料"等。materials that have been processed or can be used as evidence or authority; used in such familiar expressions as statistical data, books and reference materials, historical data, etc.: 这些是我的参考资料。These are my reference materials. 2.还指生产资料，生活资料。如土地、厂房、机器等是生产资料；衣服、食品、住房等是生活资料。而"材料"不能这样说。means of production and livelihood. (Land, workshop, machine, etc. are means of production, whereas clothes, food and houses are means of livelihood.) 材料 cannot be used in this sense: 机器是生产资料。A machine is a means of production.

〔相同点〕：都是名词。都可表示用以制造成品的东西。Syn. n. material from which an artefact can be made or derived.

51

采纳 cǎinà　采取 cǎiqǔ　采用 cǎiyòng

采纳 (accept; adopt) 指接受的意思，着重在"纳"，对象较窄。常见的只是某些抽象事物，如意见、建议、要求等。to accept, often refers to abstract things such as opinions, suggestions or demands, has a limited range of usage: 他的技术革新建议被采纳了。His suggestions for technical innovations have been accepted. / 我们应该采纳群众的建议。We should accept suggestions made by the masses.

采取 (adopt; take) 指认为合适而使用，着重在"取"。对象较广，可以是许多抽象事物如方针、政策、措施、立场、态度、原则等。refers to sth. which is considered appropriate and susceptible of being put to use. It takes a great variety of objects, including abstract nouns such as principle, policy, step, stand, attitude, etc.: 我们应该采取说服教育的办法来帮助他。We should use the method of persuasion and education to help him.

采用 (adopt; use; employ) 指认为合适加以利用，着重在"用"。对象很广，可以是一切抽象的事物，如技术、经验等；也可以是某些具体的事物，如药物、工具、稿件等。refers to sth. which can be used because of its suitability. The emphasis is on use. It can take a great variety of objects ranging from abstract things such as technique and experience to tangible things such as medicine, implements, documents, etc.: 我们工厂采用新技术。Our factory adopts new techniques.

〔相同点〕：都是动词。都表示可以采用的意思。Syn. v. to adopt.

参加 cānjiā 参与 cānyù 加入 jiārù

参加 (join; take part in; attend) 指加入某种组织或某种活动。使用范围较广，可以表示加入某个集团，如党、团、队伍、协会等，还可表示参与某种活动如工作、讨论、典礼等。to join an organization such as a party, a league, the army, an association. It also refers to participation in various activities including work, discussion, and ceremonies: 这件事你也来参加点意见吧！Come and give us your opinions on this matter too, won't you? ／他父母也参加了他的大学毕业典礼。His parents also attended his college graduation ceremony.

参与 (participate in; have a hand) (也写作"参预") 专指参加并一起活动。使用范围较窄，它的宾语常见的只是某些表示集体活动的词，如"工作、领导、运动、谈话"等，而不

53

能用于"革命"、"劳动"等。to join in sth. and to take part in activities together with others. Its range of usage is limited. Its object is usually a group activity — work, leadership, movement or talk. It cannot be used to mean taking part in revolution or labor：他参与制定规划。He participated in the drawing up of the plan.

加入 (**add; mix; put in; join; accede to**) 指参加进去，即指参加并成为其中一员。使用范围较窄，它的宾语常见的只有某些表示组织的词，如党、团、协会、行列、组织等。to join in an activity or a certain organization, to become a member thereof. Its usage is limited. It is often followed by terms referring to organizations (party, league, association, rank, etc.)：他加入了作家协会。She has joined the writers' union association.

〔相同点〕：都是动词。都有投身进去的意思。Syn. v. to participate.

仓促 cāngcù　匆匆 cōngcōng
匆忙 cōngmáng

仓促 (**hurriedly; hastily; all of a sudden**) （也写作"仓卒"或"仓猝"）着重指时间不充足。可以形容时间，也可形容行动。implies lack of time; it can refer to both time and actions: 他走得很仓促。He left in a hurry. / 不要仓促下结论。Don't jump to conclusions.

匆匆 (hurriedly) 多指急速草率，一般形容行动，如"来去匆匆"。to do things carelessly and in a hurry. It usually describes actions, as in 来去匆匆 (pay a flying visit): 他匆匆地洗完脸就走了。He gave his face a hurried wash and then left.

匆忙 (hastily; in a hurry) 着重指急急忙忙，一般只形容行动，可以说成"匆匆忙忙"。in a hurry. Generally it refers to action only. One can say 匆匆忙忙: 他匆匆忙忙吃了几口东西，又回车间去了。He bolted down a few mouthfuls of food and hurried back to the workshop.

〔相同点〕：都是形容词。表示做事急急忙忙，时间不充足。Syn. adj. to do sth. in a hurry because of lack of time.

曾经 céngjīng   已经 yǐjīng

曾经 (formerly, once) 表示从前有过某种行为或情况，事情已结束了。在句中常与"过"搭配。indicates that a certain action or situation began and finished in the past, and has no connection with the present. 过 often appears in the same clause：几年前我曾经见过她一面。I met her once several years ago. ／他曾参加过第一次世界大战。He took part in the First World War.

已经 (already) 表示事情在以前的时间发生，但不一定结束。在句中常跟"了"搭配。indicates that an action or situation began in the past but may not have ended yet. It is often combined with 了：这样已经不错了。It is good enough as it is. ／天已经黑了。It is already dark. ／这点前面已经说过了。This has been dealt with above.

〔相同点〕：都是副词。表示事情发生的时间是在以前。Syn. adv. indicating that sth. happened at a previous time.

产生 chǎnshēng 发生 fāshēng

产生 (produce; engender; emerge; come into being) 指从已有事物中生出新的事物，适用范围较广，可以是具体的，也可以是抽象的。refers to new things arising from existing ones. It has a very wide range of usage and may refer either to abstract or to concrete things：实践使我们的认识产生了新的飞跃。Practice has brought about a new leap in our knowledge. ／产生很好的结果 produce good results ／这个事

件产生很大影响。This event has exerted a great influence.

发生 (happen; occur; take place) 指原来没有的事出现了，适用对象一般是抽象的。indicates that sth. which did not exist before has come into being. It usually refers to abstract things: 那里发生了强烈地震。A violent earthquake occurred there. / 这里发生了巨大的变化。Tremendous changes have taken place here. / 故事发生在 1962 年秋天。The story takes place in the autumn of 1962.

〔相同点〕: 都是动词。都有"出现"的意思。Syn. v. to occur; to arise or to appear.

场所 chǎngsuǒ 场合 chǎnghé

场所 (place; arena) 活动的处所的意思，指具体的地点，许多人或生物能聚集的地方或处所，使用范围较小。a specific place of action where people, etc. gather. Its usage is limited: 公共场所 a public place / 娱乐场所 place of recreation / 蚊蝇孳生的场所 a breeding ground of flies and mosquitoes

场合 (occasion; situation) 指一定的时间、地点、情况的意思，使用范围较大。refers to a definite time, place and situation, and has a wider range of usage: 外交场合 a diplomatic occa-

57

〔相同点〕：都是名词，都有地点的意思。Syn. n. a place; a site.

陈列 chénliè   陈设 chénshè

陈列 (display; set out; exhibit) 着重表示按一定条理排列、展出、供人参观，对象常是模型、纪念品、文物、展览品等。to arrange things such as models, souvenirs, historicl relics and exhibits, and display them in good and pleasing order: 玻璃柜里陈列着各种矿物标本。Specimens of various minerals are on display in showcases.

陈设 (display; set out; arrange) 着重指按一定审美观点摆设、布置，供人观看、欣赏，对象常是家庭用品等。to arrange things, such as household articles so as to appeal to people's aesthetic sense: 屋子里陈设着几件工艺品。There are some ornaments arranged about the room. ／ 他屋子的陈设既朴素又大方。His room is furnished simply and in good taste.

〔相同点〕：都是动词。都有把物品摆出来供人看的意思，对象是商品、工艺品等。Syn. v. to put articles on display. These may be commodities, handicrafts, etc.

沉寂 chénjì　沉默 chénmò

沉寂 (quiet; still) 指十分寂静的意思，常用来描写环境状态。extremely quiet, often used to describe the environment or one's surroundings：沉寂的深夜 in the still of the night ／傍晚，暴风雨已经过去，四周开始沉寂下来。By evening the storm had subsided and all was quiet.

沉默 (reticent; taciturn; uncommunicative; silent) 指不说话的意思，着重指人的性格，表示不爱说笑。speechless, used especially of a taciturn or reticent character：沉默寡言的人 a reticent person ／他沉默了一会儿又继续说下去。After a moment's silence, he went on speaking.

〔相同点〕：都是形容词。表示没有声音、很安静的意思。Syn. adj. silent.

陈旧 chénjiù　破旧 pòjiù

陈旧 (outmoded; obsolete; old fashioned; out of date) 指旧的、过时的意思，是因年深月久而不新了，它可以用来形容具体事物，也可形容思想和观点落后于时代。old, outmoded, used to describe concrete things as well as ideas and mentality: 这是陈旧的观点。 This is an outmoded notion. / 这些是陈旧的设备。 This equipment is obsolete.

破旧 (old and shabby; worn-out; dilapidated) 指破损、陈旧的意思，它不但表明是不新的，而还表明是破损、破烂或不完整的，它一般用来修饰具体事物，象房舍、衣物等。shabby, damaged, worn-out, generally used to describe concrete things, such as a house or clothes: 他戴一顶破旧的草帽。 He wears a shabby straw hat. / 他只有破旧的家具。 He only has old battered furniture.

〔相同点〕：都是形容词。都指物体因时间久而有所变样、变质、亏损的意思。 Syn. adj. indicating that sth. has deteriorated with the passage of time.

沉思 chénsī　深思 shēnsī　寻思 xúnsi

沉思 (ponder; meditate; be lost in thought) 指精神贯注地思考，重在表现思考时的精神贯注。 to be lost in thought, refers in particular to concentrated thought: 为了这个问题，她坐在那里沉思了好久。 She sat there pondering over the problem for a long time.

深思 (think deeply about; ponder deeply over) 指深刻地思考，重在表现思考程度的深刻、深

入。to think deeply. The emphasis is on the depth of thinking: 这个问题值得我们深思。This matter gives us much food for thought. / 这难道不值得深思吗？Is this not worth pondering?

寻思 (think sth. over again and again) 指反复地思考的意思，多着眼于思考的程度和次数，常用于口语。to revolve sth. in one's mind, often used in spoken language, and mainly refers to frequency and depth of thinking: 我正寻思着你有无时间，下班后咱们一起吃晚饭。I am wondering whether you have time for us to have dinner together after work.

〔相同点〕：都是动词。都常作谓语，含有注意力集中，仔细思考的意思。Syn. v. generally used as predicate, to concentrate one's mind on sth. or to think of sth. carefully.

沉着 chénzhuó　冷静 lěngjìng

沉着 (cool-headed; composed; steady; calm) 一般指人的性格，不慌不忙。indicates that one is calm and collected: 我们应该沉着应战。We should meet the attack calmly. / 他沉着勇敢。He is brave and steady.

冷静 (sober; calm) 原指冷落、寂静。现在引申义一般指沉着而不感情用事，常说"头脑冷

61

静"。The root meaning is unfrequented and silent. The current, extended meaning is cool and collected, not apt to act impetuously. It is often used in the collocation 头脑冷静 (cool-headed): 他的话使我冷静下来。His words sobered me.

〔相同点〕：都是形容词。都指人在遇到某一件事情时，不慌不忙，不急躁。Syn. adj. indicating that one is not worried or vexed by circumstances.

成果 chéngguǒ　结果 jiéguǒ　效果 xiàoguǒ

成果 **(achievement; fruit; gain; positive result)** 指工作或事业的收获，好的结果，是褒义词，常用大、小、伟大、丰硕、巨大等词来形容。good result or achievement in one's or some cause; an approbatory term, often used with adjectives such as big, small, great, bountiful, tremendous, etc.: 会谈取得一些成果。The talks have yielded some positive results. / 每一粒粮食都是辛勤劳动的成果。Every single grain is the fruit of hard work. / 这是一项科研成果。This is an achievement of scientific research.

结果 **(result; outcome)** 1.指在一定阶段，事物发展所达到的最后状态，是中性词，兼指好的和坏的，可指行为的结局，也可指各种事物发展变化的结果。indicates that, at a certain stage, things have reached their final state. A neutral term, it denotes the result, good or bad, of an action, or of a development or change in a thing or object: 这样瞎吵下去不会有什么结果。Squabbling like this won't get you anywhere. / 经过一番争论，结果他还是让步了。After a heated argument he finally gave in. 2.也可做动词。有杀的意思。when used as a verb, to kill: 他结果了这条狗的性命。He killed the dog.

效果 (effect; effectiveness; result) 中性词。但以好的结果居多，坏的结果较少。可以用好、坏、大、小来形容，范围较窄，常指主观上所作所为的结果。a neutral term; it tends nevertheless to be used of good results rather than bad. 好，坏，大，小 can be used to describe 效果, referring to the outcome of behavior or actions: 试验治虫药的效果。Test the effectiveness of the insecticide. / 首次演出效果好。The first performance went off well.

〔相同点〕：都是名词。都表示事物发展到最后而产生的情况的意思。Syn. n. the consequence of a development.

成绩 chéngjì　成就 chéngjiù
成效 chéngxiào

成绩 (result; achievement; success) 指工作或学习的收获，一般用于具体的小的方面。是中性词。the result of work or study relating to some small, concrete aspect. It is neutral in tone: 他们的工作是有成绩的。Their work has been fruitful. ／ 在这次比赛中，他取得了良好的成绩。He did very well in the tournament.

成就 (achievement; accomplishment; attainment; success) 指事业上的成绩，是褒义词。an approbatory term; it refers to achievements in cause or important undertaking: 他是一个很有成就的科学家。He is an accomplished scientist. ／ 这部小说的艺术成就是公认的。The artistic merits of this novel are universally recognized.

成效 (effect; result) 指功效、效果，是褒义词。an approbatory term, efficacy or good result: 成效显著 produce a marked effect ／ 初见成效 win initial success ／ 这种药连着吃下去一定会有成效。This medicine will be effective if you keep on taking it.

〔相同点〕：都是名词。表示已经取得的收获或效果。Syn. n. results or effects achieved.

64

持续 chíxù   继续 jìxù

持续 (continue; be sustained) 指延续不断的意思，着重指动作行为或某一事情的出现，中间没有间歇。to continue without stopping, refers mainly to an action or a thing which, having once begun, goes on without interruption: 两国间的文化交流已经持续了一千多年。 Cultural interchange between the two countries has gone on for more than a thousand years. / 使原油产量持续稳定上升 keep up a steady increase in the output of crude oil

继续 (continue; go on) 指连下去，延长下去，着重指前一动作完成了，后一动作又接上来，中间可以有间歇，也可以没有间歇。to keep on doing sth. without stopping, refers mainly to an action which, upon completion, is followed by another. There may or may not be a pause in between: 会议继续到深夜。 The meeting went on till late at night. / 有些问题仍需继续研究。 Some problems require further study. / 他们第二天继续会谈。 They resumed the talks the next day.

〔相同点〕：都是动词。都含有接连、延续下去的意思。Syn. v. indicating continuation or succession.

65

充分 chōngfèn　充足 chōngzú

充分 **(full; ample; abundant)** 有尽量达到最大的限度或完全达到最大限度的意思。用于比较抽象的事物，如知识、信心等。trying as far as possible to reach, or having reached, the maximum degree; used to describe abstract things such as knowledge or confidence: 我们有充分理由相信这消息是可靠的。We have every reason to believe that the news is true.

充足 **(adequate; sufficient; abundant; ample)** 指多到能满足需要的意思，用于比较具体的事物，如光线、空气、经费等。sufficient to satisfy all requirements; used of concrete things such as light, air or funds: 这里阳光充足。It is full of sunshine here. ／ 这所学院的教育经费是充足的。The college has sufficient funds for education.

〔相同点〕：都是形容词。都有足够的意思。Syn. adj. to be sufficient.

重复 chóngfù　反复 fǎnfù

重复 **(repeat; duplicate)** 指照原来样子又来一次，着重照原样，可以是一次之后再来一次，也可以是多次。不能用来指性情。indicates that what has been done before is repeated once or many times, not used to refer to mood: 避免不必要的重复 avoid unnecessary repetition ／ 任何历史现象都不会是简单的重复。 No historical phenomenon is a mere repetition of the past.

反复 (repeatedly; again and again; over and over again; reversal; relapse) 1.指一遍又一遍，多次重复，不一定照原样，而且总是多次的。除有翻来覆去的意思之外，还有为了求深入，所以一而再，再而三地进行的意思。 indicates that sth. happens again and again or is repeated many times, although not necessarily in the original manner. It may also signify that a matter is probed deeply, to which end repeated thought, action, etc. is necessary: 反复思考 think a lot about something ／ 这个计划是经过反复讨论而产生的。 The plan was born out of repeated discussions. ／ 你的病虽然好了，可要防止反复。 You are well now, but mind you don't have a relapse. 2.还可用来指性情，这时有贬义。 used in a derogatory sense to describe a fickle, changeable state or disposition: 那家伙反复无常。 That guy is always chopping and changing.

〔相同点〕：都是形容词。都含有不止一次的意思。 Syn. adj. not only once.

67

充满 chōngmǎn 弥漫 mímàn

充满 (**full of; brimming with; permeated with**) 是中性词。表示填满和充分具有的意思，使用范围较广，可用于具体事物和抽象事物。a neutral term, to be full or in full possession of sth. It has a wide range of usage, and may refer to either concrete or abstract things: 这首诗里充满乐观主义的精神。The poem is imbued with a spirit of optimism. 大厅里充满了孩子们的笑声。The hall resounded with the laughter of children.

弥漫 (**fill the air; spread all over the place**) 是中性词。表示充满和遍布的意思，一般适用于具体事物。a neutral term, generally applied to concrete things: 烟雾弥漫 heavy with smoke

〔相同点〕：都是动词。表示布满的意思。Syn. v. to spread everywhere.

出生 chūshēng 诞生 dànshēng

出生 (**be born**) 是中性词。指胎儿从母体中分离出来，可以用于任何人。a neutral term denoting the act of birth, may be used of any person: 他出生在一个农民家庭里。He was born into a peasant family.

68

诞生 (be born; come into being; emerge) 是褒义词，一般用于领袖和有重大贡献的人。有时也用于事物，因为这些事物的产生有着重大意义，"出生"没有这种用法。approbatory term, used of the birth of leaders or people who have made major achievements, sometimes refers to the emergence of events of great significance. 出生 does not share this meaning：他在斗争的烈火中诞生。He emerged from the flames of struggle. ／新中国的诞生是一个非常重大的事件。The birth of China is a very important event.

〔相同点〕：都是动词。指人生下来的意思。Syn. v. to be born.

传授 chuánshòu　教授 jiàoshòu

传授 (pass on — knowledge, skill, etc.; impart) 指把知识、技术教给别人的意思，使用范围较广，适用于校内外，适用的对象较多。to impart knowledge and technique to others. It has a wide range of usage, and occurs in both academic and no-academic contexts, with reference to various matters：传授技术 pass on one's technical skill ／向青年传授培育良种的经验。teach young people how to cultivate good strains of seeds

教授 (instruct; teach; professor) 一般用于学校，主要指教师把知识教给学生。indicates the transmission of knowledge by a teacher to students, generally in a formal academic context: 教授历史 lecture on history 2.也可作名词用。"传授"不能做名词。unlike 传授, it may also be used as a noun meaning professor: 他是教授。He is a professor.

〔相同点〕：都是动词。含有将道理、知识、方法等教给人的意思。Syn. v. to pass on ideas, knowledge, methods, etc. to others.

垂死 chuísǐ　　垂危 chuíwēi

垂死 (moribund; dying) 更强调接近死亡，还可以形容政治制度等的没落。an emphatic expression meaning "on the brink of death". It can also describe the decline of a political system, etc.: 谁也无法挽救他的垂死的命运。Nobody can save him from his approaching doom.

垂危 (critically ill; in mortal danger) 着重指生命危险，还可以形容民族、国家的危亡。in mortal peril; it may also be applied to peoples or countries in jeopardy: 他从来没想到自己是一个垂危的病人。It never occurred to him that he was critically ill. ／为了挽救这个垂危的民族，他们曾经顽强地斗争不息。In order to save the nation from danger, they kept on struggling hard.

〔相同点〕：都是形容词。表示临近死亡的意思。
Syn. adj. approaching one's death.

错误 cuòwù　过失 guòshi

错误 (wrong; mistaken; erroneous; mistake; error; blunder) 指不正确，与客观实际不符合的意思，是就事物的性质而言，跟"正确"相对。incorrect, incompatible with reality; it refers to the nature of a matter and is the opposite of 正确 (correct)：这是错误的结论。This is a wrong conclusion. ／他犯错误了。He committed an error.

过失 (fault; slip; error; crime; offence) 指因疏忽而犯的错误，是就行为而言。an error committed by accident or inadvertence; refers to an action：这件事是大家的责任，并不完全是他一个人的过失。Everybody should take responsibility for this; it is not all his fault. ／过失杀人 man-slaughter

〔相同点〕：都是名词。表示不正确，有差错的意思。Syn. n. not right; at fault.

71

D

答应 dāying   允许 yǔnxǔ   准许 zhǔnxǔ

答应 (promise; comply with; agree) 对别人的要求表示同意。一般不用于自己对自己。to agree to other people's demands. The expression cannot be applied to a promise made to oneself: 我答应来。I promise to come. ／我答应给她一个答复。I promised her a reply. ／学校领导一口答应了我们的要求。The school administration readily complied with our request.

允许 (permit; allow) 泛指同意、许可。to permit or consent: 不允许任何破坏纪律的现象存在。No breach of discipline is permitted. ／请允许我代表全厂职工向你们致谢。Allow me to thank you on behalf of our factory.

准许 (permit; allow) 着重指批准、同意别人的要求，常用于上对下。to approve or to acquiesce to another's request, often used in reference to permission granted by a person at a higher level to one at a lower level: 领导准许我们去试一试。The leader permits us to have a try.

〔相同点〕：都是动词。表示同意别人做某种事情的

72

意思。Syn. v. to agree that sb. should do sth.

达到 dádào　到达 dàodá

达到 **(achieve; attain)** 多用于抽象活动。宾语常是抽象的名词，如理想、目的、阶段、水平等。chiefly used in an abstract sense. Its objects are abstract nouns, such as ideal, destination, stage, level, etc.: 达到世界先进水平 come up to the highest international standards ／ 达到目的 achieve (attain) the goal

到达 **(arrive; get to; reach)** 多用于具体行动。宾语多是表示处所的名词如北京，机场等。often used to describe concrete activity. The object is an expression of place, such as Beijing, the airport, etc.: 代表团于今晨到达北京。The delegation arrived in Beijing this morning. ／火车一点钟到达这里。The train gets here at one o'clock.

〔相同点〕：都是动词。表示到了目的地。Syn. v. to reach a destination.

打量 dǎliang　端详 duānxiang

打量 **(measure with the eye; look sb. up and down; size up; think; reckon; suppose)** 1.指观察人的衣着、外貌或环境等。多用于口语。to ob-

73

serve surroundings or sb.'s dress, appearance, etc., often used in spoken language：门卫上下打量着那个陌生人。The sentry looked the stranger up and down. 2.还有认为、估计的意思。to deem; to estimate：你打量她这点事都干不了吗？Do you deem her incapable of doing little job like that?

端详 (look sb. up and down) 仔细地看某个人的意思。多用于书面语体。to scrutinize sb. carefully, often used in written language：我端详了他半天，也没认出是谁。I could not recognized who he is although I had looked him up and down quite a while.

〔相同点〕：都是动词。都有观察、看的意思。Syn. v. to observe; to look.

打算 dǎsuan　盘算 pánsuan

打算 (plan; intend) 1.表示一般地考虑、计划。多用于口语。to consider or plan to do sth. in a general way, often used in spoken language：代表团打算去上海访问。The delegation plans to visit Shanghai. ／他打算当教师。He intends to become a teacher. 2.还有名词用法，指事先的想法。also used as a noun, meaning a preconceived plan：各有各的打算。Each has a plan of his or her own.

盘算 (calculate; figure; plan) 常指心里反复打算，用于费脑筋的事情上。to calculate sth.; turning it over and over in one's mind, used in connection with knotty problems: 我们盘算了一下，产量将增加百分之五。We figured that the output would increase by five percent.

〔相同点〕：都是动词。表示事先考虑、计划的意思。Syn. v. to consider or plan sth. in advance.

大胆 dàdǎn　勇敢 yǒnggǎn

大胆 (bold; daring; audacious) 着重指有勇气，没有什么顾虑，一般用于对事情的态度上，是中性词。having courage, and no misgivings, a neutral term normally used to describe an attitude towards sth.: 大胆的改革 a bold reform

勇敢 (brave; courageous) 指不怕危险和困难，有胆量。着重在无所畏惧，表示一种好的品质，是褒义词。braving danger and difficulties, and having guts; it emphasizes fearlessness. It is an approbatory term, implying fine qualities of character: 勤劳、勇敢的人民 a brave and industrious people ／ 勇敢善战 courageous and skilful in battle

〔相同点〕：都是形容词。都表示有勇气。Syn. adj.

75

having courage.

带 (take; bring) 指随身携带、拿着。to take along sth. with one: 别忘了带雨衣。Don't forget to take your raincoat along. ／请人带个话给她。Ask somebody to take a message to her. ／这本书我明天给你带来。I will bring you the book tomorrow.

戴 (put on; wear) 指放在头、面、胸、臂、手等处。宾语常是帽子、眼镜、耳环，手表等。to put sth. on one's head, neck, chest, arm, hand, etc. The object is usually hat, glasses, earring, watch, etc.: 戴上手套 put on one's gloves ／戴眼镜 wear glasses

〔相同点〕：都是动词，表示放在身上。Syn. v. to have sth. on or about one's person.

耽搁 (stopover; stay) 是拖延或停留的意思。宾语一般是指时间。It means to delay, or to remain. Its object is usually a time expression: 我去北京途中可能在上海耽搁一下。I may have a stopover at Shanghai on my way to Beijing. ／我不打算在这里耽搁很久。I won't be here

76

for long. ／ 一分钟也不能耽搁。 Not a single minute is to be lost.

耽误 (delay; hold up) 是因拖延或错过时机而误事的意思。没有"停留"的意思。宾语可指时间，也可指事情。to cause mishaps or delays in work because of procrastination or missing opportunities. It does not mean to make a stopover. The object can be either time or a thing: 耽误了整个工程 hold up (or delay) the whole project ／ 她从不为个人事情耽误工作。She never allows her private affairs to interfere with work.

〔相同点〕：都是动词。都有拖延、不得前进的意思。当它们的宾语是"时间"时，可以通用。Syn. v. to delay; to be or make unable to go on any longer. When the object is a time expression, they can be used interchangeably.

担任 dānrèn　担当 dāndāng

担任 (assume the office of; hold the post of) 指做某种工作或任某个职务的意思。对象常是一般的任务。to do certain work or assume a certain post. The object is generally an ordinary assignment or task: 担任会议主席 take the chair ／请他们担任校外辅导员。Invite them to be advisers on after-school activities.

77

担当 (take on; undertake; assume) 指接受并负起责任来，常跟"重任"配合。to agree to do sth. and take charge of it; often used of heavy responsibility：无论多么艰巨的任务，他都敢担当。No matter how arduous the task is, he dares to take it on.

〔相同点〕：都是动词。都有负责、承担的意思。Syn. v. to be responsible for; or to undertake.

担心 dānxīn 担忧 dānyōu

担心 (worry; feel anxious) 语义较轻，表示放心不下。indicates that one feels ill at ease about sth.：快给他写信，免得他担心。Write to him at once so as to set his mind at rest. ／我担心找不着座位，如果现在我们还不去的话。I am worried that we won't be able to find seats, if we don't go right away.

担忧 (worry; be anxious) 不仅放心不下，而且忧虑、发愁。一般不带宾语。to be worried and to feel anxiety and grave concern about the fate of sb. or sth. As a rule, it has no object：我们为人类的生存环境担忧。We are concerned about the environment in which human beings live.

〔相同点〕：都是动词。表示不放心，一般用于可能出现的不如意的情况。Syn. v. to be ill at

78

ease, generally used in connection with unhappy circumstances which are likely to occur.

诞辰 dànchén　生日 shēngri

诞辰 (birthday) 用于书面语体，带庄重、尊敬色彩。used in written language; conveys a serious, respectful tone：1981 年 9 月 25 日是鲁迅先生诞辰一百周年纪念日。September 25, 1981 was the 100th anniversary of Lu Xun's birth.

生日 (birthday) 适用于口语。可以用于比喻。common in spoken language, may be used metaphorically：七月一日是中国共产党的生日。July 1 is the birthday of the Communist Party of China.

〔相同点〕：都是名词。一般是指人出生的日子或每年满周岁的那一天。Syn. n. the day one was born; anniversary of someone's birth.

但是 dànshì　可是 kěshì　然而 rán'ér

但是 (but; yet; nevertheless) 常用在书面语和口语里。语气较重。used quite often in both written and spoken language, conveys a strong adversative sense：他早已年过七十，但是他精神仍然很旺盛。He is well over

79

seventy, but he remains healthy and vigorous.

可是 (but; yet; however) 多用在口语体。often used in spoken language: 他们劳动了一天，虽然很累，可是都很愉快。They were tired out after the day's work, but they all felt happy.

然而 (yet; but; however) 多用在书面语体。often used in written language: 试验失败了多次，然而他们并不灰心。Time after time the experiment failed, but they did not lose heart.

〔相同点〕：都是连词。常与"虽然"搭配。多用在后半句，或下句开头，表示前后语义的转折。Syn. conj. used in combination with 虽然, and often placed in the second half of a sentence, or at the beginning of the following sentence, to mark a transition or a turning point in meaning.

道歉 dàoqiàn　抱歉 bàoqiàn

道歉 (apologize; make an apology) 指承认错误，向人表示歉意。不能用"很"或"非常"等程度副词修饰。to admit one's mistakes and make an apology. Adverbs of degree like 很 (very) and 非常 (extremely) cannot be used with this expression: 他因在课堂上发出喧哗声而向老师道歉。He apologized to his teacher for making noises in class.

抱歉 (be sorry; feel apologetic; regret) 是觉得对不起别人，可以用"很""非常"等程度副词修饰。used when one is sorry for having done sth. wrong. 很，非常 and similar adverbs of degree can be used as modifiers：叫你久等了，很抱歉。Very sorry to have kept you waiting.

〔相同点〕：都是动词。都有觉得对不起别人而心里不安的意思。Syn. v. indicating that one feels sorry towards others and disturbed at heart.

抵偿 dǐcháng　赔偿 péicháng
补偿 bǔcháng

抵偿 (compensate for; give sth. by way of payment for) 指用价值相等的事物来偿还。着重于"抵"，就是顶替、抵消的意思。to compensate for a loss with sth. of equal value. The key element is 抵 (offset), i.e. to counteract the effect of the losses：抵偿性命 pay for one's life／用房屋抵偿 mortgage a house

赔偿 (compensate; pay for; make good) 指偿还别人受到的损失。着重在"赔"，即偿还他人的损失。to compensate for losses suffered by sb. The key element is 赔 (to pay back others for the losses)：保留要求赔偿的权利 reserve the right to demand compensation for losses／照

价赔偿 compensate according to the value

补偿 (compensate; make up) 指把损失的部分补足。to make up the portion which is lost or damaged: 补偿差额 make up a deficiency / 补偿所受的损失 compensate sb. for losses suffered.

〔相同点〕: 都是动词。表示弥补损失的意思。Syn. v. to compensate losses sustained.

抵挡 dǐdǎng　阻挡 zǔdǎng

抵挡 (keep out; resist) 指挡住压力、抵抗的意思。只指人或物，不指事情。to resist pressure; refers only to a person or thing, not to an event or business: 抵挡风寒 keep out the wind and cold / 抵挡洪水 keep the flood in check

阻挡 (stop; prevent; stand in the way) 指阻止。适用范围广。可指人，也可指事物。可以是具体的，也可以是抽象的。to hold back or to prevent. It has a wide range of usage, and can refer to people or things, concrete or abstract: 不可阻挡的历史潮流 an irresistible historical trend

〔相同点〕: 都是动词。表示阻拦，挡住的意思。Syn. v. to obstruct; to stem.

抵制 dǐzhì　抵抗 dǐkàng

抵制 (resist; boycott) 指阻止有害的事物，使它不能侵入或发生作用。着重指"约束""阻止"，多用于非武力的行为。to prevent harmful things from approaching or taking effect. The emphasis is on restraining or stopping. It is mostly used of non-violent acts：抵制错误领导 boycott erroneous leadership

抵抗 (resist; stand up to) 指用力量制止对方的进攻。着重指反抗。多用于军事方面。to check by force an offensive launched by an opponent. The emphasis is on putting up resistance. It is often used in a military sense：我们应当增强对疾病的抵抗力。We should increase our power to resist diseases. / 奋起抵抗 rise in resistance

〔相同点〕：都是动词，也可以是名词。表示反抗敌对力量。Syn. v.; n. to resist hostile forces.

动员 dòngyuán　发动 fādòng

动员 (mobilize; arouse) 1.着重指用说服、教育、或号召等方式启发人行动起来。to arouse people to action by means of persuasion, education or appeals：他作一番动员。He gives a

83

mobilization talk. 2.还有行动的意思。to act; to take action：整个医院都动员起来，抢救伤员。The whole hospital was mobilized for the emergency treatment of wounded personnel.

发动 (call into action; mobilize; arouse; launch) 1. 着重指宣传、鼓动，使全面行动起来的意思。对象较窄，一般只指群众、运动。to arouse people to take full-scale action by the use of propaganda and agitation. Its usage is rather limited and it can only refer to masses of people, campaigns, etc.：发动群众 arouse the masses to action 2.还指使开始的意思。also means to set sth. in motion：发动机器 set a machine going／发动战争 launch (unleash) a war

〔**相同点**〕：都是动词。表示启发人行动起来，自愿做某种事情的意思。Syn. v. to arouse people to action or to do sth. of their own accord.

度过 dùguò　渡过 dùguò

度过 (spend; pass) 是经历过、生活过的意思。通常用于时间方面。to have experienced a certain aspect of life, often used in relation to a period of time：他在农村度过童年。He spent his childhood in the countryside.

渡过 (cross; tide over; pull through) 常用于过江河

84

湖海。指从这岸过到那岸的意思。有时也用于通过困难、难关等方面。often used in connection with river (lake, sea) crossings. Sometimes it means to tide over a difficulty or crisis: 渡过难关 tide over a difficulty / 他们强行渡过这条河。They forced their way across the river.

〔相同点〕：都是动词。表示经历过或通过一段时间的意思。Syn. v. to have experienced or spent a period of time.

顿时 dùnshí　立刻 lìkè

顿时 (immediately; at once; forthwith) 指很快、一下子的意思。多用在书面语体，很少用于口语。very quickly; suddenly, often used in written language, seldom in spoken language: 喜讯传来，人们顿时欢呼起来。The people broke into cheers as soon as they heard the good news.

立刻 (immediately; at once; right away) 指马上的意思，表示紧接某个时候。使用范围较广，既可用于口语，也可用于书面语体。at once or immediately after a certain point of time, used in both written and spoken language: 我立刻就去。I will go right away.

〔相同点〕：都是副词。表示时间很短的意思。Syn.

85

adv. a very brief elapse of time.

多少 duōshao 几 jǐ

多少 **(how many; how much)** 1.使用范围较广，可以用于较大的数目，也可以用于较小的数目，后面可以直接跟上名词。used to describe large or small numbers of things, may be followed by a noun. This expression has a wide range of usage: 这个班有多少学生？How many pupils are there in this class? 2.表示不定的数量。used to express an indefinite quantity: 这种药我每次吃多少？How much of the medicine do I take each time? / 我跟你说过不知多少次了。I don't know how many times I have told you about this. / 不论有多少困难，都不能阻止我们前进。No matter what the difficulties, nothing can stop our advance.

几 **(how many; a few; several; some)** 使用范围较窄，除了用于"十、百、千、万、亿"之前，一般用于十以内的数目。后面一般要跟上量词，不可直接跟名词。refers as a rule to a number below ten, may also be placed before ten, hundred, thousand, ten thousand and a hundred million. It is followed by a measure word, never directly by a noun. The range of usage of the term is limited: 几天可以完工？

How many days will it take to finish the project? / 我要说几句话。 I want to say a few words. / 这里有十几本中文书。 There are a dozen or so Chinese books here. / 今天有几十个人来参加这个会。 Today dozens of people came to attend the meeting.

〔相同点〕：表示询问数目，也可以表示不定数目。有时通用。 Syn. used in asking how many and may also indicate an indefinite number. Sometimes used interchangeably.

夺取 duóqǔ   掠夺 lüèduó

夺取 **(capture; seize; wrest)** 是用武力强取的意思，是中性词。对象可以是具体的，也可以是抽象的事物。 a neutral term, to take by force or by power. Its object can be concrete or abstract：夺取敌人的据点 capture an enemy stronghold.

掠夺 **(plunder; rob; pillage)** 是公开抢劫的意思，是贬义词，对象往往是具体的财物。 a pejorative term, it means to rob sb. of sth. publicly. Its object is usually property in some form：封建统治者，长期在这里掠夺矿产资源。 The feudal rulers had plundered mineral resources over a long period of time. / 这些强盗掠夺成性。 Depredation has become second nature to these robbers.

〔相同点〕：都是动词。表示以势力强夺的意思。

Syn. v. to capture sth. by force.

E

恶果 èguǒ   后果 hòuguǒ

恶果 (evil consequence; disastrous effect) 是贬义词。专指坏的结果和下场。程度比"后果"重。pejorative term; bad result. It is stronger than 后果：有些国家不注意环境保护，对人民健康已经造成了严重的恶果。Some countries do not pay attention to environmental protection, which has disastrous result for people's health.

后果 (consequence; aftermath) 是中性词。有时指将产生的结果，但常用来表示坏的结果。a neutral term, refers usually but not necessarily to a bad result：检查制度不严，会造成严重的后果。A lax checking system may have serious consequences. ／ 后果不堪设想。 The consequences would be too ghastly to contemplate. ／ 承担后果 accept the consequences

〔相同点〕：都是名词。表示事情的不好的结果。Syn. n. the bad result of sth.

89

遏止 èzhǐ　遏制 èzhì　制止 zhìzhǐ

遏止 **(check; hold back)** 用强力阻止。对象常是力量强大、来势迅猛的事物。to stop sth. or sb. by force. Its object is usually sth. which moves rapidly and violently: 这是不可遏止的洪流。This is an irresistible tide.

遏制 **(keep within limits; contain)** 指尽力控制、不让其发展的意思。对象常是自己某种情绪（喜、怒、哀、乐）等，有时是敌人或某种力量。to do all one can to bring sth. under control and prevent its further development. The object is usually one's own emotion—joy, anger, grief or happiness, sometimes an enemy or other force: 遏制愤怒的情绪 check one's anger / 遏制的政策 policy of containment

制止 **(check; curb; prevent)** 指强迫使之停止，不允许继续行动。使用的范围较广，可以用于较大的对象或较小的对象。to bring a halt to sth. by force, not allowing it to continue its action. The object may be great or small: 制止流沙 stop sand from drifting / 制止通货膨胀 check (halt) inflation / 我做了一个手势，制止他再说下去。I made a gesture to stop him from saying any more.

〔相同点〕：都是动词。有阻止的意思。Syn. v. to

stop or to prevent sth. from happening.

二 èr   两 liǎng

二和两有以下区别：二(two) and 两(two) differ in the following six ways:

二 **(two, different)** 1. 用于读数目字时，用"二"。二 is the Chinese name of the numeral 2; 2. 用于表序数时，放在"第、初"后面时，用"二"。to form the ordinal number, 二 is used after 第 or 初; 3. 用于小数和分数时用"二"。二 is used in decimals and fractions; 4. 在多位数字中用"二"。In numerals of more than two digits, 二 is used (but see 两 1); 5. 在传统度量衡单位（尺、寸、斗、升、斤、里、亩）前，多半用"二"。二 is used with traditional units of weight and measure (尺、寸、斗、升、斤、里、亩); 6. 一般不直接用于名词前，当你说"二门""二队"时，那是表示序数。The cardinal number 二 is not directly placed before a noun. In collocations such as 二门 or 二队，二 is an ordinal number.

两 **(two, a few, some)** 1. 常用于"千""万""亿"前面。It is often placed before 千(thousand)，万(ten thousand) and 亿 (a hundred thousand); 2. 在"半"前用"两"。It is used before 半(half)；3.常用于量词（个、双、本、只、把、匹、张等）和度量衡单位（吨、公里、公斤、克、平方米等）的前面。It is often used before measure words（个、双、本、只、把、匹、张）and new units of weight and measure（吨、公里、公斤、克、平方米）。"二"还可当"不同"讲。如"二心"。二 also can indicate difference, e.g. 二 心 (disloyalty; half-heartedness)。"两"还可当"一些"讲，表示不准确的数字。两 can also mean some, a few or an inexact number：我想讲两句话。I would like to say a few words. ╱ 这事过两天再说。Let's leave it at that for a couple of days.

F

发表 fābiǎo　宣告 xuāngào　宣布 xuānbù

发表 (publish; issue)　1.指公开出版。to publish sth.:发表文章 publish an article ／发表社论 carry an editorial 2.宾语常是表示言论的词。The object often indicates an expression of opinion：发表意见 state one's views.

宣告 (declare; proclaim)　宾语常是小句或某些动词(以表示重大事物的居多)，如"国家的诞生、计划破产、旧制度的灭亡"等。具有郑重的色彩。The object of 宣告 is a subordinate clause or verb denoting a major event such as the birth of nation, the miscarriage of a plan or the collapse of an old system. Its tone is solemn：宣告破产 declare bankruptcy (go bankrupt) ／宣告成立 proclaim the founding of a state, organization, etc.

宣布 (declare; proclaim; announce)　宾语除了名词(如法令、罪行、名单、结果等)以外，还常是某些动词或小句，如开会，开幕、弃权……等。常用于口语。The object of 宣布 may be a noun such as law, crime, list, result, etc., or a verb or subordinate clause, such as hold

93

a meeting or inauguration, abstain from voting, and so on. It is often used in spoken language: 宣布独立 declare independence ／ 宣布会议开始 declare a meeting open ／ 宣布一件事 make an announcement

〔相同点〕：都是动词。表示把事情公开出来让大家知道的意思。Syn. v. to make a matter publicly known.

发达 fādá　发展 fāzhǎn

发达 (developed; flourishing) 是形容词。表示兴旺的状况，指事物已充分发展或事业的兴盛的意思。adj. in a flourishing state, e.g. a flourishing business, a flourishing cause, etc.: 发达国家 developed countries ／ 工商业很发达。Industry and commerce are flourishing. ／ 肌肉发达 have well developed muscles

发展 (develop; expand; grow) 是动词。表示进展、变化的过程，着重在变化。v. indicates a process of advancement and change, the accent being on change: 发展经济，保障供给 develop the economy and ensure supplies ／ 用发展的眼光看人 look at a person with an eye to the course of his or her development

〔相同点〕：都表示扩大、开展的意思。Syn. v. to expand, develop.

发觉 fājué　发现 fāxiàn

发觉 (find; detect; discover) 表示知道原先不知道的事。是指由于外物刺激人的感官（听觉、视觉等）而觉察到。to realize, to become aware of things hitherto unknown through a sensory stimulus: 我们已发觉他很不可靠。We have discovered him to be quite untrustworthy.

发现 (find; discover) 指看到或找到原先没有看到的事物或规律。使用范围比"发觉"广。to find out or discover things or principles hitherto unknown. The usage of the term is wider than that of 发觉: 我没有发现什么情况。I didn't notice anything. ／敌机被我们的雷达发现了。Enemy planes were picked up by our radar. ／发现问题，解决问题 discover problems and solve them

〔相同点〕: 都是动词。表示开始认识到、了解到、感觉到隐藏的或没注意到的事物。Syn. v. referring to the moment of comprehension, knowing or perceiving things that were previously hidden or had escaped one's notice.

发明 fāmíng　创造 chuàngzào

发明 (invent; invention) 着重指创造性的思维活

95

动，研究出世上没有的东西。常作名词用。refers mainly to creative thinking or inventing sth. which did not exist before, often used as a noun: 印刷术是中国首先发明的。Printing was first invented in China. / 最新发明 the latest invention

创造 (create; produce; bring out) 着重指实践活动。名词用法较少。refers mainly to a practical activity, seldom used as noun: 创造奇迹 work miracles / 创造有·利条件 create favorable conditions

〔相同点〕：1.都可作动词。表示前所未有的制造。对象可以是某些物品、方法、理论等。Syn. to bring sth. new into being. The object can be a thing, method, theory, etc.; 2.都可作名词。表示首先制造的前所未有的东西。常连用有时也可换用。n. referring to the creation of sth. previous non-existent. They can be used interchangeable or jointly.

烦燥 fánzào　急躁 jízào

烦躁 (be fidgety; be agitated) 是烦闷、着急的意思。常由一件事引起，时间较短。anxious and irritable. The feeling is often aroused by a single circumstance of brief duration: 某些动物烦躁不安，可能是地震前的预兆。When certain animals feel agitated and uneasy, it may be a sign of an impending earthquake.

急躁 (**irritable**; **irascible**; **impetuous**; **rash**; **impatient**) 指由于不如意而马上激动不安。可以用来形容性格，而"烦躁"却不行。refers to an agitated state of mind caused by some dissatisfaction. The term usually describes a trait of character. 烦躁 is, however, not used this way: 防止急躁情绪 guard against impetuosity ／产生急躁情绪 give way to impatience

〔相同点〕: 都是形容词。表示心绪不安、着急的意思。Syn. adj. to be in a disturbed state of mind or extremely anxious.

妨碍 fáng'ài 妨害 fánghài

妨碍 (**hinder**; **hamper**; **impede**; **obstruct**) 指一种障碍使事物不能顺利进行。refers to some obstacle hindering the smooth development of things: 妨碍生产的发展 hamper the growth of production ／这不应妨碍我们两国之间良好关系的发展。This should not present an obstacle to the development of good relations between our two countries. ／妨碍工作 hinder one's work

妨害 (**impair**; **jeopardize**; **be harmful to**) 是"有害于"的意思。着重指事物受到损害。harmful or detrimental to; with emphasis on sth. sustaining harm：妨害健康 be harmful to one's health

〔相同点〕：都是动词。都表示不利于事物发展的意思。Syn. v. to be disadvantageous to the development of things.

分辨 fēnbiàn　区别 qūbié

分辨 (**distinguish; differentiate**) 多用于容易相混、不易区分的事物。to distinguish between two or more things: 分辨真假 distinguish truth from falsehood ／ 你很难分辨谁是工人，谁是学生。You can hardly tell who are workers and who are students.

区别 (**distinguish; differentiate; make a distinction between; difference**) 用分辨的地方大都可以换成"区别"。如目的和手段、任务和义务、权利和义务等。区别 can usually be replaced by 分辨，but is more suited to describing things related to each other or regarded as a unit, such as end and means, tasks and duties, rights and obligations: 这两个词在意义上没有区别。There is no difference in meaning between the two words. ／ 把两者区别开来 differentiate one from the other ／ 区别对待 deal with each case on its merits ／ 区别好坏 distinguish between good and bad

98

〔相同点〕: 都是动词。都表示把两个以上的人或事物区分开的意思。Syn. v. to distinguish between two or more things.

分别 fēnbié　分离 fēnlí　离别 líbié

分别 (**part; leave each other; differentiate; difference; respectively; separately**) 1.一般指人与人之间分开、离开一段时间。normally indicates a separation of a period of time: 他们分别不久又见面了。They met again after a short separation. 2.多用于有明显区别的事物, 如黑白、是非、里外、优劣等。often used in reference to things that are clearly distinguished from each other, such as black and white; right and wrong; inside and outside; superior and inferior, etc.: 分别善恶 distinguish good from evil / 两者之间没有什么分别。There is no difference between the two. 3.还可以是副词, 表示分头、各自、或不同的意思。used as adverb; to proceed separately or differently: 他们分别代表本国政府在协定上签字。They signed the agreement on behalf of their respective governments.

分离 (**separate; sever**) 1.不如"分别""离别"常用。有时特指人与人的被迫离散。used less often than 分别 or 离别, sometimes indicates that people are forced to separate from each other: 旧社会害得他卖儿卖女、骨肉分离。The old society forced him to sell his children and sever himself from his own flesh and blood. 2.还有把事物分开的意思。to keep things apart: 从空气中把氮分离出去。Separate nitrogen from air.

离别 (part for a long period; leave; bid farewell) 除了用于人与人之外，还可用于人与地方，能带宾语。而"分别"、"分离"则不能。离别 means that people leave each other or leave a place. Unlike 分别 and 分离，it can be followed by an object：我离别故乡已经两年了。It has been two years since I left my home town.

〔**相同点**〕：都是动词。都有表示人与人之间在一段时间里分开、离开的意思。Syn. v. denoting a period of time of separation between people.

分派 fēnpài　分配 fēnpèi

分派 (assign — to different persons; apportion) 着重指分别指定或派人去办。一般用于上级对下级，多带有命令性，对象较窄。to appoint or dispatch a person to do sth. It is generally used of a direction by a superior to a lower ranking person and is imperative in tone. The range of possible objects is limited: 队长给各个组都分派了任务。 The team leader has assigned tasks to all the groups.

分配 (distribute; allot; assign) 着重指按计划安排，按一定标准分开。对象较广，不一定用于上级对下级，还可以是时间、地方等。emphasizes arrangement of things according to plan or distribution of things according to certain criteria. It takes a wide range of objects, and does not necessarily apply to the assignment of work by those in authority. It may refer to time and place: 分配住房 allot accommodation ／ 她被分配到医院工作。 She was assigned to work at a hospital. ／ 他们的收入按贡献分配。 Their income is allocated according to the contributions they make.

〔相同点〕: 都是动词。都表示分给的意思。对象常是工作、任务、人或财物等。Syn. v. to give; to distribute. The object may be a task, duty, person, wealth, etc.

愤慨 fènkǎi　愤怒 fènnù　气愤 qìfèn

愤慨 (indignation) 除表示生气之外，还带有不平的意思。多用于书面语言。refers to feelings of anger and indignation, particularly

101

righteous indignation at some injustice, often used in written language: 表示愤慨 express one's indignation

愤怒 (indignation; anger; wrath) 表示激动到极点，非常生气。常用在文艺作品中。indicates extreme agitation and furious anger, often used in literary language: 激起了群众的极大愤怒 rouse the masses to great indignation ／ 愤怒的烈火在胸中燃烧 burn with anger

气愤 (indignation; furious) 表示生气、愤恨的意思。多用于口语。anger or resentment, often used in spoken language: 对于这种蛮横态度，大家都感到气愤。Everybody was indignant at such an overbearing manner.

〔相同点〕：都是形容词。表示因极不满而感情激动、生气的意思。Syn. adj. describing feelings of excitement or anger owing to extreme dissatisfaction with sth.

风景 fēngjǐng　景色 jǐngsè　景物 jǐngwù

风景 (scenery; landscape) 意义范围较小，一般只指可供观赏的，而且着眼于整个景象。has a narrow range of meaning; generally indicates beautiful scenery, and refers to the whole of a landscape: 以风景优美著称 famous for its scenic beauty ／ 西湖风景如画。 The West Lake is as beautiful as a painting. ／ 昆明是座风景美丽的城市。 Kunming is a picturesque city.

景色 (view; scene) 意义范围更小，一般只指有特色的风景，多着眼于色彩。indicates scenery with special characteristics and emphasizes color. The range of meaning is even narrower: 深秋的景色 a late autumn scene ／ 海上看日出景色特别美丽。 At sea one can enjoy a particularly beautiful view of the sunrise.

景物 (scenery) 意义范围较大，可以指供观赏的，也可以指不供观赏的自然物。多着眼于物体。 has a wide range of meaning; does not necessarily imply scenic beauty; generally refers to the elements of a landscape: 车子开得飞快，路旁的景物一闪而过。 The car was running so fast that the scenery on either side flashed past.

〔相同点〕：都是名词。都表示供人们观赏的山水、花木、建筑物、自然现象等的意思。Syn. n. referring to mountains, rivers, flowers, woods, buildings and natural scenes and beauty spots.

风气 fēngqì　风尚 fēngshàng　风俗 fēngsú

风气 (general mood; atmosphere; common or estab-

103

lished practice）着重指习气，是现时流行的较普遍的爱好、习惯。是中性词，多用于口语。refers mainly to a general mood or practice, which may be a popular pursuit or habit in vogue. It is neutral in tone and mostly used in spoken language: 全厂出现了大搞技术革新的风气。It has become the regular practice in the factory to go in for technical innovations.

风尚 (prevailing custom or practice) 着重指在一定时期中大家崇尚、尊重的风气和习惯。是褒义词，多用于书面语体。established practice or general mood enjoying general approval during a certain period of time, mostly used in written language as an approbatory: 勤俭节约的风尚 a habit of diligence and frugality

风俗 (custom) 指社会发展中长期沿袭下来的礼节、习惯等的总和。不能作动词。"风俗"是指某个地区、某个民族、某个国家、某个社会，长期沿袭下来的生活方式和社会风尚。the sum total of etiquette and custom handed down as society develops, it refers to the way of life and social custom followed since earlier times in a certain region, nationality, country or society. It cannot be used as a verb: 中国有些过春节的风俗可以追溯到一两千年的史迹中去。Some of the Chinese Spring Festival customs can be traced back one or two thousand years. / 他去云南调查一些少数民族的风俗习惯。 He went to study the customs of some of the minority nationalities of Yunnan province.

〔相同点〕：都是名词。表示社会上一时形成的习俗的意思。 Syn. n. customs that prevail in society during a certain period of time.

肤浅 fūqiǎn   浮浅 fúqiǎn   浅薄 qiǎnbó

肤浅 (superficial; shallow) 着重指局限于表面的认识。常形容看法、理解、了解、体会、体验、观察、研究等。 refers mainly to cognition of a superficial kind; very often used of opinions, comprehension, understanding, experience, observation and research, etc.: 根据我自己的一点肤浅体会，我认为首先要培养学生的强烈求知欲。 According to my own experience which is very slight, I think we should first try to foster students' academic curiosity.

浮浅 (superficial; shallow) 泛指浮在表面，有"肤浅"和"浅薄"的意思。不如"肤浅"和"浅薄"常用。浮浅 means "floating on the surface" and is synonymous with both 肤浅 and 浅薄, although less often used than the two other terms: 他们的认识还浮浅得很。 Their understanding of it is still very superficial.

105

浅薄 (meagre) 着重指知识少，修养差。常形容知识、思想、内容等。having insufficient knowledge or ill-trained, often used to describe knowledge, thought and subject matter: 他的历史知识很浅薄。He has a very meagre knowledge of history.

〔相同点〕：都是形容词。表示认识的深度不够或认识的程度不深的意思。可以形容知识、言论、学识等，或者从这些角度去形容人。Syn. adv. indicating that the depth of degree of understanding is not sufficient. They may describe cognition, speech, learning or people considered from the point of view of these.

G

改变 gǎibiàn　转变 zhuǎnbiàn

改变 (**change; alter; transform**) 是指比较具体的事物的更动和变化。to alter or change concrete things: 这艘船改变了航线。The ship changed its course.

转变 (**change; transform**) 是指由一种情况变到另一种情况，一般指抽象事物。indicates that one situation or state of affairs is changed into another; usually refers to abstract things: 把一种能转变为另一种能 transform one form of energy into another / 经过尖锐的思想斗争，他转变了。Intense mental struggle has brought about a change in him.

〔相同点〕：都是动词。都有更动、变化的意思。Syn. v. to alter, to change.

干净 gānjìng　清洁 qīngjié

干净 (**clean, neat and tidy; completely; totally**) 1.可以指没有杂质或多余的东西。也可比喻思想、语言、文章。indicates that sth. is free from impurity or superfluity. It may be used

107

figuratively in connection with ideas, language and literary works: 把院子扫干净 sweep the yard clean / 屋子收拾得干净 The room is neat and tidy. / 把谷子扬干净 winnow the grain thoroughly 2.还可以比喻一点儿不剩。 indicates that there is nothing left: 忘得干干净净 have completely forgotten

清洁 (clean) 一般只指没有尘土、油污等脏物。只形容环境和物品等。refers to the absence of dust or dirt, used to describe environment, objects etc.: 整齐清洁 clean and tidy / 人人要注意清洁卫生。 Everybody should pay attention to cleanliness and hygiene.

〔相同点〕: 都是形容词。表示没有尘土、油污等脏物。Syn. adj. without dust or dirt.

感激 gǎnjī　感谢 gǎnxiè

感激 (feel grateful; be thankful; feel indebted to) 着重指心情激动，并用好的情意回敬对方。indicates the grateful feelings aroused by help from others, as well as their expression: 感激涕零 shed grateful tears / 不胜感激 be deeply grateful / 我非常感激你的批评和帮助。 I am greatly indebted to you for your criticisms and help.

感谢 (thank; be grateful) 着重指酬谢、报答。多

108

半指用言语或行动，有时指用情意。to show thanks to sb. by word or deed, or sometimes through one's feelings of gratitude alone: 表示衷心感谢 express heartfelt thanks / 非常感谢你的帮助。Thank you very much for your help. / 感谢信 letter of thanks

〔相同点〕：都是动词。都有得到好处或帮助后，用好意回敬对方的意思。Syn. v. to express gratitude to others for help, or kindness.

干 gàn 搞 gǎo 做 zuò

干 **(do; work)** 1.着重指非常卖力气地做。denotes working with all one's might and main: 叫我干什么都行。I don't mind what I do. / 咱们干吧。Let's get started. / 他们都在干活呢。They are all at work. 2.在"担任"的意义上，"干"只用于某种职务。口语中常用。It may be used with expressions referring to a kind of work or a specific task, but not with the title of a profession. It is often used in spoken language: 他是干医务工作的。He works in the medical field.

搞 **(do; carry on; be engaged in; get hold of; secure; get)** 1.着重指用一定智力，采取一定方式、方法去做。mainly refers to performing activities which call for certain knowledge

109

or a certain method: 搞调查研究 conduct investigation and research / 搞生产 engage in production / 他是搞建筑的。He is an architect (or civil engineer, etc.)。/ 搞阴谋诡计的人注定要失败。Those who go in for intrigues and conspiracy are doomed to failure。2.还有"办"和"弄"的意思。to attend to; handle or manage: 你去给我们搞点吃的东西。Go and get us something to eat. / 把事情搞清楚 to arrive at a clear understanding of the question

做 **(make; produce; manufacture; do; act; engage in; become)** 1.没有什么特殊的含义，就是表示从事某种工作或活动。to do work or perform activities, without any particular implications: 做生意 do business / 大事做不来，小事又不做 be unable to do great things and look down on small ones 2.在当"担任"讲时，"做"不限于担任某种职务，还可以表示充当某种角色，作为某种身份。如"做主人的"等。It can be used with an expression referring to a type of work, and also with a job title or term indicating professional status, as in 做主人 (be the master): 后来她做保育员了。Later she became a child-care worker. / 今天开会由你做主席。You will be the chairperson at today's meeting.

〔相同点〕：都是动词。1.都表示从事某种工作或活

110

动。有时通用。Syn. v. to do work or to carry out some activities. They are sometimes interchangeable. 2."干"和"做"都可以表示担任。干 and 做 both have the meaning of holding a post.

高兴 gāoxìng　喜悦 xǐyuè　愉快 yúkuài

高兴 (glad; happy; cheerful; be willing to; be happy to)　1.着重形容精神情绪的状态，既愉快又兴奋。as an adjective, it describes a happy and elated state of mind：小强高高兴兴地上学去了。Xiao Qiang cheerfully went off to school. 2.还有动词意义和用法，表示乐意、喜欢的意思。as a verb, to "be willing" or "have a liking for"：他们高兴得太早了。They rejoiced too soon. / 你不高兴去就甭去了。You don't have to go if you are not in the mood.

喜悦 (happy; joyous)　着重形容心情欢喜。多用于书面语体。an intense expression of happiness, often used in written language：怀着万分喜悦的心情 with a feeling of immeasurable joy

愉快 (happy; joyful; cheerful)　着重形容心情、精神、不仅喜悦而且畅快、痛快。describes a state of mind which is happy, delighted and carefree：心情愉快 be in a cheerful frame of

111

mind / 祝你在中国逗留期间过得愉快。I hope you will have a pleasant stay in China.

〔相同点〕：都是形容词。都表示人在满意时感到快意、舒畅的意思。Syn. adj. expressing the idea that someone feels pleased and happy because of a satisfaction obtained.

歌唱 gēchàng　　歌颂 gēsòng

歌唱 (sing) 1.一般只指用歌曲、诗歌来赞美。多用于文学作品中。如歌唱领袖。to praise people in song or poetry, often used in literary language; for example, to sing the praise of a leader: 歌唱我们的祖国 sing in praise of our motherland 2.还有"唱歌"的意思。to sing a song: 尽情歌唱 sing to one's heart's content

歌颂 (sing the praise of; extol; eulogize) 不仅可用歌曲、诗歌赞美，也可以用文章、言语等。更强调"颂扬"这一层意思。as well as poetry and song, this may also refer to prose panegyrics; it stresses the sense of eulogy: 歌颂英雄 extol heroes

〔相同点〕：都是动词。都有用歌曲，诗歌等形式颂扬好人好事的意思。Syn. v. to praise good people and good deeds in poetry and song.

112

根据 gēnjù　依据 yījù

根据 (on the basis of; according to; in the light of; in line with) 1.偏于强调结论或言行的根本来源。口语和书面语体都常用。refers to the source of an action or a conclusion, often used in both spoken and written language: 根 据 天 气 预 报 according to the weather forecast / 根据同名小说拍摄的影片。A film based on the novel of the same title. 2.做名词时，比"依据"常用。It is more often used as a noun than 依据：说话要有根据。One should avoid making assertions without good grounds.

依据 (according to; in the light of; on the basis of; judging by; basis; foundation) 1.偏于强调结论或言行的凭据。多半用于书面语体，更多用于法令文件、科技语体。This term stresses evidence or authority for a conclusion, speech or deed. Often used in written language, it is found especially in laws, decrees, and official documents as well as in scientific and technical writings: 提供科学依据 provide scientific basis 2.作名词时，比"根据"少见。As a noun, it is less used than 根据：当时我们没有什么蓝图可以作依据。We did not have any

113

blueprints to go by at that time.

〔相同点〕：都是介词和名词。表示把某种事物作为结论的前提或言行的基础。Syn. prep. n.; indicating that sth. is used as a premise for certain conclusions or the basis for speech or action.

功夫 gōngfu　时间 shíjiān

功夫 (time; workmanship; skill; art; work; labor; effort) 1.多用于表示花费的时间和精力。time and energy used in doing sth.: 他三天功夫就学会了滑冰。It took him only three days to learn to skate. / 花了好大功夫 put in a lot of work 2. 也指本领、造诣。skill or accomplishment: 他的文章很有功夫。His article reveals his talent and skill as a writer.

时间 (the concept of time; duration of time; a point in time) 只用于做事占用的一段时间，或是不做事空闲的一段时间。a period of time spent in doing sth. (or doing nothing): 时间与空间 time and space / 这项工程需要多少时间？How long will it take to finish this project?

〔相同点〕：都是名词。表示占用的一段时间。Syn. n. a period of time occupied.

114

功绩 gōngjì　功劳 gōngláo　功勋 gōngxūn

功绩 (merits and achievements; contribution) 常指较大的贡献和成就，多用于重大事业上。常说"丰功伟绩"。great achievement or contribution in relation to a great cause, often used in the collocation 丰功伟绩 (great achievement or signal contributions): 为我们的事业建立不朽的功绩 make immortal contributions to our cause

功劳 (contribution; meritorious service; credit) 泛指贡献。多用于一般的事情上，也可以用于较大的事业上。常说"汗马功劳"。contributions to a great cause or a more ordinary matter. The expression 汗马功劳 is used to mean distinction won in a battle or contributions made in one's work: 她的功劳可不小啊。She has certainly made no small contribution. ／绝不能把一切功劳归于自己。One must never claim all the credit for oneself.

功勋 (exploit; meritorious service) 专指特殊的重大的贡献，多用于国家和人民的重大事业上。常说"不朽的功勋"。great feats of exceptional merit. The term is used in relation to major events in the history of a country and the life of its people. The expression 不朽功勋 mean-

115

ing immortal feats is often used: 为国家立下了不朽的功勋 have performed immortal feats for the country

〔相同点〕: 都是名词。表示对事业的贡献的意思。Syn. n. contributions to a cause.

公平 gōngpíng　公正 gōngzhèng

公平 (fair; just; impartial; equitable) 指处理事情合情合理，不偏袒哪一方面。常与"正直"一起连用。handling matters fairly and reasonably, showing no partiality to either side, often used with 正直 (upright, fair-minded; honest): 公平合理 fair and reasonable / 买卖公平 be fair in buying and selling / 太不公平了。It is grossly unfair.

公正 (just; fair; impartial; fair-minded) 指公平正直，没有私心。主要指人的品格，常与"无私"一起用。fair and honest, without selfish motives, refers chiefly to human character. It is often used with 无私 (unselfish): 历史将对这些人作出最公正的判断。History will pass the fairest judgment on such people.

〔相同点〕: 都是形容词。都有不偏袒的意思。Syn. adj. showing no partiality.

公约 gōngyuē   契约 qìyuē   条约 tiáoyuē

公约 (convention; pact; joint pledge) 可以指国家之间的，是三个国家或三个以上的国家订立的，也可以指个人之间的，即内部成员之间订立的。a treaty concluded between three or more countries or an agreement reached by individuals or amongst members of an organization: 北大西洋公约 The North Atlantic Treaty / 服务公约 service pledge (observed by workers in the service industries)

契约 (contract; deed) 多指个人之间的，一般只用于出卖、抵押、租赁等事情。contract signed by individuals, for such matters as sales, mortgage and leases: 租船的契约 chartering contract

条约 (treaty; pact) 多指国家之间的，是两个国家或两个以上国家订立的。a treaty concluded between two or more countries: 互不侵犯条约 mutual non-aggression treaty / 多边条约 multi-lateral pact

〔相同点〕：都是名词。表示共同订立的有关某种权利或义务的文书的意思。Syn. n. document jointly signed by certain parties pertaining to reciprocal right and obligations.

117

鼓励 gǔlì 怂恿 sǒngyǒng

鼓励 (encourage; urge) 是激动、勉励的意思。常指劝人做好事。to impel and encourage, often refers to persuading sb. to do good things：他对我们讲了许多鼓励的话。He said a lot to encourage us. / 精神鼓励和物质鼓励相结合 combining moral encouragement with material reward

怂恿 (instigate; incite; egg sb. on; abet) 一般指唆使他人做坏事，并且是在背地里鼓动。是贬义。a pejorative term, it refers to inducing sb. to do things bad or to covert instigation：这些坏事是谁怂恿你干的？Who put you up to all these dirty tricks?

〔相同点〕：都是动词。都有鼓动人去做某一件事的意思。Syn. v. to arouse sb. to do sth.

关切 guānqiè 关注 guānzhù

关切 (be deeply concerned; show one's concern over) 表示关心、爱护的意思，着重表示深切的感情。to be solicitous; to cherish; particularly indicates deep feeling：表示严重关切 show grave concern over / 获悉贵国遭受地震，我们极为关切。We are deeply concerned

118

at the news that your country has been struck by an earthquake.

关注 (follow with interest; pay close attention to; show solicitude for) 指特别关心、重视，着重表示特别重视的意思。一般用于事情。to show special concern or pay special attention, normally used with reference to things: 我们对这个地区的情况十分关注。We follow with interest the development of the situation in this area.

〔相同点〕：都是动词。都表示关心的意思。Syn. v. to be concerned about.

规矩 guiju　规则 guīzé

规矩 (rule; established practice; custom; well–behaved; well–disciplined) 1.表示长期延续下来的行为标准、习惯、礼节。比较通俗，多用于口头语体。long established rules, customs and etiquette, often used in informal spoken language: 损坏东西要赔，是我们的老规矩。To pay compensation for damage incurred is a long–established rule with us. 2.也可作形容词。表示行为端正老实或表示合乎标准的意思。adj. well–behaved or up to standard: 他的字写得规矩。His handwriting shows care and training.

规则 (rule; regulation; regular) 1.多半指具体规定的办法、规章、有的形成条文。specific rules, regulations or methods, which may constitute the articles of a code. 交通规则 traffic regulations 2.可作形容词，表示合乎一定方式的或整齐的意思。如"规则动词""规则图形"。as an adjective, it means that sth. conforms to a definite shape, and is arranged in an orderly manner, such as a regular verb, regular figure, etc.: 这条河流的水道原来很不规则。The course of this river used to be quite irregular.

〔相同点〕：都是名词。表示必须遵守的法则、习惯、或制度、章程。Syn. n. rules, customs, systems, regulations which should be followed.

果断 guǒduàn　　武断 wǔduàn

果断 (resolute; decisive) 是褒义词。表示处理事情时能够及时地、坚定地作出决定的意思。to deal with matters with quick and firm decision, an approbatory term: 办事果断 handle affairs in a decisive manner／他果断地作出决定。He resolutely makes a decision.

武断 (arbitrary; decision; subjective assertion) 是贬义词。表示考虑问题，处理事情不顾客观实

120

际，不采纳别人的意见，只凭主观判断，就轻易下结论的意思。a pejorative term, to deal with matters without regard for objective realities or without considering other's opinions and to draw rash conclusions: 他很武断。He is very arbitrary. / 我们不能武断地下结论。We should not draw conclusions arbitrarily.

〔相同点〕：都是形容词。都有作事决断，不犹豫的意思。用来表示判断和处理事情的态度。Syn. adj. acting resolutely and without hesitation; refers to an attitude displayed in making judgments or in handling affairs.

果然 guǒrán 居然 jūrán 竟然 jìngrán

果然 (really; as expected; sure enough) 表示事实与预料的一致的意思。indicates that events turned out as was expected: 果然名不虚传 really a well-deserved reputation / 敌人果然中了我们的埋伏。Just as we expected, the enemy was caught in our ambush.

居然 (unexpectedly; to one's surprise; go so far as to; have the impudence to) 表示出乎意料，即预料与结果相反的意思。既可用于好的方面，也可用于坏的方面。beyond one's expectations or with a result contrary to one's expectations. It can have positive or negative con-

121

notation: 这么重的担子，他居然挑着走了 10 公里。Who would have thought he could carry such a heavy load for 10 kilometers. / 你怎么居然相信这种谣言。How could you believe such a rumour?

竟然 (unexpectedly; to one's surprise; actually; go so far as to) 表示有点出乎意料之外的意思，即预期和结果相反。当表示不应当这样而这样的意思时，常用于不好的方面。to go beyond one's expectation, to have a result contrary to one's expectation. When indicating that sth. did not turn out as expected, it generally has a negative connotation: 竟然不顾事实 go so far as to disregard the facts / 真没想到他竟然敢当面撒谎。It never occurred to me that he would dare to tell a barefaced lie.

〔相同点〕：都是副词。都有表示预料和结果之间的关系的意思。经常作状语。Syn. adv. referring to the relation between expectations and results, often used as adverbials.

过程 guòchéng 历程 lìchéng

过程 (course; process) 泛指一切事情进行所经过的程序。意义范围大。indicates the process of any event, action; has a wide range of usage: 我们应该缩短制作的过程。We should shorten the manufacturing process. / 在讨论过程中 in the course of discussion

历程 (course) 专指人们经历的较长的不平凡的过程，一般用于书面语体。意义范围小。refers especially to a long and unusual process; often used in written language. The scope of its meaning is limited: 回顾战斗的历程 look back on the course of the struggle

〔相同点〕：都是名词。表示经过的程序的意思。Syn. n. a process.

H

害怕 hàipà　惧怕 jùpà

害怕 (be afraid; be scared) 指遇到困难、危险等心中不安或发慌的意思。多用于口语。to feel apprehension and dread when facing danger and difficulties, often used in spoken language: 没有什么可害怕的。There is nothing to be afraid of. / 他提心吊胆，连自己的影子都害怕。He is scared of his own shadow.

惧怕 (fear; dread) 指心里恐惧的意思。程度较重，多用于书面语。indicates an intense feeling of fear; often used in written language: 他会因惧怕你——甚至恼恨你而用对付敌人的手段对付你。He will treat you as he would an enemy because he is afraid of you, or rather, he hates you.

〔相同点〕: 都是动词。都有怕的意思。Syn. v. to fear.

含糊 hánhu　模糊 móhu

含糊 (ambiguous; vague; careless; perfunctory) 1.着重指模棱两可、不明确。常形容语言及其表

达的意思。ambiguous; vague, often used to describe language or mode of expression: 含糊其词 talk ambiguously／在原则问题上不能含糊。One must not be vague on matters of principle. 2.还表示不认真、马虎的意思。careless, not conscientious: 这件事一点儿也不能含糊。We will have to handle the matter with meticulous care. 3.还表示示弱的意思（多用于否定形式）。showing weakness (often used with a negative expression): 以毫不含糊的语言作出回答 answer in clear and unequivocal terms

模糊 (blurred; indistinct; dim; vague; blur; obscure; confuse; mix up) 1.着重指不分明的意思。常形容具体东西的外形、也形容感觉、印象、记忆、神态、认识等。indistinct, relates to the shape of a concrete thing, or to feelings, impressions, memory, manner and knowledge: 她对这个问题还有一些模糊的认识。She still has some confused ideas about this question.／字迹模糊了。The handwriting was blurred. 2.还表示混淆的意思。to mix up: 不能模糊了阶级界限。Class distinctions must not be obscured. 3.还有使模糊不清的意思。to make sth. unclear: 泪水模糊了他的双眼。Tears blurred his eyes.

〔相同点〕：都是形容词。表示不清楚、不清晰的意思。Syn. adj. not clear; indistinct.

好象 hǎoxiàng 似乎 sìhu

好象 (seem, be like) 1.除了表示不十分肯定的语气外，还表示委婉否定的语气，后半句常用"实际上""实质上"等词。Besides expressing uncertainty, it is a euphemistic way of making a negative statement, the latter part of which contains such expressions as 实际上（in fact）or 实质上（really）：他看上去好象是中国人，但实际上是日本人。He looks Chinese, but he is actually Japanese; 2.表示比喻，有 A 象 B 的意思。后面可与"似的""一般""一样"搭配。多用于口语。It is used in similes, in which A is likened to B, often followed by 似的 or 一般。This usage is common in spoken language：他们好象是多年的老朋友似的。They seem to have been close friends for many years.

似乎 (it seems; as if; seemingly) 不能表示比喻，后面不常与"一般""一样"搭配，多用于书面语。is not used in similes, nor is it followed by 一般 or 一样。It is often used in written language：他的意思似乎另有所指。It seems he was referring to something else. / 似乎明天要起风。It looks as if it will be windy tomorrow.

126

〔相同点〕：都表示不十分肯定的意思。Syn. showing the absence of complete certainty.

和蔼 hé'ǎi 和气 héqi

和蔼 (kindly; affable; amiable) 指态度温和、容易接近。多用于上对下，长对幼。常用于书面语。gentle in manner and easy to approach; used of the behavior of a person in high position or an older person towards his or her juniors; it is frequently used in written language: 和蔼可亲 affable and genial ／ 态度和蔼 amiable

和气 (gentle; kind; polite; amiable) 主要指对人的语言及态度等不高傲，不粗暴，使人感到亲切。常用于口语。refers mainly to language and attitude — not supercilious or rude, but conveying an impression of cordiality and kindness; often used in spoken language: 她说话和气。She speaks civilly ／ 不要伤了和气。Don't hurt people's feelings.

〔相同点〕：都是形容词。表示态度温和的意思。Syn. adj. describing a gentle, kind attitude.

合作 hézuò 协作 xiézuò

合作 (cooperate; collaborate; work together) 着重

指共同合力地从事同一工作。参加者一般没有主次之分。to make a united effort to carry out a common task as equal partners: 我们应当互相合作。We should cooperate with each other. / 这幅画是他们合作的。This painting is their joint work.

协作 (cooperate; coordination; combined) 着重指配合、协助完成某一工作的意思，有时有主次之分。refers to the accomplishment of a task through coordination between those playing primary and secondary roles: 双方协作得很好。The two sides cooperated well. / 这是几个厂协作的产物。This is a product of the combined efforts of several factories.

〔相同点〕: 都是动词。表示为了共同目的，一起完成某项工作或任务的意思。Syn. v. to work together in order to reach a common goal.

宏大 hóngdà 庞大 pángdà

宏大 (grand; great) 多着眼于规模，着重指宏伟。常形容建筑物、理想等，带有称赞的感情色彩。indicates the scale of sth., with special reference to magnificence, grandeur; often used in connection with architectural constructions and ideals. It has a laudatory tone: 建设宏大的科学技术队伍 build a

128

mammoth force of scientific and technical personnel. / 宏大的志愿 great aspirations / 规模宏大 on a large scale

庞大 (**huge; colossal; enormous; gigantic**) 着眼于形体或总体等方面，指过大或大而不当。是中性词。describes the shape, overall appearance, etc. of sth. which is exceptionally or inappropriately large. It is neutral in tone: 这个国家的政府机构庞大。This country has an unwieldy governmental apparatus. / 庞大的正规军 a massive regular army

〔相同点〕：都是形容词。表示非常大，不同一般的意思。Syn. adj. great, extraordinary.

后悔 hòuhuǐ   忏悔 chànhuǐ

后悔 (**regret; repent**) 指事后懊悔的意思。to feel regret after the event: 他后悔不已。He is overcome with regret. / 后悔莫及 too late to repent

忏悔 (**repent; be penitent; confess one's sins**) 本是宗教的专门术语。后来使用范围扩大，表示认识过去的错误、决心改过的意思。originally a religious term, which has since expanded its scope to cover regret for mistakes committed and the determination to correct them: 他回想过去，深感痛心，决心忏悔，

129

重新做人。When he thought of the past, he felt sorry and decided to reform himself.

〔相同点〕：都是动词。都有悔恨自己做错了事的意思。Syn. v. to regret having done sth. wrong.

忽略 hūlüè　疏忽 shūhu

忽略 (neglect; overlook; lose sight of) 一般指没注意到，而且多指全面思考中的疏漏的意思。一般是无意的，有时指不注意，是有意的。to fail to pay attention to sth; usually refers to negligence of some particular aspect in making overall considerations. It generally indicates accidental oversight, but may also refer to ignoring sth. intentionally: 我们在注意主要矛盾的同时，不要忽略次要矛盾。While paying attention to principal contradiction, we should not overlook secondary contradictions.

疏忽 (showing carelessness; negligence; oversight) 一般只指粗心大意、马虎的意思，是无意的。常不带宾语。常说"实在太疏忽了。" indicates unintentional negligence or carelessness, does not generally take an object. It is frequently heard in the expression 实在太疏忽了 meaning "It is really too careless": 疏忽大意就可能造成事故。Carelessness is liable to cause accidents. / 我一时疏忽，搞错了。I made the

130

mistake through an oversight.

〔相同点〕：都是动词。表示没有注意到的意思。
Syn. v. fail to pay attention to.

滑稽 huáji　诙谐 huīxié　幽默 yōumò

滑稽 **(funny; amusing; comical)** 指逗人发笑的意思，也指因愚蠢惹人发笑的意思。refers to sth. funny or foolish that causes laughter: 那个丑角的表演非常滑稽。That clown's performance was funny. / 我觉得他很滑稽。I think he is very comical.

诙谐 **(humorous; jocular)** 指意使人感到有趣，引人发笑。多用于褒义。常用于书面语。refers to sth. amusing; an approbatory term often used in written language: 他是个诙谐的作家。He is a humorous writer.

幽默 **(humor)** 指作品或言行使人感到有趣发笑，而且意味深长。是褒义词，是英语"humor"的音译。denotes sth. which not only amuses people but also implies a deeper significance. An approbatory term, it is the Chinese transliteration of the English word humor: 很有幽默感 to have a good sense of humor / 他是富有幽默感的人。He is a man with much humor.

〔相同点〕：都是形容词。表示有趣而引人发笑的意思。可以形容言语。Syn. adj. amusing;

131

may be used to describe language.

华丽 huálì　壮丽 zhuànglì

华丽 (magnificent; resplendent; gorgeous) 着重指外表有光彩、漂亮。除了形容建筑、陈设之外，还常形容装饰、衣着、花朵、文章风格、词句等。indicates splendid and beautiful appearance. Besides architectural constructions and furnishings, it may describe ornament, dress, flowers, writing, language, etc.: 华丽的宫殿 a magnificent palace / 服饰华丽 gorgeously and richly dressed / 华丽的词藻 flowery language, ornate diction

壮丽 (majestic; magnificent; glorious) 着重指雄壮、雄伟、色彩庄重。常形容城市或山河的景象、诗文、画面或歌曲的气势。magnificent, grand and solemn in color or tone. The expression usually describes cities, mountains and rivers, or the grandeur of poetry, essays, pictures or songs: 壮丽的景色 magnificent scenery / 一篇壮丽的史诗 a magnificent (glorious) epic

〔相同点〕：都是形容词。指建筑物等特别美丽。Syn. adj. referring to buildings, etc. of particular beauty.

132

化装 huàzhuāng　化妆 huàzhuāng

化装 (make up; disguise oneself)　指改变装束或容貌，着重在改变原来的样子。to alter one's dress or appearance. The emphasis is on transforming the original appearance: 他去化装侦察。He went reconnoitring in disguise. / 化装师 makeup artist

化妆 (make up)　指修饰容貌、进行打扮的意思。着重在打扮得更美，但不改变原来的样子。to use cosmetics so as to improve one's appearance or to enhance one's beauty. The emphasis is laid on beautifying the appearance without however transforming it into sth. different: 她喜欢化妆品。She likes cosmetics. / 她喜欢化妆。She likes to make up.

〔相同点〕：都是动词。都有修饰外貌的意思。Syn. v. to embellish one's appearance.

怀念 huáiniàn　想念 xiǎngniàn

怀念 (cherish the memory of; think of)　感情较深沉。带敬重或庄重色彩，常用于书面语。refers to deep feeling, implies respect or solemnity; often used in written language: 怀念已故的亲人 to cherish the memory of a deceased family member or of a loved one / 怀念远方的友人 think of a friend who is away in a distant place

想念 (**remember with longing; long to see again; miss**) 常用于口语。often used in spoken language: 我们都很想念奶奶。We all miss grandma very much. / 侨胞想念祖国。Overseas Chinese cherish the memory of their homeland.

〔相同点〕：都是动词。都表示不能忘怀、希望见到的意思。Syn. v. indicating that one cannot forget sth. or sb. that one wishes to see again.

豢养 huànyǎng　饲养 sìyǎng　喂养 wèiyǎng

豢养 (**feed; groom; keep**) 原指喂养牲畜，现常用它的引申义，表示收买利用的意思，只用于贬斥敌人，含贬义。originally, to keep an animal; in its extended meaning, it refers to buying over and making use of sb., and is used in denouncing an enemy. It is derogatory in tone: 敌人豢养的走狗 a lackey kept by the enemy

饲养 (**raise; rear**) 指喂养动物，只适用于动物，中性词。a neutral term, applied only to keeping animals: 饲养牲畜 raise livestock / 动物园的饲养员 an animal keeper in a zoo

喂养 (**feed; raise; keep**) 是哺食、养育的意思。指给幼儿或动物东西吃，使其长大。是中性词。to feed or bring up; refers to the feeding and rearing of children or animals; a neutral term: 为了进行研究工作，他还喂养了几只兔子，在它们身上进行试验。 For research purposes, he kept rabbits, on which he conducted experiments.

〔相同点〕：都是动词。都有养育的意思。Syn. v. to bring up; to rear.

回顾 huígù　回忆 huíyì

回顾 **(look back; review)** 指回过头来看。现在引申义指看一看过去一个阶段的情况。to look back on sth. or sb., often extended to refer to a retrospect of the events of a former epoch: 回顾历史 review history / 1979 年的回顾 1979 in retrospect

回忆 **(call to mind; recollect; recall)** 指回想的意思。着重指回想经历过的事情的当时情况。使用范围较小，一般回忆的是亲自经历的事。to think back; more especially, to summon up a past state of affairs as it was at the time. Its range of usage is limited, and generally confined to recalling events one has experienced oneself: 童年的回忆 recollections of childhood / 战争年代的回忆 reminiscences of the war years / 回忆对比 recall the past and contrast it with the present

135

〔相同点〕：都是动词。表示对过去的事情的回想。Syn. v. to think back to the past.

会见 huìjiàn　接见 jiējiàn

会见 (meet with) 更多指彼此相见，有时可用于上级对下级。 refers to meetings between persons, sometimes used of a meeting between one in a high position and his or her juniors: 周恩来总理那次与我们的会见是叫人永远难忘的。 Our meeting with Premier Zhou Enlai was unforgettable.

接见 (receive sb.; grant an interview to) 比"会见"更多用于上级对下级。 used more often than 会见 in describing an audience granted by people in high position to people in low position: 国家元首接见外宾。 The head of state receives foreign guests.

〔相同点〕：都是动词。表示跟别人见面的意思。多用于郑重的或外交场合。Syn. v. to meet sb.; often used of solemn occasions or in diplomatic contexts.

活动 huódòng　运动 yùndòng

活动 (move about; exercise; activity; manoeuvre) 1. 指让身子随便动一动。 to move the body without rule or method, to move about: 站起

来活动。Stand up and move about. 2.指群众性的行动和个人的行动或工作，还可用于文娱、军事等方面 refers to activities by masses of people, individual work or activities for recreational or military purposes: 他从事科学活动。He goes in for scientific pursuits.

运动 (**motion; movement; sports; athletics; exercise; campaign; drive**) 1.多指按一定的技巧、规划和方法活动。to engage in physical activity according to a certain technique rule or method: 运动是物质的存在方式。Motion is the mode of existence of matter. / 游泳是我喜爱的运动。Swimming is my favorite sport. 2.指群众性的行动，它的目的明确，规模大。mass activity with a clearly-defined purpose performed on a large scale: 群众运动 mass movements / 爱国卫生运动 patriotic public health campaign

〔相同点〕: 1.都是动词。表示作健身动作的意思。Syn. v. go in for physical exercise. 2.可以作名词。表示有目的、有组织的行动。n. purposeful, organized action.

活泼 huópo 活跃 huóyuè

活泼 (**lively; vivacious; vivid**) 指生动、自然、不呆板。主要指性格，有时也用来指文字。to be lively and spontaneous; refers mainly to dispo-

137

sition, sometimes also to literary style: 天真活泼的孩子 lively children / 文字活泼 written in a lively style

活跃 (brisk; active; dynamic; enliven; animate; liven up; invigorate) 指行动活泼、积极、气氛热烈。主要用来指行动，有时也用来形容气氛。 refers to action that is lively and energetic, sometimes used to describe a warm atmosphere: 市场活跃 business is brisk / 活跃文娱生活 enliven cultural and recreational activities

〔相同点〕：都是形容词。都有灵活、不呆板的意思。Syn. adj. quick and flexible.

138

J

基本 jīběn　根本 gēnběn

基本 (elementary; basic; main; essential; basically; in the main; on the whole) 1.作名词时，不如"根本"常用，有时含有基础的意思。n. less often used than 根本；sometimes synonymous with 基础 (basis): 基本知识 elementary knowledge 2.作形容词时，语义较轻，语气不如"根本"强。adj. has a lighter tone than 根本: 基本工资 basic wage / 基本条件 main conditions 3.作副词时，表示大体上的意思。adv. on the whole: 这部电影基本上是好的。This film is good on the whole.

根本 (basic; fundamental; essential; cardinal; at all; simply; radically; thoroughly) 1.作名词时，含有根源的意思。常用"从根本上"这一格式。n. the source of things, often used in the phrase 从根本上: 从根本上改变农村缺医少药的现象 put an end once for all to the lack of doctors and medicine in the rural areas / 千头万绪抓根本。Faced with a great variety of problems, one must concentrate on what is of basic importance. 2.作形容词时，语义较重，语

139

气较强。adj. It strikes a deeper note than 基本 and the tone is stronger。根本原因 root cause 3.作副词时，表示本来、从来、完全、彻底的意思，多用于否定句。adv. originally; always; completely; thoroughly, often used in a negative clause：我根本就不赞成你的主张。I don't agree with you at all. / 奴隶主根本不把奴隶当人看待。The slave owner simply did not treat the slaves as human beings. / 问题已经得到根本解决。The problem has been settled once and for all.

〔相同点〕：1.都是名词。表示最重要部分或最主要部分的意思。Syn. n. the most important part of sth. 2.也可以用作形容词或副词。表示最重要的或起决定作用的意思。adj., adv. the most important or playing a decisive role.

激动 jīdòng　感动 gǎndòng

激动 (excite; stir; agitate) 着重指感情的强烈冲动或冲动的状态。可以说"激动人心"、"心情激动"等。refers chiefly to a strong emotional impulse or a state of excitement. One may say 激动人心 (inspiring; stirring) or 心情激动 (thrilled)：令人激动的场面 an inspiring scene / 他激动地说："是他救了我。"He said with feeling, "It's he who saved me."

140

感动 (move; touch) 着重指感情的共鸣、同情或敬佩。是褒义词。an approbatory term; indicates that one's feelings are stirred by sympathy or admiration：感动得流下了眼泪 moved to tears / 深为他的精神所感动 deeply touched by his spirit

〔相同点〕：都是动词。都有使思想感情起变化的意思。Syn. v. to stir one's emotions.

讥讽 jīfěng   讽刺 fěngcì

讥讽 (ridicule; satirize) 表示讥笑并讽刺对方的意思。一般用于书面语。to mock and sneer at others, generally used in written language：他毫不理睬某些人的讥讽，继续进行试验。Completely ignoring the ridicule of certain people, he went on with his experiments.

讽刺 (satirize; mock) 指用夸张、反语、含蓄等手法嘲笑对方。书面语和口语都常用。to laugh at others with exaggerated irony or implicit criticism, often used in written and spoken language：这是一部讽刺封建文人的作品。This is a satire on feudal scholars.

〔相同点〕：都是动词。表示用刺激的话来笑话对方的意思。Syn. v. to make fun of others with provocative words.

141

几乎 jīhū   简直 jiǎnzhí

几乎 (nearly; almost; practically) 表示接近于、差点儿的意思。语气较轻。nearly; almost. The tone is lighter: 他几乎一夜没睡。He lay awake almost the whole night. / 故乡变化太大了，我几乎认不出来了。My hometown had changed so much that I could hardly recognize it.

简直 (simply; at all) 表示干脆就是、完全如此的意思。语气较重，也较肯定。带有夸张的意味。expresses the idea sth. simply is so, or that it is completely so. Rather emphatic and affirmative in tone, it implies some exaggeration: 我简直不能想象有这种事。I simply couldn't imagine such a thing. / 这个星期简直没有一个好天。We have had no fine weather at all this week. / 简直跟新的一样 as good as new

〔相同点〕：都是副词。都有对事物表示强调的意思。还表示差不多的意思。Syn. adv. used for emphasis, and sometimes with the meaning of "nearly".

讥笑 jīxiào   嘲笑 cháoxiào   嗤笑 chīxiào

讥笑 (sneer at; deride; ridicule; jeer) 指讥讽和嘲笑，词义比"嗤笑"和"嘲笑"重一些。to sati-

142

rize and ridicule. It is stronger than 嗤笑 and 嘲笑：他喜欢讥笑别人。 He likes to sneer at others.

嘲笑 **(ridicule; deride; jeer at; laugh at)** 指用言辞取笑对方。一般的取笑，有善意的，也有恶意的。 to make verbal fun of sb. with good or bad intention: 我觉得该做的，就不怕别人嘲笑，坚持做下去。 When I believe that what I am doing is right, I will persist in it without fear of ridicule.

嗤笑 **(laugh at; sneer)** 指轻蔑地笑。意思偏重在轻视。 to laugh at sb. with disdain. Its emphasis is on contempt for the person: 我们不应当嗤笑他，应该耐心地帮助他。 We should not sneer at him, but help him.

〔相同点〕：都是动词。指不怀好意地笑话别人的意思。 Syn. v. to laugh at others maliciously.

急忙 jímáng　连忙 liánmáng

急忙 **(in a hurry; in haste; hurriedly; hastily)** 着重在"急"，表示因心里着急而行动加快。Emphasizing on impatience, it implies that one does things in haste because of a sense of urgency: 你干吗这样急急忙忙的？ Why are you in such a hurry? / 她背起药箱急忙朝病人家里跑去。 She flung the medical kit over her shoulder

143

and hurriedly set out for the patient's home.

连忙 (promptly; at once) 着重表示动作接得很紧，很迅速。indicates that actions occur in quick succession：他连忙道歉。He hastened to apologize.

〔相同点〕：都是形容词。都有紧急、匆忙的意思。Syn. adj. urgent; hastily.

计划 jìhuà　规划 guīhuà

计划 (plan; program; project; map out;) 指工作或行动以前预先拟定的具体打算。一般都比较周密、具体、使用范围较广。a project for work or other action, prepared in advance, and usually specific and well-conceived. It has a wide range of usage：这是切实可行的计划。This is a feasible plan. / 计划好了再动手干。Map it out before you start. / 我们计划下周出发。We plan to leave next week.

规划 (program; plan) 指比较全面的长远的发展计划的意思。着重于全局性的问题。a comprehensive long-term plan of development; used particularly with reference to overall situations：我们要有长远规划。We must have a long-term program. / 生产规划 production plan

〔相同点〕：都是名词，也都可以做动词。表示有预先拟定工作或行动的步骤和方法的意思。

Syn. n.; v. indicating that measures and methods for work or other actions are drawn up in advance.

家乡 jiāxiāng　故乡 gùxiāng

家乡 (hometown; native place) 家庭世代居住的地方，自己现在可能居住在那里，也可能不居住在那里。常用于口语。a place where a family has lived for many generations and where it is possibly, but not necessarily still residing; often used in spoken language: 家乡话 native dialect / 这是他的家乡菜。This dish is a speciality of his hometown.

故乡 (native place; hometown; birthplace) 出生地方，或曾经长期居住过的地方，自己现在已经不住在那里。常用于书面语。a birthplace or place where sb. has lived for a long time although he or she is no longer living there; often used in written language: 我非常热爱自己的故乡。I love my hometown very much.

〔相同点〕：都是名词。表示老家所在的地方的意思。Syn. n. the place where one was born or habitually lives.

家属 jiāshǔ　家族 jiāzú

家属 (family members; family dependents) 只指某人的家庭成员。他们有亲近的血缘或夫妻关系。refers only to immediate family members including husband and wife or those related to each other by ties of blood: 工人家属 families of workers / 他的家属 his family members

家族 (clan; family) 意义范围大，包括同一姓氏的、血缘关系不太近的几辈人。has a broad range of meaning; includes members of a clan bearing the same surname and those only remotely related to each other by blood and may extend to several generations: 这是一个大家族。This is a big clan.

〔相同点〕: 都是名词。表示一家人的意思。Syn. n. people belonging to one family.

坚定 jiāndìng　坚决 jiānjué

坚定 (firm; staunch; steadfast; strengthen) 1.着重于思想方面，指拿定了主意不动摇。常形容立场、观点或目光等。never vacillating in one's thinking once one has made up one's mind; often refers to stance or viewpoint: 坚定的意志 constancy of purpose / 坚定的步伐

firm strides 2.还有动词用法和意义。表示使坚定。v. to make firm: 坚定了攀登科学技术新高峰的决心 strengthen one's resolve to scale new heights in science and technology

坚决 (firm; resolute; determined) 着重于态度和行动方面，指认准目标，下定决心，不犹豫，不迟疑。常形容某些行动，如支持、反对、拥护、斗争等。跟"犹豫"相对。used of attitudes and deeds. It means that when one's mind is set on a goal, one does not hesitate or waver. It is often used to qualify certain actions, e.g. support, oppose, uphold, struggle. It is the opposite of 犹豫 (hesitate): 我们坚决完成任务。We will carry out the task without fail. / 他很坚决。He stood firm.

〔相同点〕：都是形容词。表示决不动摇的意思。Syn. adj. not vacillating under any circumstances.

检查 jiǎnchá　检验 jiǎnyàn

检查 (check up; inspect; examine; self-criticism) 指对工作、事情、物品加以检点，查看的意思。使用范围大。可以是较具体的事物如身体、产品等，也可以是较抽象的事物，如思想，工作等。是指查找问题、错误，看是否符合要求。to examine or check work, goods, etc. It has a wide range of usage and may refer to concrete things such as products, or abstract entities such as ideas or work. It means to check for problems or mistakes, and to see whether the things examined conform to certain requirements: 检查身体 have a physical examination / 把练习检查一遍再交。 Look over your exercises before handing them in. / 作检查 criticize oneself

检验 (test; examine; inspect) 指对东西或事情用一定的标准去衡量。常用于抽象的事物如理论、思想等。也可用于具体的事物如仪表。 to measure according to certain criteria; often used in relation to abstract things (theories, ideas, etc.) as well as concrete ones such as instruments: 严格检验产品质量 maintain strict quality controls / 社会实践及其效果是检验主观愿望或动机的标准。 The criteria for judging subjective intention or motive are social practice and its effects.

〔相同点〕：都是动词。表示仔细地看的意思。 Syn. v. to examine carefully.

简单 jiǎndān　　简略 jiǎnlüè

简单 (simple; uncomplicated; commonplace; ordinary; oversimplified, casual) 1. 主要指事物内

容。跟"复杂"、"详细"相对。使用范围广，能形容语言、设计等。简单 refers mainly to simplicity of content, and is the opposite of 复杂 (complicated) and 详细 (detailed). It has a wide range of usage and may describe language, design, etc.: 这机器构造简单。The machine is simple in structure. 2.指能力或经历平凡，一般跟"不"连用。refers to ability or experience that is unexceptional; in this sense, it is usually combined with 不 (not) to mean "out of the common run.": 她的枪法这么准，真不简单。It is a marvel that she is able to shoot with such accuracy. / 这家伙鬼点子特别多，可不简单。This fellow is no simpleton; he is full of tricks. 3.指草率、不细致。perfunctory; not careful enough: 简单地看问题 take a naive view / 文章我只是简单地看了看。I only skimmed through the article.

简略 (simple; brief; sketchy) 指的是不详细，只有要略的意思。用来指口头或书面表达的内容，跟"详细"相对。simple and sketchy; used in spoken and written language in reference to the contents of sth. It is the opposite of 详细 (detailed, minute): 他提供的材料过于简略。The material he supplied is too sketchy.

〔相同点〕：都是形容词。都有不充分、不周全、不复杂的意思。Syn. adj. not full; not

149

thorough; not complex.

俭朴 jiǎnpǔ   俭省 jiǎnshěng

俭朴 (**thrifty and simple; economical**) 指朴素，常用来形容生活作风。plain and frugal; often used to describe a style of life: 衣着俭朴 dress simply / 生活俭朴 lead a thrifty and simple life

俭省 (**economical; thrifty**) 着重指"省"，尽量少用的意思。the key element is 省 (economize); it indicates that one uses sth. as sparingly as possible: 过日子俭省 live economically

〔相同点〕：都是形容词。表示使用财物很有节制、不浪费的意思。Syn. adj. to use materials, money and other forms of property economically and without waste.

骄傲 jiāo'ào   自豪 zìháo   傲慢 àomàn

骄傲 (**arrogant; proud; conceited; take pride in; pride**) 1.一般情况下"骄傲"是贬义词，有自以为了不起、瞧不起别人的意思。a pejorative term, conceited or looking down upon others: 我们永远不能骄傲。We should never become arrogant. 2.用褒义时，常指值得自豪的人或事物。an approbatory term, often refers to a just cause for self-esteem: 老科

学家为青年的成就感到骄傲。The old scientist takes pride in the achievements of his young colleagues. 3.还有确实了不起的意思。truly phenomenal: 这真是我们民族的骄傲。This is in truth the pride of our nation.

自豪 (have a proper sense of pride or dignity; be proud of sth.) 是褒义词。表示因自己或别人取得伟大成就而感到光荣。an approbatory term, proud of great successes achieved by oneself or other persons: 我们为祖国的伟大成就而感到自豪。We are proud of the great achievements of our motherland. / 自豪感 sense of pride

傲慢 (arrogant; haughty) 1.重点在"慢"，指看不起别人，态度冷淡、怠慢、没有礼貌。The key element is 慢, which describes a contemptuous, cold attitude: 他的态度很傲慢。He adopts an arrogant attitude. 2.用于褒义时，表示自尊而不可侮。an approbatory term, indicating that sb. has a strong sense of self-esteem and will brook no insults: 他的四方脸孔冷如铁块，带有自信、傲慢和威严难犯的神气，使左右不敢正视。His cold square face with its air of self-confidence, arrogance and dignity made one afraid to look him in the eye.

〔**相同点**〕：都是形容词。都有褒义，表示自尊。Syn. adj. as approbatory terms, they convey

151

the meaning of self−respect.

交换 jiāohuàn　交流 jiāoliú

交换 (exchange; swap) 表示双方各拿出自己的物品或某种意见给对方。着重在"换"，即互换的意思。expresses the idea that two persons present things or suggestions to each other, the key element is 换 (exchange)：交换意见 exchange views ／ 用小麦交换大米 barter wheat for rice

交流 (exchange; interflow; interchange) 指经常不断地或多次地互相给予。一般用于抽象的事物，如思想、经验、文化等。frequent or continuous exchange of ideas, experiences, culture or other abstract things：交流经验 exchange experiences ／ 经济和技术交流 economic and technical interchange

〔相同点〕：都是动词。表示彼此把自己有的东西给对方的意思。Syn. v. indicating that a person gives sth. and receives sth. else in return.

矫正 jiǎozhèng　改正 gǎizhèng

矫正 (correct; put right; rectify) 对象多半指不正确的姿势、动作、发音、语言或其他偏差。适用对象较窄。used in reference to incorrect

152

posture or movement, pronunciation, language or other such deviations. Its range of usage is limited：矫正视力 correct defects of vision ／ 矫正口吃 correct a stammer／ 矫正偏差 correct a deviation

改正 (correct; amend; put right) 对象多半指缺点、错误或问题等。运用对象较广。used of shortcomings, mistakes or problems. Its range of usage is wide：改正错误 correct one's mistakes

〔相同点〕：都是动词。都有把不正确的改为正确的意思。Syn. v. put right what is wrong.

教导 jiàodǎo　指导 zhǐdǎo　辅导 fǔdǎo

教导 (instruct; teach; give guidance) 有教育和引导的意思，指明方向。带尊敬色彩。用于长对幼，上级对下级。to instruct and lead or to point out a direction. It conveys a sense of respect, and is used of instructions given by older people to their juniors or by leaders to the subordinates：在老师的教导下，他有很大进步。He has been making great progress under the teacher's guidance.／ 母亲的教导记心间 bear in mind mother's teachings

指导 (guide; direct) 是指点的意思。给予指导的可以是人，也可以是事物。to give directions.

153

That which directs can be a person or an abstract entity: 老农指导青年干农活。The old peasants instructed the youths in farm work.

辅导 (**give guidance in study or training; coach**) 是指导和帮助的意思，多用于学习方面。to guide and help, generally in reference to study: 学习这篇文章，你给我们辅导、辅导，好吗？Could you give us some guidance in studying this article? 辅导孩子们练武术 coach the children in Wu Shu exercises

〔相同点〕：都是动词。都有启发、帮助的意思。Syn. v. to enlighten, to help.

教室 jiàoshì   课堂 kètáng

教室 (**classroom; schoolroom**) 专指供上课用的房间。使用范围较小。a room where a class meets. It has a limited range of usage: 这是我们的教室。This is our classroom.

课堂 (**classroom; schoolroom**) 除指用来上课的房间外，还可以泛指进行各种教学活动的场所，使用范围较大。常说："课堂纪律"等。apart from being used to refer to a room where a class meets, it can be used in a more abstract sense, or generally to refer to a location where teaching and learning take place. It has a wide range of usage. One often refers to "classroom discipline", etc.: 课堂讨论 classroom discussion / 课堂作业 classwork

〔相同点〕: 都是名词。指专供上课用的房间。Syn. n. a room where a class meets for a lesson.

解除 jiěchú　废除 fèichú　破除 pòchú

解除 (remove; relieve; get rid of) 着重指解去，去掉。对象常是束缚或压在身心上的东西，如痛苦、顾虑、危险、武装等。to get rid of sth. The object is sth. that oppresses the body or mind such as pain, worry, or danger. It can also be used in connection with weapons: 解除职务 remove someone from his or her post / 解除武装 disarm / 旱情已经解除。The dry spell is over. / 解除顾虑 free one's mind of apprehensions

废除 (abolish; abrogate; annul; repeal) 着重指取消、废止。对象常是不合理的或没用的东西，如制度、法令、条约等。to abrogate; to abolish. The object of this term is usually a law, decree, treaty or system which is unreasonable or useless: 废除一切不平等条约 abrogate all unequal treaties / 废除烦琐的礼节 do away with tedious formalities

破除 (do away with; get rid of; eradicate; break with) 着重指揭穿、打破。对象常是原来被

人特别重视的、或信仰的、蒙蔽人的东西，如迷信、成见、思想、习惯等。to do away or break with sth. The object of this term is usually sth. that people had faith in or respect for, which has turned out to be deceptive such as superstition, prejudice or custom: 破除迷信 do away with superstition／破除情面 not spare anybody's feelings

〔相同点〕: 都是动词。表示完全去掉不好的或没用的东西的意思。Syn. v. to get rid completely of what is bad or useless.

界限 jièxiàn　界线 jièxiàn

界限 (demarcation line; dividing line; limits; bounds; end) 1.主要指事物性质的区别。distinction between the nature of things: 打破植物、动物的界限 to get rid of the distinction between plants and animals 2.还指尽头和限度的意思。end or limit: 潜水员潜到超过危险界限的深水中去了。The diver went into the deep water beyond the danger limit.

界线 (boundary line) 主要指不同地区的分界。也可指事物性质的区别。the dividing line of different areas, may also refer to distinctions between the nature of things: 机场界线灯 boundary light／他把球踢过了界线。He kicked the ball over the boundary.

〔相同点〕：都是名词。表示不同事物的分界的意思。Syn. n. the dividing line between different things.

进步 jìnbù　先进 xiānjìn

进步 (advance; progress; improve; progressive) 1.着重于思想领先。指对社会发展起促进作用，常用来形容包含思想的事物，如言论、作品、书刊、艺术等。refers to the vanguard of progressive thought or to sth. which impels forward the development of society; frequently used of opinions, literature, newspaper and periodicals, art, etc.：进步势力 progressive forces 2.还有动词意义和用法，指人或物向前、向好的方向发展。跟"退步"相反。as a verb, indicates that sb. or sth. is moving forward in the right direction. It is the opposite of 退步 (retrograde)：你的发音很有进步。Your pronunciation has greatly improved.

先进 (advanced) 着重指思想或水平领先。"先进"是指比一般进步快、水平高。跟"后进"相对。indicates that ideas or standards are in the vanguard. It refers to extraordinarily rapid progress or an exceptionally higher level, and is the opposite of 后进 (lagging behind)：

157

先进经验 advanced experience／后进赶先进。
Those falling behind strive to catch up with the
more advanced.

〔相同点〕：都是形容词。表示在前列的，领先的，
值得学习的，与"落后"相对。Syn. adj. in the
forefront or in the vanguard and worth emu-
lating; the opposite of 落后 (backward).

进攻 jìngōng　进击 jìnjí　进犯 jìnfàn

进攻 (**attack; assault; offensive**)　是中性词 1.我们
对敌人或敌人对我们都可以用。a neutral
term; it can be used either of an enemy or of
oneself: 做好进攻准备 get ready to take the offensive 2.还指在斗争或竞赛中发动攻势，常
用于体育、思想等方面。to launch an offen-
sive during a struggle or contest, often used in
the context of sports or ideology: 发起全面进
攻 launch an all-out offensive

进击 (**advance on**)　是中性词。是进攻、攻击的意
思，具有较强的进攻精神，不用于言论等方
面。a neutral term; to launch a powerful attack or assault. It is not used of verbal at-
tacks: 我们的士兵勇敢地向敌人进击。Our
soldiers advanced bravely against the enemy.

进犯 (**intrude into; invade**)　是贬义词。表示进攻侵
犯的意思。对象多是指地方，只用于敌对

158

我。a pejorative term, to intrude into or invade. It is only applied to an enemy attack. Its object is often a place name: 打败进犯敌人 beat back the invading enemy / 全歼进犯之敌 wipe out the invading enemy

〔相同点〕: 都是动词。表示攻打敌人的意思。Syn. v. to attack the enemy.

精力 jīnglì　精神 jīngshen

精力 (energy; vigor; vim) 兼指精神和体力。refers to mental vigor and physical strength: 精力充沛 very energetic / 集中精力解决主要矛盾 concentrate one's effort on solving the main contradiction

精神 (vigor; vitality; drive; spirit; mind; consciousness; essence; gist) 1.不兼指体力。常与振作、饱满、好、坏等词搭配。is not used of physical energy; often qualified by adjectives indicating the state of one's spirits: 精神饱满 full of vitality 2.还有形容词的用法和意义，意思是"有生气"。When used as an adjective, it means animated, vivacious: 那孩子大大的眼睛，怪精神的。That child with big eyes is certainly full of life. 3."精神"与"物质"相对。这时"精神"读 "jīngshén". spiritual, mental; the opposite of "物质" (material), pronounced "jīngshén"：给予精神上的支持 give moral support / 作好精神准备 be mentally prepared 4.还有宗旨的意思，指主要意义。这时"精神"读"jīngshén". purport; indicating the main idea of sth., pronounced "jīngshén"：译者没有体会原文的精神。The translator failed to fully understand the essence of the original.

〔相同点〕：都是名词。指人表现出来的活力。Syn. n. vigor displayed by sb.

纠正 jiūzhèng　更正 gēngzhèng

纠正 **(correct; put right; redress)** 指改正错误的意思，对象多指偏向、过失等。to correct faults. The object is usually a deviation, mistake, etc.：纠正不正之风 put right unhealthy tendencies / 纠正错误 correct a mistake / 纠正姿势 correct one's posture / 问题处理不当的，应予纠正。Cases which have not been handled properly should be rectified.

更正 **(make corrections)** 一般指改正消息、语言文字和演算的错误。refers to the correction of errors in news reports, language, or mathmatical calculations：更正文章中的错误 make corrections in articles

〔相同点〕：都是动词。都有改变不正确的意思。Syn. v. to change what is incorrect.

决 jué 绝 jué

决 **(decide; determine; definitely; certainly; under any circumstances)** 强调的是一定、肯定。"决不"的意思是"一定不"或"肯定不"。stressing the idea of certainty, positiveness or definiteness. 决不 indicates certainly not, assuredly not: 决非恶意 with no malice whatsoever / 我们不达目的决不罢休。 We will never give up until the goal is reached.

绝 **(extremely; most; absolutely; in the least; by any means; on any account)** 强调的是绝对。"绝不"就是"绝对不"或"全然不"的意思。the emphasis is on the concept of absoluteness. When used with 不, it means absolutely not: 绝大错误 monstrous error / 绝好的机会 an excellent opportunity / 绝无此意 have absolutely no such intentions

〔相同点〕：都是副词。用在"不、无、非"等否定词前面，表示无论如何。Syn. adv. used before negative particles, such as 不，无，and 非；indicating "in any case", "whatever happens".

K

看 kàn　瞧 qiáo　望 wàng

看 **(see; look at; watch; read; think; call on; visit; depend on)** 泛指视线接触的一切。refers generally to all acts involving vision：看电视 watch TV／我看报。I read the newspaper.／你看这个人可靠吗? Do you think this person is reliable?／我明天去看他。I shall go to see him tomorrow.／明天是不是去，得看天气。Whether we shall go or not tomorrow will depend on the weather.

瞧 **(look; see)** 多用于口语。有时指仔细地看。often used in spoken language; sometimes means to look carefully：等着瞧吧 wait and see／你瞧着办吧。You can do as you see fit.／仔细瞧一下儿 look at it carefully

望 **(gaze into the distance; look over; call on; visit; hope; expect; reputation; prestige)** 一般指往远处望看，有时指不仔细地看，有时指带着希望或失望等心情看。usually refers to looking into the far distance; sometimes refers to looking at sth. casually; may imply hope or disappointment：放眼望去 look ahead as far as

162

the eye can reach／望了他一眼 shot a glance at him／望送回 hoping you will return as soon as possible

〔相同点〕：都是动词。都有使视线接触人或物的意思。Syn. v. to look or glance at sb. or sth.

看法 kànfǎ　观点 guāndiǎn　见解 jiànjiě

看法 (a way of looking at a thing; view) 泛指人们对事物的某种认识。one's views on a certain matter. 对这个问题有两种不同的看法。There are two different views on this question.

观点 (point of view; viewpoint; standpoint) 1.着重指人们从一定的立足点得出的一种正式的、稳定的认识。a formal and settled standpoint: 阐明观点 explain one's position／阶级观点 class viewpoint 2.还指观察、处理事物时所处的位置、立足点、着眼点。position; standpoint; or perspective from which one observes or addresses matters: 你的观点是什么? What is your position?

见解 (view; opinion; standpoint) 着重指自己对事物的理解，是经过思考、分析或研究得出的一种比较正式、比较稳定的认识。one's understanding of a matter — a formal and settled view arrived at through reflection, analysis or research: 对这个问题他没有提出任何

163

新的见解。He did not put forward any new ideas on the subject. / 这只是我个人的见解。That is just my own opinion.

〔相同点〕：都是名词。都表示对事物的一种认识。Syn. n. one's view of a matter.

考查 kǎochá　考察 kǎochá

考查 (examine; check) 着重指依据一定的标准去考核、检查。"考查"的对象多半是人们的所作所为，如成绩、学习、业务等。to examine or check sth. according to certain criteria. The objects of examination are human activities such as achievements, study, professional competence, vocation, work, etc.：考查学生成绩 check students' work / 实习生顺利地通过了考查。The trainees checked out all right.

考察 (inspect; make an on-the-spot investigation; observe and study) 1.指规模较大的调查研究。to study or investigate on a large scale：他们去南极考察了。They have gone on an expedition to the Antarctic. / 他们正进行野生植物考察。They are making a survey of wild plants. 2.又指细致深刻地分析观察问题，目的是收集材料，弄清问题的本质。对象多半是山川、地形、地质等。to inspect or observe sth. in great detail in order to collect data or illumi-

nate the essence of a problem. The object
may be mountains and rivers, topography,
geology, etc.: 考察水利工程 investigate water
conservancy projects

〔相同点〕: 表示用一定的标准来了解和弄清事物的
情况 Syn. v. to try to arrive at a clear understanding of sth. through investigation according to certain criteria.

考虑 kǎolǜ　斟酌 zhēnzhuó

考虑 (think over; consider) 指思索问题。对象较
广，还可以是较大的事情。to think over
problems; takes a wide range of objects, and
may refer to important matters: 让我考虑一
下再答复你。Let me think it over before I give
you an answer. / 这方面的情况你考虑了吗?
Have you taken this aspect of the matter into account?

斟酌 (consider; deliberate) 着重指根据具体情况反
复思索看是否可行或是否适当。对象常是小
事情及文章的内容和词句等。to think a mat-
ter over and over to determine whether it is
workable or appropriate. The object is often
a minor matter, or the content or language of
a written text: 再三斟酌 consider carefully again
and again / 斟酌情况作适当调整 make appro-

priate adjustments in the light of circumstances

〔相同点〕：都是动词。都表示仔细地想的意思。
Syn. v. to think sth. over seriously.

渴望 kěwàng　盼望 pànwàng

渴望 **(thirst for; long for; yearn for)** 着重指如饥似
渴地希望。语气比"盼望"重。to feel a strong
desire for sth. It is stronger in tone than 盼
望：许多青年渴望参军。Many young people
long to join the army.

盼望 **(hope for; long for; look forward to)** 着重指怀
着深情地希望。语气比"希望"重。to hope
for sth. with depth of feeling. Its tone is
stronger than that of 希望：他日夜盼望回
家。Day and night he looked forward to returning
home.

〔相同点〕：都是动词。表示要满足某种愿望、从内
　　　　　心发出一种要求的意思。Syn. v. to seek for
　　　　　the satisfaction of a desire; to yearn for sth.

克制 kèzhì　抑制 yìzhì

克制 **(restrain; hold back)** 主要指用力量控制自己
思想感情的冲动。常用于对自己，不用于别
人对自己。to control one's impulses; refers
to self-imposed restraint only; not to re-

166

straints imposed by others: 克制自己的感情
restrain one's feelings / 表现很大的克制 exercise great restraint

抑制 (**restrain; control; check**) 主要指把某种情绪压下去的意思。对象可以是自己的思想感情，还可以是力量等。常用于对自己，不用于别人对自己。to suppress one's emotions, etc.; the object can be either a feeling or a physical phenomenon. Like 克制，it refers to a self−imposed constraint: 抑制自己的愤怒 contain one's anger / 眼泪抑制不住直往下流 be unable to hold back one's tears

〔相同点〕: 都是动词。都有用一种力量对思想感情或某种行动加以限制的意思。Syn. v. to restrain one's ideas, feelings or actions by force.

空洞 kōngdòng 空虚 kōngxū

空洞 (**empty; hollow; devoid of content**) 指没有内容或内容不充实，多用于文辞表达方面。devoid of content or lacking solid content; mostly used in connection with literary expression: 空洞的理论 empty theory / 空洞的词句 empty phraseology

空虚 (**hollow; void**) 指力量不足，包括物质力量和精神力量。lacking either physical or spiritual strength: 生活空虚 lead a life devoid of mean-

ing / 敌人后方空虚。The enemy rear is weakly
defended.

〔相同点〕：都是形容词。都表示内容不充实的意
思。Syn. adj. having no solid content.

夸奖 kuājiǎng　夸耀 kuāyào

夸奖 (praise; commend) 是褒义词。有称赞的意
思。常用于表扬、称赞别人。an approbatory
term; to praise; generally used in the sense of
praising others: 师傅夸奖他进步快。The mas-
ter praised him for his rapid progress.

夸耀 (brag about; show off; flaunt) 有炫耀、显示的
意思，是贬义词，常用于向别人显示自己。a
pejorative term; to show off or make a
display; used in the sense of bragging about
oneself to others: 她从不夸耀自己。She never brags. / 夸耀他的见识 show off his knowledge and experience

〔相同点〕：都是动词。都表示把好处说出来，让
人家知道的意思。Syn. v. to praise someone's
strong points in order to make them known to
others.

168

L

拉拢 lālong　笼络 lǒngluò

拉拢 (draw sb. over to one's side; rope in)　1.本义是用力收拢的意思。to draw towards oneself by exerting physical force: 第四次把网拉拢来的时候，他觉得太重了，简直拉不动。When he drew the net in for the fourth time, he felt it was too heavy to haul for him. 2.引申义指用不正当的手段把别人拉到自己方面来，共同进行不正当的活动或阴谋活动。The extended meaning is to draw sb. over to one's side by improper means in order to carry on improper or conspiratorial activities: 宗派主义者总拉拢一些人，排挤一些人。Sectarians are always drawing some people in and forcing others out. / 不要受坏人拉拢！Don't get roped in by bad people!

笼络 (win sb. over by any means; rope in)　指用欺骗手段取得别人信任，并使别人为自己利用。to win the confidence of sb. by deceitful means, and make use of him or her: 笼络人心。try to win people's support by hook or by crook

169

〔相同点〕：都是动词。表示用某种不正当的手段把别人拉到自己方面来加以利用的意思，是贬义词。Syn. v. to draw sb. over to one's side by improper means and make use of him or her; pejorative terms.

牢固 láogù　稳固 wěngù
坚固 jiāngù　巩固 gǒnggù

牢固 (firm; secure) 着重指特别牢，经久不变。常形容建筑物等具体的东西。describes sth. especially firm and durable, often used in connection with concrete things such as buildings: 地基很牢固。The foundations are very firm.

稳固 (firm; stable) 着重指安稳、不易动摇。常形容某些抽象事物，有时也形容某些具体的东西。refers to sth. which is very steady, firm and not easily moved; often used to describe both abstract and concrete things: 稳固的基础 solid foundation / 稳固的政权 a stable government

坚固 (firm; solid; sturdy; strong) 着重指物质结合紧密，物品结实。常形容某些具体的东西或建筑物，如房屋、桥梁、床、车等。of solid or compact structure; describes concrete things such as buildings, bridges, beds and

vehicles。坚固耐用 sturdy and durable / 坚固的
工事 strong fortifications / 这座桥造得很坚
固。This bridge is very solidly built.

巩固 (consolidated; strong; solid; stable; consolidate; strengthen; solidity) 着重指在原有基础上更加
不易破坏，不易动摇。常形容抽象事物，如政
权、友谊、团结等。还有动词意义，表示使巩
固的意思。indicates that the original foundation is strengthened, making it even more difficult to destroy or move; often used in reference
to abstract things such as political power,
friendship or unity. When used as a verb, it
means to make sth. more solid。巩固的国防
strong national defence / 巩固阵地 to consolidate
a position / 巩固我们的友谊 to strengthen our
friendship

〔相同点〕: 都是形容词。表示不易破坏的意思。能
形容"基础"。Syn. adj. not easily destroyed;
used to describe foundations.

黎明 **límíng**　凌晨 **língchén**　拂晓 **fúxiǎo**

黎明 (dawn; daybreak) 意义范围较广。可指天快
亮的时候，也可指天刚亮的时候，还常用于
比喻。has a wide range of usage; indicates
daybreak or, sometimes, just before daybreak,
sometimes also used metaphorically：从黎明到

171

夜晚 from dawn till dusk / 天刚黎明。The day was just dawning.

凌晨 (in the small hours; before dawn) 意义范围更广。可以指半夜以后不久到天明的各个时候，有时在"凌晨"后注明具体时间。may refer to any period of time from shortly after midnight till daybreak. It has an even wider range of usage, and is sometimes followed by an expression of definite time：火车将于明日凌晨四时半到达。The train arrives at half past four tomorrow morning.

拂晓 (before dawn) 意义范围较窄，指天快亮的时候。常用于指军事行动的时间。indicates only the point of daybreak, often refers to the timing of a military operation：拂晓前发起总攻。Start the general offensive before dawn.

〔相同点〕：都是名词。表示天亮前后的意思。常用于书面语。Syn. n. the time around daybreak; often used in written language.

礼拜 lǐbài　星期 xīngqī

礼拜 (Sunday; week; religious service) 1. 多用于口语。"礼拜"也是星期天或礼拜日的意思。often used in spoken language with the same meaning as 星期天 or 礼拜日 (Sunday)：今天礼拜几？What day is it today? / 今天是礼拜

天。Today is Sunday. 2.原指宗教徒向神行礼。originally refers to religious worship: 做礼拜 go to church

星期 (week) 一般用于书面语，特别是新闻语体或其他正式的场合。used in written language, especially in journalistic writing, and in more formal speech: 今天星期几? What day is it today? / 星期天休息 Sunday is a holiday.

〔相同点〕：都是名词。作息时间单位，七天一个周期，一般可以通用。Syn. n. time unit of work and rest, usually interchangeable.

历来 lìlái　向来 xiànglái　从来 cónglái

历来 (always; constantly; all through the ages) 后面多跟肯定形式，很少跟否定形式。多用于书面语，语气不及"向来"、"从来"那么强。often followed by an affirmative statement, seldom by a negative one; mostly used in written language; its tone is not as strong as that of 向来 and 从来: 历来如此 This has always been the case. / 这些岛屿历来都是中国的领土。These islands have been Chinese territory from time immemorial.

向来 (always; all along) 后面既可跟肯定形式也可跟否定形式。在口语和书面语中都常用。followed by an affirmative or a negative

173

statement, used in both written and spoken language: 我向来不抽烟。I never smoke. / 向来如此。It has always been so.

从来 (**always; at all times; all along**) 后面跟否定形式居多，也跟肯定形式。口语和书面语均常用。followed by a negative statement, or occasionally by an affirmative one, used in both written and spoken language: 我从来没见过他。I have never seen him before. / 世界各国人民从来都是互相支持的。The people of all countries have always supported each other in struggle.

〔相同点〕：都是副词。都有从过去到现在一直是这样的意思。常通用。Syn. adv. unchanging or unceasing from the past up to the present; used interchangeably.

力量 liliang　力气 liqi

力量 (**physical strength; power; strength; force**) 1.表示力气的意思。(physical) strength: 团结就是力量。Union is strength. 2.表示能力的意思。ability: 尽一切力量完成任务 go all out to accomplish the task 3. 表示作用或效力的意思。function or effect: 这种农药力量大。This pesticide is very effective.

力气 (**physical strength; effort**) 只表示人或动物筋肉产生的效能。the physical strength of human beings or animals: 他很有力气。He is very strong. / 不费力气是学不了的。You cannot learn without making an effort.

〔相同点〕：都是名词。都有劲头的意思。Syn. n. physical strength.

临时 línshí　暂时 zànshí

临时 (for a short time; at the time when sth. happens; temporary; provisional) 1.表示临到事情发生的时候，这时是副词。adv. at the time just before sth. happens, at the last moment: 事先作好准备，免得临时忙乱。Arrange everything in advance so that you won't be in a rush at the last moment. 2.表示非正式的、非固定的、非经常的意思。如"临时工"等。informal; irregular, for example 临时工 (casual workers): 临时法庭 provisional court / 临时主席 interim chairman

暂时 (temporary; transient) 只表示短时间之内的意思。within a limited period of time: 这件事暂时就这样定了吧。Let's make it a tentative decision. / 比赛的胜负是暂时的，而友谊是长久的。The results of contests are transient, but friendship is lasting.

〔相同点〕：都是形容词。表示短时间，不长久的意思。Syn. n. a short period of time.

灵活 línghuó 灵巧 língqiǎo

灵活 (**nimble; agile; quick; flexible; elastic**) 主要指活泼，机灵。常形容人们反应敏锐，以及运用规律和执行方针、政策不机械等。lively and clever, used to describe people who have quick reactions or are flexible in administering laws or in implementing principles and policies: 手脚灵活 dexterous and nimble / 灵活机动的战略战术 flexible strategy and tactics

灵巧 (**dexterous; nimble; skilful; ingenious**) 主要指灵便、精巧、不笨拙的意思。常用以形容人们手艺、技术高超。nimble; ingenious; not clumsy, often used to describe cunning workmanship or exceptional skill: 做得真灵巧。It is most ingeniously made. / 她的体操动作准确而灵巧。Her movements in callisthenics were precise and nimble. / 一双灵巧的手 a clever pair of hands

〔相同点〕: 都是形容词。都表示活泼、机智、不呆板。Syn. adj. lively; resourceful; not rigid.

伶俐 línglì 聪明 cōngming

伶俐 (**clever; bright; quick-witted**) 除指智力强以外，还指动作灵活。如常说"口齿伶俐"。常用来形容青少年，特别是少年儿童，有时也

176

形容小动物。of high intelligence; quick-witted and prompt to act. 口齿伶俐 (clever and fluent) is often used to describe young children, and sometimes also small animals: 孩子真伶俐。What a clever child!

聪明 (intelligent; bright; clever） 常形容人，有时借用来形容动物。口语和书面语都常用。describes people and sometimes also animals; used in both spoken and written language: 聪明能干 bright and capable / 聪明反被聪明误。Clever people may be victims of their own cleverness. / 聪明一世，糊涂一时。Smart as a rule, but this time a fool.

〔相同点〕：都是形容词。表示智力强，思维能力超过一般的意思。Syn. adj. possessing high intelligence or extraordinary mental ability.

流畅 liúchàng　流利 liúlì

流畅 (easy and smooth） 使用范围较窄，多半形容文章或作品的语言文字。has a narrow range of usage; mostly applied to the language used in literary works: 文笔流畅 write with ease and grace / 这篇文章读起来很流畅。The essay reads very smoothly.

流利 (fluent; smooth） 1.使用范围较广，不限于形容书面语言，也可以形容说话快而且清楚。

has a wider range of usage; describes written language and also quick, clear speech: 她说一口流利的英语。 She speaks fluent English. / 她文章读得流利。 She read the article fluently. 2.还指灵活、不凝滞的意思。 nimble; not clumsy: 她字写得流利。 She writes an easy, flowing hand.

〔相同点〕：都是形容词。都表示语言很通顺。Syn. adj. applied to clear, easy speech and writing.

流浪 liúlàng　流落 liúluò

流浪 (roam about; lead a vagrant life) 指漂泊不定，没有固定的住所。 to drift about, having no permanent dwelling place: 流浪街头 roam the streets

流落 (wander about destitute) 指虽然身在他乡，却暂时有落脚的地方。 to wander in a place far away from home, able nonetheless to find a place to stay: 流落他乡 wander destitute far away from home

〔相同点〕：都是动词。都有飘流在外，无家可归的意思。 Syn. v. to drift about without a home to go to.

178

流亡 liúwáng　逃亡 táowáng

流亡 (be forced to leave one's native land; go into exile) 着重指流落他乡，生活不安定。to wander destitute far away from home, living an unsettled life: 他前后两次被迫流亡国外。He was twice forced into exile abroad.

逃亡 (become a fugitive; flee from home; go into exile) 着重指外逃的意思。to flee from one's home to some other place: 解放前，他逃亡到日本一直呆了十年。Before liberation he fled to Japan where he stayed for 10 years.

〔相同点〕：都是动词。表示因灾害或政治、经济等原因，离开本乡或本国去谋生或从事政治、文化活动的意思。Syn. v. leave one's native place or one's country due to natural calamity or for political and economic reasons, and go elsewhere to make a living or to engage in political or cultural activities.

屡次 lǚcì　一再 yīzài

屡次 (time and again; repeatedly) 强调动作或活动的次数多。语气比"一再"轻。indicates that actions and activities taken place very frequently. Its tone is lighter than that of 一再: 屡次打

179

破全国纪录 repeatedly break the national records

一再 (**time and again; again and again; repeatedly**)
强调动作或活动的重复、反复。语气比"屡次"重。denotes the repetition of an action or activity. Its tone is stronger than that of 屡次：
一再宣称 declare time and again ／一再表示感谢 express one's gratitude again and again

〔相同点〕：都是副词。表示一次又一次。Syn. adv. again and again.

M

毛病 máobìng　　缺点 quēdiǎn　　缺陷 quēxiàn

毛病 **(trouble; mishap; breakdown; defect; shortcoming; fault; mistake)** 1.常指较小的习惯性缺点，语气较轻。常用于口语。small habitual failing. It is light in tone and often used in spoken language：他的毛病是性急。The trouble with him is that he is impetuous. 2.还指器物出了故障或指工作的失误。indicates a (mechanical) defect or breakdown or an error in one's work：发动机出了毛病。There is something wrong with the engine.

缺点 **(shortcoming; defect; weakness; drawback)** 着重指欠缺的意思。跟"优点""成绩"相对。语气较重，意义较肯定。口语和书面语都常用。indicates that sth. is lacking; contrasts with 优点 (merit) and 成绩 (achievement), has a strong tone and conveys a definite judgment, frequently used in both spoken and written language：克服工作中的缺点 overcome shortcomings in one's work /这种药的主要缺点是败胃。The chief drawback of the medicine is that it spoils your appetite.

缺陷 (defect; drawback; flaw; blemish) 表示不完满的意思，多用来指人生理上的毛病或社会组织的某些缺点。indicates that sth. is imperfect; refers mainly to physical defects or shortcomings in a social organization: 不要嘲笑人家的生理缺陷。Don't laugh at others' physical defects. / 这个计划有些缺陷。The plan has some shortcomings.

〔相同点〕：都是名词。表示不完美的，不完备的意思。Syn. n. imperfection, incompleteness.

美丽 měili 漂亮 piàoliang

美丽 (beautiful) 1.指给人以美感的。arousing a sense of beauty: 美丽的姑娘 a beautiful girl 2.还有美好、使人感到高尚的意思。多用来形容花朵、远景、青春等。indicates that sth. is of great excellence and inspires people with noble feelings, often used to describe flowers, scenery, youth, etc.: 美丽的花朵 beautiful flowers / 美丽富饶的国家 a beautiful and richly-endowed country

漂亮 (handsome; good-looking; pretty; beautiful; remarkable; brilliant; splendid) 1.着重指外表好看。使用范围较窄，常形容具体事物，不形容抽象事物。having a fine exterior; has a narrow range of usage and is not used to describe abstract things: 打扮得漂漂亮亮的 be smartly dressed 2.还指超出一般的，出色的，精彩的意思。uncommon; remarkable; brilliant: 守门员这个球救得真漂亮。The goalie made a beautiful save. 3."漂亮话"指华而不实的话。漂亮话 refers to high-sounding words without real substance: 那个人爱说漂亮话。That man is a mere talker.

〔相同点〕：都是形容词。表示好看的意思。可以形容人和事物，如衣服、建筑、花朵、山河、图画等。Syn. adj. good looking, describing people and things — clothes, buildings, flowers, rivers, mountains and pictures, etc.

美满 měimǎn　圆满 yuánmǎn

美满 (happy; perfect; satisfactory) 着重指美好、完美的意思。常用来形容生活、社会、家庭、婚姻等。常做定语。glorious; perfect; often used to describe life, society, family, marriage, etc.; usually functions as an attributive: 美满的生活 a happy life / 美满的婚姻 happy marriage

圆满 (satisfactory; successful; complete) 着重指完备周全或完全符合所希望的意思。常用来形容答案、结果、理由，完成等，常作状语。complete and thorough; wholly meeting one's

183

desires; modifies answer, result, reason, etc.,
often used as an adverbial: 圆满的成功
complete success / 圆满的答案 a satisfactory
answer / 问题圆满地解决了。 The problem has
been solved satisfactorily.

〔相同点〕: 都是形容词。表示事情完美, 使人满意
的意思。 Syn. adj. consummate and satisfying.

秘密 mìmì 神秘 shénmì 机密 jīmì

秘密 (**secret; clandestine; confidential**) 指不公开,
不让大家知道的意思, 也可以做名词用, 如
保守秘密。 kept hidden from others, not
made known to the public; also used as a
noun in collocations such as 保守秘密
(keep secret): 秘密会议 secret meeting / 秘
密活动 clandestine activities / 探索海底秘密
explore the secrets of the ocean

神秘 (**mysterious; mystical**) 有使人摸不透, 高深
莫测的意思。 不能做名词。 inscrutable;
unfathomable; not used as a noun: 神秘人物
a mysterious person / 哲学并不神秘。 Philoso-
phy is no mystery.

机密 (**secret; classified; confidential**) 指重要而秘
密。也可以做名词用。多用于庄重的场合和
比较重要的事情。 often used to describe sth.

184

that is very important and confidential, also used as a noun; generally refers to matters of great consequence: 严守国家的机密 strictly guard state secrets／机密文件 classified papers

〔相同点〕：都是形容词。都有事物内部情况尚未被人们了解的意思。Syn. adj. indicating that the inner reality of sth. is not known.

密切 mìqiè 亲密 qīnmì

密切 (close; intimate; intently; closely) 1.着重指关系近，使用范围广，常形容人的关系和事物的关系。refers to a close relationship, widely used to describe relations between people, things or circumstances: 密切两国关系 build closer relations between the two countries／密切注视 pay close attention to; watch closely

亲密 (close; intimate) 着重指感情好的意思。使用范围较窄。一般只形容人的关系，感情。refers to emotional closeness, normally only between people. Its range of usage is narrow: 亲密的战友 close comrade-in-arms／亲密无间 be on very intimate terms with each other

〔相同点〕：都是形容词。表示关系近，感情好的意思。Syn. adj. closely connected to another or cherishing intimate, warm feelings.

185

明白 míngbai   清楚 qīngchu

明白 **(clear; obvious; plain; frank; unequivocal; understand; realize; know)** 1.作形容词时，着重指明显易懂。使用范围较窄。一般只形容内容、意思、道理、任务、话语等较抽象事物。adj. clear and easy to understand; describes only abstract matters such as subject matter, ideas, reasons, tasks, language, etc.: 他讲得明白易懂。He spoke clearly and simply. 2.作动词时，着重指由不了解到了解的意思。v. refers to the process of coming to understand sth.: 我不明白你的意思。I can't understand what you mean. / 我忽然明白了。The truth suddenly dawned on me. 3.作形容词时还有两个意义：a. 表示公开的，不含糊的意思。b. 表示聪明，懂道理的意思。as an adjective it has two meanings: a. public; unambiguous; b. intelligent; understanding the whys and wherefores of things: 他明白表示不赞成这个提议。He stated clearly that he didn't agree with the proposal. / 明白事理 have good sense

清楚 **(clear; be clear about; understand)** 1.作形容词时，着重指清晰，有条理的意思。使用范围较广，还能形容历史、思想、声音等事物。adj. clear; distinct; presented in an orderly

186

way; modifies history, idea, sound, etc.: 他的话说得不清楚。He didn't speak clearly. ／把工作交代清楚 explain one's job clearly on handing it over 2.作动词时，着重指清晰地了解的意思。一般不带宾语。v. to know sth. clearly; does not normally take an object: 头脑清楚 a clear head 3.作形容词时，还可表示对事物了解很透彻的意思，跟"糊涂"相对。adj. understanding thoroughly the implications of sth., the opposite of 糊涂（muddle-headed）：这个问题你清楚不清楚？Are you clear about this issue?

〔相同点〕：1.都可做形容词。有不含糊，有条理的意思。Syn. adj. be unambiguous, or presented in an orderly way. 2.都可做动词。有懂得，了解的意思。v. to understand

名誉 míngyù　荣誉 róngyù

名誉（**fame; reputation; honorary**）是中性词。1.指个人或集体的名声的意思。a neutral term., the reputation of an individual or a collective: 名誉好 have a good reputation ／闹名誉地位 be out for fame and position 2.还有只担任名义，不负实际责任的意思。describes a position which is purely titular and has no duties attached to it: 名誉主席 honorary

187

chairman

荣誉 (honor; credit; glory) 是褒义词。指个人或集体由于对社会有了贡献，从而在社会上有了好名声。an approbatory term, indicating that a person or a collective enjoys a good reputation owing to contributions made to society: 为祖国赢得荣誉 win honor for one's country / 爱护集体的荣誉 cherish the good name of the collective / 荣誉感 sense of honor

〔相同点〕：都是名词。都有名声的意思。Syn. n. reputation.

陌生 mòshēng   生疏 shēngshū

陌生 (strange; unfamiliar) 从来不认识或先前认识而现在已经很不熟悉的意思。使用范围较窄，一般用于人和地方，有时用于语言，内容等，程度较重。indicates that sth. or sb. has become unfamiliar to one. Its range is generally limited to people and places, though it is sometimes used to modify language, subject matter, etc. The tone is strong: 陌生人 strangers / 在会场上我看到许多陌生的面孔。I saw many unfamiliar faces at the meeting. / 尽管我们初次见面，但并不感到陌生。Although this was only our first meeting, we didn't feel like strangers.

生疏 (not familiar; out of practice; rusty; not as close as before) 1.常表示不熟悉，没有接触过或很少接触过的意思。使用范围较广。可用于人、地方、语言、内容、工作等。程度较轻。to be unfamiliar, or to have little contact with sth., widely used in connection with people, places, language, subject matter, work, etc. The tone is less intense：人地生疏 be unfamiliar with the place and the people 2.还可表示技术和技艺等掌握得不熟悉（因长期荒废）或用得不纯熟。indicates that one is out of practice. 他的英文有点生疏了。His English is getting rusty. 3.表示感情淡薄的意思。shows that one's affection is becoming attenuated：多年不来往，我们的关系生疏了。We have not been in touch with each other for years, so we are not as close as we used to be.

〔相同点〕：都是形容词。表示不熟悉的意思，表示对人或对事物没有接触过的意思。Syn. adj. to be unfamiliar or to have had no contact with sb. or sth.

溺爱 nì'ài　宠爱 chǒng'ài

溺爱 (spoil; dote on) 过分地爱，无原则的爱，有姑息、纵容的意思。对象较窄，一般只指对孩子、学生。to show excessive, unprincipled love, indulgence to the point of connivance. Usually the objects are children or students: 做父母的应该正确对待自己的子女，不要溺爱他们，要严格要求他们。Parents should treat their children in a proper way. They mustn't dote on them, but be strict with them.

宠爱 (make a pet of sb.; dote on) 着重指另眼相看，偏爱，或指受到赏识。对象较广，多指对孩子、学生或下级，偶尔用于某事物。refers to favoritism and partiality, or to sb.'s being in another's good graces. The objects are mainly children, students or subordinates, only occasionally things: 别把孩子宠爱坏了。Don't spoil the child. / 他小时候很聪明，爱好读书，所以，很受老师的宠爱。As a boy, he was very clever and interested in books, so he became the teacher's pet.

〔相同点〕：都是动词。都有过分地爱，包括娇惯，纵容的意思。通常是指上对下的爱，都是贬义词。Syn. v. to love to an excessive degree, to the extent of spoiling and conniving, referring to love for one in a subordinate position or parental love for children; pejorative terms.

凝视 níngshì　注视 zhùshì

凝视 (gaze fixedly; stare) 着重指目光集中在具体事物的一点上，是表示比较长久地看着某一具体事物的意思。to concentrate one's eyes on one point or on a concrete object, i.e. to look at sth. for a long time: 凝视天空 to gaze into the sky

注视 (look attentively; gaze at) 1.着重于全神贯注，精神集中，指眼光集中，留神地看的意思。应用范围比"凝视"广。可指具体事物，也指抽象事物。to look at sth. attentively, with absorption; emphasizes mental concentration. Its range of usage is wider than that of 凝视。It can take both concrete and abstract objects: 久久注视着陌生人的脸 look fixedly at the stranger's face for a long time 2. 还有注意、重视的意思。to pay attention to or to take sth. seriously: 密切注视着会议的进展 closely follow the progress of the conference

〔相同点〕：都是动词。都表示集中注意力看的意思。Syn. v. to look at sth. with concentration.

浓厚 nónghòu　深厚 shēnhòu

浓厚 (dense; thick; strong; pronounced) 着重指成分多，密度大。常形容烟、气、色等具体东西，以及思想、兴趣（不用来形容感情）等抽象事物。indicates density and high concentration; used to describe physical phenomena like smoke, air and color as well as thought and interest, (but not feeling): 浓厚的云层 thick clouds / 浓厚的地方色彩 pronounced (marked) local color / 孩子们对中国的历史兴趣很浓厚。The children take a great interest in Chinese history.

深厚 (deep; profound; solid; deep-seated) 着重指深度大，常形容感情、同情、友谊等抽象事物。emphasizes depth; often describes such abstract things as feeling, sympathy and friendship: 深厚的感情 deep (profound) feelings / 他们在反对入侵的共同敌人的斗争中结下了深厚的友谊。They established a profound friendship in their struggle against the invasion by their common enemy.

〔相同点〕：都是形容词。表示程度深，不淡薄的意思。Syn. adj. indicates intensity; not thin,

192

weak or unsubstantial.

O

偶尔 ǒu'ěr 偶然 ǒurán

偶尔 (once in a while; occasionally) 表示某种事情发生的次数少，时间不定，或某种现象是少见的。跟"经常"相对。indicates that sth. happens infrequently and irregularly or is a rare phenomenon. It is the opposite of 经常 (often)：我们偶尔见面。We see each other once in a long while.

偶然 (accidental; fortuitous; chance) 1.着重表示事情的发生是意外的，是在规律之外的，跟"必然"相对。indicates that sth. happens by chance and does not conform to any pattern. It is the opposite of 必然 (inevitable)：偶然现象 accidental phenomena／偶然遇见一个老朋友 meet an old friend by chance 2.表示并非必然时，还常作定语，谓语。not inevitable; in this case often used as an attributive or a predicate：偶然误差 accidental error

〔相同点〕：都是副词。表示不经常的意思，都可作状语。Syn. adv. not often, used as adverbials.

P

胖 pàng　肥 féi

胖 (fat; stout; plump) 指脂肪多、肉多。只用来形容人。excessively fat and fleshy; describes human beings only：他胖起来了。He is getting fat or He is putting on weight.

肥 (fat; loose-fitting; loose; large) 1.一般只指含脂肪多。常用来形容牛、羊、猪、马等动物，或它们的肉。有时用于形容人，常含贬义。having too much fat; describes livestock such as cows, sheep, pigs and horses as well as meat, sometimes used to describe persons, in a strongly pejorative sense：这肉太肥了。The meat is too fatty. 2. 还有宽大的意思，常形容衣服。loose, used of clothes：这条裤子太肥了。These trousers are too baggy.

〔相同点〕：都是形容词。表示含脂肪多，跟"瘦"相反。Syn. adj. having too much fat, the opposite of 瘦 (thin).

平常 píngcháng　平凡 píngfán

平常 (ordinary; common; generally; usually; ordinarily; as a rule）着重指不特别的意思。常形容人或事物。not out of the ordinary; often used in reference to people, things and events：这种现象很平常。This is quite a common phenomenon. 2. 还有"平时""往常"之类的意思。ordinarily; as a rule：平常我很少进城。I don't go to town much as a rule. / 这个词儿平常很少用。This word is seldom used on ordinary occasions.

平凡 **(ordinary; common)** 指不奇特或不出色的意思，跟"伟大，非凡"等相对。"平凡"的否定说法是"不平凡"，含有褒义。语气比"平常"重。undistinguished, not remarkable; the opposite of 伟大 (great) or 非凡 (outstanding). Its negative form, 不平凡, is a term of approbation. It is stronger than 平常：他在平凡的岗位上做出不平凡的成绩。He has achieved extraordinary successes at an ordinary post.

〔相同点〕：都是形容词。表示普通，一般的意思。Syn. adj. common; general.

普遍 pǔbiàn 广泛 guǎngfàn

普遍 **(universal; general; widespread; common)** 指面比较全的，形容事物具有的共性。emphasizes comprehensiveness, universality：我们的

196

城市已经普遍用上煤气灶了。Gas stoves are now in common use in our city. / 这是普遍的真理。This is a universal truth.

广泛 (extensive; wide-ranging; wide-spread) 着眼于"广"。The emphasis is on vastness：我们进行了广泛的交谈。We had a wide-ranging conversation. / 我们广泛征求意见。We solicit opinions from all sides.

〔相同点〕：都是形容词。都指人们活动涉及的方面多，范围广。Syn. adj. referring to large-scale, wide-ranging activites and phenomena.

朴实 pǔshí   朴素 pǔsù

朴实 (simple; plain; sincere and honest; guileless) 着重指讲究实际，不求虚浮的意思。用于两方面：1.思想、感情等实在。concerned with realities; not superficial, it is used in two ways: 1. of thought, feeling, etc. which are honest and dependable：朴实无华 simple and unadorned / 文风朴实 simple style of writing 2. 做事或作风踏实、不浮夸。2. of an action or mode of operation which is down-to-earth and unostentatious：朴实的工作作风 a down-to-earth style of work

朴素 (simple; plain) 着重指讲究自然、保持原样

197

的意思。用于三方面：1.指衣着、陈设等不讲装饰。concerned with naturalness or striving after original purity. It is used in three ways: 1. referring to clothing or furnishings which are unadorned：衣着朴素 simply dressed 2.指思想感情等自然，不做作。2. referring to thought and feeling that are natural and unaffected：他养成朴素的生活作风。He cultivates the habit of simple and plain living. 3.生活不奢侈 3. refers to a way of life which is without luxury and extravagance：朴素的生活 simple life

〔相同点〕：都是形容词。表示不加修饰的意思。能形容衣着、陈设、语言、作品、思想、感情等。Syn. adj. unadorned, used to describe clothes, furnishings, language, works of literature and art, thought, feeling, etc.

198

Q

欺负 qīfu   欺侮 qīwǔ   欺压 qīyā

欺负 (bully; treat sb. high-handedly) 一般包含侵犯或侮辱的意思。程度可重可轻。书面语和口语都常用。usually implies humiliation, infringement upon someone's rights; the degree of gravity can vary; used in both written and spoken language: 大国不应当欺负小国。Big nations should not bully small ones.

欺侮 (bully; treat sb. high-handedly) 着重指侮辱，多指用轻慢的态度对待别人，程度较轻，多用于口语。to humiliate sb., to treat sb. with contempt; implies a less serious offence, often used in spoken language: 我们是工人，是这个厂的主人，谁也不敢来欺侮我们。We are workers, masters of the factory. Nobody dares bully us.

欺压 (bully and oppress; ride roughshod over) 着重指压迫，依仗权势欺负人，程度比"欺负"重。to oppress, victimize by abusing one's power. The tone is stronger than that of 欺负: 地主欺压农民。The landlords oppressed the peasants. / 军阀欺压老百姓。The warlords bullied the common people.

〔相同点〕：都是动词。都表示用蛮横无理的手段侵犯、压迫或侮辱的意思。Syn. v. to oppress, infringe or insult sb., in a rude or unreasonable manner.

期间 qījiān　时代 shídài

期间 (**time; period; course**) 专指有明显界限的一段时间。可以是较长的，也可以是较短的一段时间。a clearly delimited period of time, either long or short: 会议期间 in the course of the conference

时代 (**times; age; era; epoch**) 指历史、社会、国家、民族发展中的一段时间，一般是较长的一段时间。an era or age in the development of a society, country or people: a historical epoch. It refers to a relatively long period: 反映我们时代的面貌 reflect the feature of our age／青年时代 one's youth／开创一个新时代 usher in a new era

〔相同点〕：都是名词。都表示一段时间的意思。Syn. n. a period of time.

奇怪 qíguài　古怪 gǔguài

奇怪 (**strange; surprising; odd**) 1.是中性词。常形

容人、自然现象等。使用范围较广。a neutral term, commonly used to describe people, natural phenomena, etc., has a wide range of usage: 陨石雨是一种自然现象，没有什么可奇怪的。A meteorite shower is a natural phenomenon. There is nothing strange about it. 2.还有一个动词意义，表示出乎意料，难以理解，"以为奇怪"的意思 v. to be inexplicable, unexpected; to be surprised: 真奇怪，他们至今还一无所知。It is most surprising that they should still be in the dark. / 整个事情使我们感到十分奇怪。The whole thing is a great surprise to us.

古怪 (eccentric; odd; outlandish; grotesque) 多半形容人的性情、性格、脾气、声音、衣着、样子、活动等，有时也形容文章、问题。常含贬义、使用范围较窄。often used to describe character, temperament, voice, clothing, style or activities, sometimes describes literary works or questions or matters at issue. It is often pejorative, and has a comparatively narrow range of usage: 古怪的脾气 eccentric character / 他的样子长得很古怪。He has a weird appearance.

〔相同点〕：都是形容词。表示跟平常的不一样。Syn. adj. out of the ordinary, bizarre.

其他 qítā 其余 qíyú

其他 (other; else) 着重在"他"，表示别的，另外的意思。使用范围较广。 emphasizes the sense of otherness, means another, besides or in addition. The range of usage is wide: 还有其他事情要我做吗? Is there anything else you want me to do? / 除了工厂，其他地方也需要人。 Besides factories, people are needed in other places.

其余 (the rest; the remainder; the other) 着重指余下的意思，所指的范围比较明确。 The key element is 余 (remaining); it refers to a finite set of things or people: 这个班只有三个男学生，其余的都是女学生。 There are only three male students in this class. The rest are women students.

〔相同点〕: 都是代词。都有除此之外的意思。Syn. pro. apart from this.

奇特 qítè 独特 dútè

奇特 (peculiar; queer; singular) 着重指不常见，不平凡的意思。 uncommon, out of the ordinary: 山顶上有棵千年古树，长得非常奇特。 On top of the mountain grows an oddly shaped thousand-year old tree.

独特 (unique; distinctive; sui generis) 着重在 "独"，强调不仅特殊，而且独一无二（唯一）的意思。The key element is 独 (only or single); it indicates that sth. is not only special but unique：他有独特的风格。He has a unique style.

〔相同点〕：都是形容词。都说明事物很特殊。Syn. adj. indicating sth. has marked peculiarities.

启程 qǐchéng   出发 chūfa

启程 (set out; on a journey) 多用于较远的行程开始。人或车、马等都可用，常见于书面语。used frequently in written language to indicate the start of a rather long journey (for people, vehicles, horses, etc.)：一艘商船从费城启程开往广州。A merchant ship left Philadelphia for Guangzhou.

出发 (set out, off; start from; proceed from) 使用范围较广。1.表示离开原来所在的地方到别的地方去。to leave the place where one is staying in order to go elsewhere. It has a wide range of usage：医疗队今晚就要出发了。The medical team is leaving tonight. 2. 表示考虑或处理问题时以某一方面为起点。to proceed from a certain standpoint in considering or dealing with matters：一切从人民的利益出

发。 Proceed in all cases from the interests of the people.

〔相同点〕：都是动词。指人离开所在的地方，去另一个地方。Syn. v. indicating that one leaves the place where one is staying to go elsewhere.

启发 qǐfā　启示 qǐshì

启发 (arouse; inspire; enlighten) 不是直接指出结论，而是通过一定的事例让对方思考，然后领悟。to make sb. think and understand by examples taken from events, without directly drawing any conclusions: 老科学家的报告给了我们很大启发。The old scientist's lecture greatly inspired us.

启示 (enlightenment; inspiration; revelation) 直接揭示出事物道理，还指诱导、开通思想的意思。to reveal the truth of a matter directly; or to lead sb. to enlightenment or to a fresh understanding: 我从他的经验中得到很大的启示。I gained a good deal of enlightenment from his experience.

〔相同点〕：都是动词，也都可以做名词。表示开导、指点，使人有所了解、领悟的意思。Syn. v.; n. to instruct and advise sb. so as to make them comprehend and understand.

企图 qǐtú   妄想 wàngxiǎng

企图 (attempt; try; scheme) 是中性词，多用于贬义。是打算、图谋的意思。a neutral or pejorative term; to plan, to plot: 敌军企图突围，但未得逞。The enemy failed in their attempt to effect a breakthrough.

妄想 (vain hope; wishful thinking) 是贬义词，着重表示狂妄的或不能实现的打算或想法的意思。常有名词用法。a pejorative term, to make presumptuous and unrealizable plans. Sometimes it can be used as a noun: 他们妄想侵占别国领土。They delude themselves that they can invade and occupy the territory of other countries. / 他妄想侵占公有土地。He vainly hopes to seize public land.

〔相同点〕：都是动词。表示不怀好意地打算或谋划的意思。Syn. v. to plan or scheme with evil intent.

气概 qìgài   气魄 qìpò

气概 (lofty quality; mettle; spirit) 着重指在对待重大问题上表现出的态度。an attitude shown towards important events: 不畏强暴、敢于斗争的英雄气概。the heroic spirit of daring to struggle against brute force

气魄 (boldness of vision; breadth of spirit; daring)
着重指气量、敢作敢为的魄力，也指非凡的
气势。magnanimity, daring and resolution in
action; and having outstanding verve and
momentum: 我们有改天换地的气魄。We
have the daring to reshape nature.

〔相同点〕：都是名词。都表示人的魄力的意思。
Syn. n. daring and resolution.

气候 qìhòu 天气 tiānqì

气候 (climate; situation) 1.表示在一个地区经过多
年观察概括出来的气象情况。the long-term,
prevalent meteorological situation of a certain area：海洋性气候 oceanic climate 2.比喻
动向、情势或结果、成就。metaphorically
used to mean trend, situation, or result,
achievement: 政治气候 political climate / 成
不了气候 not to get anywhere

天气 (weather) 专指一定区域、一定时间内的气
象情况。the meteorological situation of a
certain area at a certain time: 天气预报
weather forecast / 天气要变。The weather is
changing.

〔相同点〕：都是名词。都表示一个地区的气象情
况。Syn. n. the meteorological situation of a

certain area.

气派 qìpài 气势 qìshì

气派 (**manner; style; air**) 着重指作风和风度，是中性词。a neutral term, indicating elegant style, demeanour: 东方气派的建筑物 architecture in oriental style / 她打扮得很入时，颇有现代气派。She dresses fashionally, with quite a modern air.

气势 (**momentum; imposing manner; verve**) 着重指精神力量及声势，能用于褒义，也能用于贬义。moral force or impetus used as an approbatory or pejorative term: 气势雄伟的长城 the imposing Great Wall / 看起来气势汹汹，实际上十分虚弱。Fierce in appearance but feeble in reality.

〔相同点〕：都是名词。都表示人的言行所显示出的总的精神状态。Syn. n. one's state of mind shown in one's words and deeds.

恰当 qiàdàng 适当 shìdàng

恰当 (**proper; suitable; fitting; appropriate**) 表示因准确而合适。indicates suitability as a result of being precise or accurate: 他的发言恰当地表达了我们的心情。What he said in his speech conveyed our feeling. ／采取恰当的措施 adopt appropriate measures

适当 (**suitable; proper; appropriate**) 表示对事物处理能切合实际或符合发展情况，常做状语。 indicates that matters are handled in accordance with realities or with the development of objective circumstances; often used as an adverbial modifier: 适当的工作 a suitable job ／我们要适当调整一下明天的工作安排。 We shall adjust the arrangement for tomorrow's work accordingly. ／适当的时候 in due course

〔相同点〕：都是形容词。都有适宜、合适的意思。 Syn. adj. suitable; appropriate.

恰好 qiàhǎo　　恰巧 qiàqiǎo　　正好 zhènghǎo

恰好 (**just right; as luck would have it**) 着重指正合适。多用于时间、空间、数量等方面。 emphasizes appropriateness; used in reference to time, space, number, etc.: 这块布恰好够做一件衬衣。 This piece of cloth is just the right length for a shirt. ／他恰好这时赶到。 He arrived in the nick of time.

恰巧 (**by chance; fortunately; as chance would have it**) 着重指凑巧。多用于时间、机会、条件等方面。 emphasizes coincidence; often used in reference to time, opportunities, conditions, etc.: 那天恰巧我也在那里。 I just happened to be there that day, too. / 雨恰巧在我们动身前停了。 Fortunately the rain stopped before we set out.

正好 (just in time; just right; just enough; happen to; chance to; as it happens) 多用于口语，语气较轻。 often used in spoken language, and light in tone: 你来得正好。 You have come just in time. / 这正好证明我们的作法是对的。 That only goes to prove that our approach is correct. / 小王正好从那儿路过。 Xiao Wang happened to be passing by. / 我身边正好有五块钱。 As it happens, I have five yuan with me.

〔相同点〕: 都是副词。都是表示巧合的意思。Syn. adv. indicating sth. happens by coincidence.

签订 qiānding 缔结 dìjié

签订 (conclude and sign) 是签署订立的意思，运用范围较广。 widely used of agreements, treaties, etc.: 签订条约 sign a treaty / 签订协定的各方 the parties signatory to the agreement

缔结 (conclude; establish) 有庄重的感情色彩，常用于外交方面。 more solemn in tone, often used in diplomatic connections: 缔结条约 conclude a treaty / 缔结邦交 establish diplomat-

〔相同点〕：都是动词。都有订立的意思。常用于公
文中。Syn. v. to conclude (a treaty, agreement), often used in official documents.

前后 qiánhòu　左右 zuǒyòu

前后 (around a certain time; about; from beginning to end; altogether) 1.可放在时间名词之后。不能放在表示度量衡或其他数量词之后。used with nouns relating to time, but not with measure words or numeral-classifier compounds: 春节前后 around Spring Festival 2.表示处所范围时比"左右"具体而确定。When it indicates location, it is more concrete and definite than 左右：房子前后都有树。There are trees both at the front and at the back of the house.

左右 (left and right; about; more or less) 1.常放在基数词+时间名词之后，可用在度量衡及其他数量词的后面，表示概数。often used with various expressions of time and sometimes with measure words and numerical-classifier compounds; denotes an approximate number: 八点钟左右 around eight o'clock／一个月左右 a month or so／十块钱左右 about 10 yuan 2.表示处所范围

时，不如"前后"具体、确定。When it indicates the limit of location, it is not as concrete and definite as 前后：主席台左右都站满了人。There are people standing on either side of the rostrum.

〔相同点〕：都是方位词。都表示时间或处所的大概范围的意思。Syn. position words to indicate the general limits of time or location.

抢救 qiǎngjiù 挽救 wǎnjiù

抢救 (rescue; save; salvage) 指在紧急危险的情况下援助和救济的意思。to help or succour sb. in danger or in an emergency：他们尽了全力抢救被水淹的庄稼。They went all out to salvage the flooded crops. 抢救病人 give emergency treatment to a patient ／ 抢救无效 all rescue measures proved ineffectual

挽救 (save; remedy; rescue) 指设法使情况好转或恢复原状的意思。"挽救"的对象是人或者组织等。to improve a situation or restore it to its former state. The objects can be people or organizations, etc.：挽救病人的生命 save the patient's life ／ 想出一个有效的挽救办法 think out an effective remedy

〔相同点〕：都是动词。都有救助的意思，也都是褒义词。Syn. v. to succour, both are

approbatory terms.

强迫 qiǎngpò   强制 qiángzhì

强迫 **(force; compel; coerce)** 指施加压力使对方服从的意思。to exert pressure on sb. in order to make him or her submit: 强迫命令 resort to coercion and commandism / 强迫敌机降落 force the enemy plane to land

强制 **(force; compel; coerce)** 常指用政治、经济或其他力量压制或限制的意思。to suppress or restrict by political, economic or other force: 强制手段 compulsory means (or coercive measures) / 强制性命令 mandatory order / 不能强制人们接受一种艺术风格或一种学派。/ People cannot be compelled to accept one particular style of art or school of thought.

〔相同点〕：都是动词。都表示用力压服的意思。Syn. v. to force sb. to do sth.

勤劳 qínláo   勤勉 qínmiǎn

勤劳 **(diligent; industrious; hardworking)** 着重指劳动多而不怕辛苦，带庄重色彩，与"懒惰"相反。describes one who works a great deal and is not afraid of hardship. It is serious in tone and is the opposite of 懒惰 (lazy): 勤

劳的双手 an untiring pair of hands ／勤劳勇敢
的中国人民 the valiant and industrious Chinese
people

勤勉 (diligent; assiduous) 着重指努力用功，要求
自己不断尽力。多用于学习、工作方面，常
用于书面语，与"懈怠"相反。describes one
who works hard, energetically, and always
demands the utmost of him or herself; often
used of study and work, common in written language. It is the opposite of 懈怠
(slack)：勤勉好学 diligent and eager to learn

〔相同点〕：都是形容词。都表示不辞劳苦，尽力多
作的意思。Syn. adj. sparing no pains; doing
one's best.

轻易 qīngyì　容易 róngyì

轻易 (easily; lightly; rashly) 1.指没有什么阻碍，
费力不大的意思。meeting no hindrance or
accomplished with little effort：胜利成果不是
轻易得来的。The fruits of victory were not easily
won. 2.指处事的态度不够慎重、随便，甚至
轻率的意思。be careless, casual or even rash
in dealing with a problem：他不轻易发表意
见。He does not give an opinion lightly. ／不要
轻易地下结论。Don't draw hasty conclusions.

容易 (easy; easily; likely; liable; apt) 1.是不难、不

费力的意思。not difficult; effortless: 这台机床容易操作。The lathe is easy to operate. / 说起来容易，做起来难。It is easier said than done. / 这容易引起误会。This is liable to cause misunderstanding. 2. "容易"跟"好"结合，构成修辞上的反语。"好容易"实际上就是不容易，很费劲。When 容易 is combined with 好, it is an ironical formula which actually means not easy at all or requiring great effort: 他好容易才买到这本书。He had great difficulty in buying the book.

〔相同点〕：都是形容词。都有不难的意思。Syn. adj. not difficult.

轻便 qīngbiàn　简便 jiǎnbiàn

轻便 (light; portable) 指轻巧，方便的意思，着重于不笨重，常用于具体事物。indicates that sth. is light and convenient to use and carry. The main idea is that the object is not heavy. It is normally used to describe things: 轻便铁道 light railway / 轻便桥 portable bridge

简便 (simple and convenient; handy) 指简单、方便的意思，着重于不繁杂，多用于抽象事物。simple and convenient; emphasizes lack of difficulty and complexity, often used to describe abstract things: 简便的方法 a simple and convenient method / 操作简便 easy to operate

〔相同点〕：都是形容词。都含有方便的意思。

Syn. adj. convenient.

情况 qíngkuàng   情形 qíngxing

情况 **(circumstances; situation; condition; state of affairs)** 一般指事情呈现出的各种状态、样子。generally refers to a state of affairs, or configuration of circumstances: 这 种 情 况 必 须 改 变 。This state of affairs must be changed. / 他们的情况怎么样? How do matters stand with them?

情形 **(circumstances; situation; condition; state of affairs)** 表示呈现出的具体形态，特别指有形的，它的意义和范围比"情况"广。specific circumstances, especially those which have a concrete form. It has a wider range of meaning and usage than 情况: 两个班的情形大不相同。Conditions in the two classes differ greatly. / 大家看了这种情形非常气愤。People felt indignant at this state of affairs.

〔相同点〕：都是名词。表示事情呈现出的状态和样子。Syn. n. the state of affairs.

情绪 qíngxù　心情 xīnqíng

情绪 (**morale; feeling; mood; sentiments; depression; moodiness; the sulks**) 指因不同的遭遇引起的感情变化。 refers to emotional changes, moods brought about changes in the circumstances: 防止急躁情绪 guard against impetuousness / 情绪不高 in low spirits / 闹情绪 in a fit of depression

心情 (**frame of mind; mood**) 指人在一定时期的内心情感。 refers to a person's emotional state, frame of mind over a certain period of time: 心情愉快 be in a good mood / 心情沉重 with a heavy heart / 心情不一样，感受也不同。 People feel differently about things in different frames of mind.

〔相同点〕: 都是名词。指人的感情活动。 Syn. n. human moods, emotions.

庆祝 qìngzhù　祝贺 zhùhè

庆祝 (**celebrate**) 着重表示快乐、喜庆或纪念等，方式是用某种群众性的活动，如集会等。有时只是用语言表示祝愿。 generally, to mark a special occasion by mass activities or festivities such as rallies, demonstrations and performances; sometimes refers to purely verbal forms of celebration. 庆祝国庆 celebrate National Day / 我们大家来庆祝她十八岁的生日。We all came to celebrate her 18th birthday.

祝贺 (congratulate; felicitate) 着重表示良好的愿望，方式一般是用语言、文字等。对象一般是群众、集体或个人的喜事，使用范围较广。to extend one's congratulations, on the occasion of a joyful event, which may concern either a collective or an individual. It has a wide range of usage. 祝贺演出成功。Congratulate the artists on their successful performance. / 祝贺两国建交。Acclaim the establishment of diplomatic relations between the two countries.

〔相同点〕：都是动词。指以一定的方式为共同的喜事表达美好的心意。Syn. v. to express in a certain form one's pleasure on account of a happy event jointly enjoyed.

屈服 qūfú 降服 xiángfú

屈服 (surrender; yield; knuckle under) 指迫于外界压力而服从。to submit to an external force. 我们决不向困难屈服。We will not yield to difficulties.

降服 (yield; surrender) 本义是投降、归附的意思，是文言词。在现代汉语中，常用它的引申义，含有自动认输的意思。originally, to capitulate; to submit to the authority of another; in the current extended meaning, to admit oneself beaten: 降服敌人 make the enemy surrender

〔相同点〕：都是动词。都含有服从的意思。Syn. v. to obey.

取消 qǔxiāo　撤消 chèxiāo

取消 (cancel; call off; abolish) 泛指废除，去掉，不一定通过命令，也不一定是强制的。对象较广，不限于上级对下级。to cancel or annul; sometimes, but not necessarily through orders, or coercion from above. It takes a wide variety of objects: 取消了他的会员资格 deprive him of his membership / 取消禁令 lift a ban / 取消一次会议 cancel （call off） a meeting

撤消 (cancel; rescind; revoke) 多指用命令撤掉。有时表示正式撤回。对象是机构、职务、决议、命令、处分、制度、意见等。to rescind sth. by order; or, sometimes, to recall or withdraw in a formal manner. It takes objects denoting organizations, resolutions, jobs, orders, punishments, systems and opinions: 撤消了他的职务 dismiss a person from his or her post / 政府撤消了这个法令 The government repeals this

218

decree.

〔相同点〕: 都是动词。都有去掉某种组织等的意思。Syn. v. to abolish a certain organization.

去世 qùshì 逝世 shìshì 死 sǐ

去世 **(die; pass away)** 只指成年人死去，不如"逝世"庄重、只用于人。used only in reference to the death of adult human beings. The tone is not as solemn as that of 逝世: 他的爷爷去世了。His grandfather died.

逝世 **(pass away; die)** 专指长者，伟大人物或可敬的人与世长辞，是文言词的沿用，只用于人，有严肃庄重的色彩。refers to the passing away of the elderly, or of distinguished or respected people; a continued usage of a classical Chinese term. It is solemn in tone, and used only of human beings: 那个国家的总统逝世了。The president of the country died.

死 **(die)** 一般指生物失去生命，可以用于人、动物或植物。refers to the death of any living thing, including people, plants, and animals: 如果你不浇水，这些植物就要死了。If you don't water those plants, they will die.

〔相同点〕:都是动词。表示失去生命。Syn. v. to die.

趣味 qùwèi　兴趣 xìngqù

趣味 (interest; delight; taste; liking; preference) 多指事物特性使人愉快，使人感到有意思，有吸引力。special features of sth. which inspire delight or interest：趣味无穷 be of infinite interest

兴趣 (interest) 一般指人对某种活动喜好的情趣。generally indicates interest in, fondness for, certain activities：我对下棋不感兴趣。I am not interested in chess.

〔相同点〕：都是名词。都表示吸引人的情趣。Syn. n. sth. that attracts one's interest.

全部 quánbù　整个 zhěnggè

全部 (whole; complete; total; all;) 着重指总和。the sum total; in total：他要求赔偿全部损失。He demands full compensation for the loss incurred. ／ 粮食全部自给 completely self-supporting in food grain

整个 (whole; entire) 着重指整体。refers to the whole of an entity：整个会场响起热烈的掌声。The whole hall resounded with applause. ／ 整个上午 the whole morning ／ 整个社会 the whole of society

〔相同点〕：都是形容词。表示全部包括在内的意思。Syn. adj. all-inclusive.

220

权力 quánlì　权利 quánlì

权力 (power; authority) 表示一种可以统治、支配别人的权柄（主要是职权）。the power to rule and dominate others; refers mainly to official powers or authority: 这是他权力范围以内的事。This matter comes within his jurisdiction. / 权力下放 delegate power to the lower levels / 国家权力机关 organ of state power

权利 (right) 表示在规定范围内可以享受的职权和利益，跟"义务"相对。the rights and interests one can enjoy within certain prescribed limits, in contradistinction to 义务(duty): 劳动的权利 the right to work / 受教育的权利 the right to education

〔相同点〕：都是名词。表示一定的支配权和使用权。Syn. n. the right to control and use.

确定 quèdìng　决定 juédìng

确定 (define; fix; determine; definite) 着重表示明确而肯定。emphasizes that sth. is established in a clear-cut and definite way: 确定开会的日期和地址 fix the time and place for a meeting / 确定会议的宗旨 define the aims of the conference

决定 (decide; resolve; make up one's mind) 着重表示

221

对如何行动拿出主意，也可以做名词。to make up one's mind on how to act. It can also be used as a noun: 他决定去学习。He decided to go and study. / 他一时决定不了。He cannot make up his mind for the moment. / 这是一项新的决定。This is a new decision.

〔相同点〕：都是动词。表示对如何行动做出主张。Syn. v. to make a decision on how to act.

确实 quèshí 切实 qièshí

确实 (true; reliable; really; indeed) 着重表示的确、确凿，没有虚假。in truth; conclusive and true: 这确实是个很好的建议。This is really a very good suggestion. / 他确实来过。Yes, he did come.

切实 (feasible; practical; realistic; conscientiously; earnestly) 着重表示真切、实在，没有浮夸。real; practical; feasible: 切实有效的办法 practical and effective measures / 我们要切实保障安全生产。We must take all necessary measures to ensure safety in production. / 切实可行的计划 a feasible plan

〔相同点〕：都是形容词。表示实在的意思。Syn. adj. real.

222

R

热情 rèqíng　热心 rèxin

热情 (enthusiasm; zeal; warmth; warm) 着重于感情的热烈与奔放。常用于对人，也可用作名词。emphasizes warm and unconstrained feeling; often used in reference to warm-hearted people; can be used as a noun：他对旅客非常热情。He is very warm-hearted towards the passengers. / 我热情支持这个倡议。I fervently support this proposal.

热心 (enthusiastic; ardent; earnest) 表示对人对事态度积极主动、有兴趣、肯尽力。indicates an enthusiastic, concerned attitude to people and things; a positive, active commitment：热心科学 enthusiastic in promoting science / 他热心地为青年人传授技术。He makes earnest efforts to pass on his technical skill to young people.

〔相同点〕：都是形容词。表示感情热烈、诚挚的意思。前面可加上"很、最"等副词。Syn. adj. indicating sincere and ardent feeling; can be preceded by 很 (very) or 最 (extremely).

223

人民 rénmín　公民 gōngmín

人民 (the people) 范围较小。指以劳动群众为主体的社会基本成员，在不同的国家和各个国家的不同历史时期，有不同的内容。"人民"后面不能加"们"，前面一般不加表示小数目的数量词。the basic members of society, in particular, the laboring people. It may take on different connotations according to the country and historical period in the context of which it is used. 人民 is never followed by 们, and cannot normally be preceded by words denoting small numbers：人民来信 letters from the masses／人民政府 the people's government

公民 (citizen) 泛指具有某国国籍，并根据该国的宪法和法律规定，享有权利和承担义务的人。the nationals of a country, who have certain rights and obligations as laid down in the constitution and laws of that country：公民权 civil rights／公民投票 referendum

〔相同点〕：都是名词。指国家或社会的基本成员。Syn. n. the basic constituent members of a country or a society.

224

认识 rènshi　知道 zhidao

认识 **(know; understand; recognize; get to know; understanding; knowledge; cognition;)** 着重强调能确定某人或某事物，是这个而不是别的。有分辨，识别、懂得、了解的意思。emphasizes the ability to identify a person or thing as being this and not that. It means to distinguish, recognize and understand the difference: 你在哪儿认识她的？Where did you get to know her? / 认识世界，改造世界 understand the world and change it / 我们要正确认识当前的形势。We should have a correct understanding of the current situation. / 感性认识 perceptual knowledge

知道 **(know; realize; be aware of)** 指对事实和道理有了解。to understand, to be intellectually aware of facts and principles: 我不知道这件事。I know nothing about it. / 你的意思我知道。I know what you mean.

〔**相同点**〕：都是动词。表示能够确定某种事物是这个而不是别的。Syn. v. to be able to define sth. as this and not that.

225

认为 rènwéi 以为 yǐwéi

认为 (think; consider; hold; deem) 表示对人或事物作出的某种判断或看法。indicates that one has arrived at a certain judgment or viewpoint regarding people or things: 你认为怎么样？What do you think of it? / 这件事我们认为有必要跟你们说清楚。We deem it necessary to make this clear to you.

以为 (think; believe; consider) 着重表示对人或事物的设想或推断。indicates that one envisages or infers sth. about sb. or sth.: 我还以为是她的。I thought it was hers. / 他以为那样作比较好。He considers it better to do it that way. / 我们以为你不来了，就把票给小王了。We thought you weren't coming, so we gave your ticket to Xiao Wang.

〔相同点〕：都是动词。都有表示自己对事情的判断和看法的意思。Syn. v. used to express one's judgment or views concerning a circumstance or event.

荣幸 róngxìng 幸运 xìngyùn

荣幸 (honored) 指光荣而且运气好。一般只指遇到引以为荣的事。glorious and fortunate, used to express the idea that one has been done a great honor: 今天很荣幸能参加你们的晚会。 It is a great honor for me to be here at your party. / 如蒙光临, 不胜荣幸。 We shall be greatly honored by your gracious presence.

幸运 (good fortune; good luck; fortunate) 指好运气, 碰上出乎意料的好机会。 refers to good luck or to receiving an extremely good opportunity: 他很幸运能有机会去这个有名的大学学习。 He was very lucky to get the chance to go to this famous university.

〔相同点〕: 都是形容词。表示运气好, 形容碰上称心如意的事。 Syn. adj. having good luck, indicating that sth. highly desirable or gratifying happens to sb..

软弱 ruǎnruò　懦弱 nuòruò

软弱 (weak; feeble; flabby) 是中性词。指缺乏力量和力气的意思, 和 "坚强" 相对。 a neutral term; indicates lack of strength and energy, the opposite of 坚强 (strong): 他病后身体很软弱。 He is much enfeebled by his illness. / 软弱无能 weak and incompetent

懦弱 (cowardly; weak) 是贬义词。指胆小怕事, 缺乏勇气的意思。 a pejorative term; timorous and overcautious; lacking courage: 她以前比

227

较懦弱，现在勇敢多了。 She used to be quite spineless, but now she has gained a lot of confidence.

〔相同点〕：都是形容词。都含有不坚强的意思。
Syn. adj. not strong.

S

扫除 sǎochú   排除 páichú   消除 xiāochú

扫除 **(cleaning; clean up; clear away; remove; wipe out)** 指去掉肮脏的东西或有害的事物。着重表示象扫掉尘土那样除掉。to get rid of dirt or of sth. which is harmful; stresses the concept of eliminating, as one would sweep away dust: 大扫除 general cleaning／扫除前进路上的障碍 remove the obstacles from the way forward

排除 **(get rid of; remove; eliminate; expel)** 着重表示努力排开，大力除掉。to eliminate, to remove sth. with great effort: 排除故障 fix a breakdown／排除私心杂念 get rid of all selfish ideas

消除 **(eliminate; dispel; remove; clear up)** 着重表示使不利的事物逐渐减少以至消失。to reduce sth. which is unpleasant or detrimental until it disappears: 消除分歧 eliminate differences／消除误会 clear up a misunderstanding

〔相同点〕：都是动词。都有去掉，使之不再存在的意思。Syn. v. to get rid of sth.

煽动 shāndòng　鼓动 gǔdòng

煽动 **(instigate; incite; stir up; whip up)** 是贬义词，指挑起别人不满情绪，怂恿别人进行某种活动。a pejorative term, to stir up sb.'s dissatisfaction and incite him or her to action：一小撮敌人企图煽动群众闹事。A handful of enemies tried to stir up trouble among the people.

鼓动 **(agitate; arouse; instigate; incite)** 是中性词，指鼓励、动员别人行动起来。a neutral term, to encourage sb. to take action：做宣传鼓动工作 conduct propaganda and agitation／这些坏事是谁鼓动你干的？Who put you up to all these dirty tricks?／鼓动群众 arouse the masses

〔相同点〕：都是动词。都含有激发起人的情绪，使其行动起来的意思。Syn. v. to rouse sb. to action.

商量 shāngliáng　讨论 tǎolùn

商量 **(consult; discuss; talk over)** 表示就某一件事交换意见。用于一般的具体事情，使用范围较广。to exchange views; often used in relation to ordinary concrete affairs; has a wide range of usage：我们得找他商量一下。We ought to talk it over with him.／这件事好商量。

230

This can be settled through discussion.

讨论 (discuss; talk over) 指就某一问题交换意见或进行辩论。可用于一般的事情，也可用于重要的事情。如政治，军事等方面。to exchange views on or to debate a certain problem; used of ordinary matters, as well as important ones such as political and military affairs, etc.: 参加讨论 join in the discussion / 他们聚在一起讨论下一步干什么。They put their heads together to discuss what to do next.

〔相同点〕：都是动词。都有商讨的意思。Syn. v. to discuss; to deliberate over sth.

申明 shēngmíng　声明 shēngmíng

申明 (declare; state; avow) 是陈述理由，含有解释、申辩的意思。to state reasons; to explain or to argue a case: 申明自己的立场 state one's position

声明 (state; declare; announce; statement; declaration) 郑重宣布，说明自己的立场、观点、态度。还可做名词用。to solemnly state one's position, viewpoint and attitude. It can be used as a noun: 庄严声明 solemn statement / 联合声明 joint statement

〔相同点〕：都是动词。都表示把一件事情说出来让人知道。Syn. v. to state sth., in order to

231

make it known to others.

慎重 shènzhòng　郑重 zhèngzhòng

慎重 **(cautious; careful; prudent; discreet)** 表示谨慎小心仔细的意思，跟"冒失""轻率"相对，主要形容言行的态度。prudent and careful; the opposite of 冒失 (rash) or 轻率 (reckless); used mainly to describe the manner of action or speech: 采取慎重的态度 adopt a prudent policy／处理这件事必须慎重。The matter has to be handled with great care.

郑重 **(serious; solemn; earnest)** 着重表示严肃的、正式的意思，跟"随便"相对，用来形容言行的态度和方式。serious and formal, the opposite of 随便 (careless, casual); used to describe attitudes and ways of speaking and acting: 郑重表示 solemnly state／郑重声明 solemnly declare／态度郑重 be serious in one's attitude

〔相同点〕：都是形容词。表示态度严肃、谨慎、不轻举妄动的意思。Syn. adj. indicating a serious and cautious attitude.

生命 shēngmìng　性命 xìngmìng

生命 **(life)** 意义范围较广，泛指一切生物具有的

232

活动能力。有比喻用法，如"政治生命"等。 has a wide range of meaning, refers to the ability to act, move and grow in all things alive; can be used figuratively, e.g. of political life:他为祖国的解放献出了年青的生命。He gave his young life for the liberation of his motherland. / 学习古人语言中有生命的东西 learn whatever is alive in the classical Chinese language

性命 (life) 意义范围窄，多指人或动物的生命。一般不用于比喻，多用于口语。has a narrow range of meaning; refers to the life of human beings and animals. It is rarely used figuratively, and is very common in spoken language:这是性命攸关的事。This is a matter of life and death.

〔相同点〕：都是名词。表示人或动物所具有的活动能力。Syn. n. the ability to act, move, grow, etc. possessed by animals and human beings.

生活 shēnghuó 生计 shēngjì

生活 (life; live; livelihood) 1.表示人们为了生存和发展而进行的各种活动的意思，使用范围大，可以用做动词。activities undertaken by people in order to live and develop themselves. It has a wide range of usage, and

233

can be used as a verb: 生活方式 way of life / 我们的生活不断提高。 Our life has been steadily improving. / 生活得不错 lead a happy life / 生活必需品 daily necessities

生计 (means of livelihood; livelihood) 单指人赖以生存的物质条件，使用的范围小。不可做动词。 the material conditions on which human beings rely for existence. Its scope of usage is limited, and it cannot be used as a verb: 另谋生计 try to find some other means of livelihood

〔相同点〕: 都是名词。都指人们吃饭、穿衣等维持生命的活动和条件。 Syn. n. the activities and conditions on which people depend to sustain life, such as food and clothing.

失望 shīwàng　绝望 juéwàng

失望 (lose hope; disappointed) 1.表示因为感到没有希望而失去信心的意思。 indicates discouragement: 试验的再次失败使他感到失望了。 He felt discouraged because his experiment had failed once again. 2.还表示因希望没有实现而不愉快的意思。 indicates disappointment because one's hope or wish has failed to materialize: 他没有借到所急需的钱而失望地离开朋友的家。 He left his friend's

234

home in disappointment because he had not man-
aged to borrow the money he needed badly.

绝望 (give up all hope; despair) 是希望断绝的意
思。indicates absolutely that all hope is lost：
这 是 一 种 绝 望 情 绪。 This is a feeling of
despair. / 绝望的挣扎 desperate struggle

〔相同点〕：都是形容词。表示没有希望的意思。也
都 可 以 作 动 词 和 名 词。 Syn. adj. hopeless,
can be used as a verb or a noun.

施行 shixíng 实行 shixíng

施行 (put in force; execute; apply; perform) 1.指法
令、规章等公布后，从某时起生效。refers to
the time when decrees or rules come into
force, after being promulgated：本条例自公
布之日起施行。 These regulations come into
force upon promulgation. 2.按照某种法令或办
法去做。对象可以是手术、方法等。to do
sth. according to laws or special procedures.
It can refer to surgical operations, methods to
be followed, etc.：李大夫给这个非洲朋友施
行了针灸治疗。 Dr. Li performed acupuncture
treatment on the African patient.

**实行 (put into practice; carry out; practise; imple-
ment)** 是实现，使思想上的东西变成现实的
意思，对象可以是理论、方针、计划等。to

235

realize a conception; for example, to put theory, policy or plan into practice: 在人民内部实行民主。 Democracy is practised within the ranks of the people. ／实行经济改革 carry out economic reform

〔相同点〕：都是动词。表示用行动来实现，对象可以是规定、制度、政策等。Syn. v. to put into effect. The objects can be regulations, systems, policies, etc.

时常 shícháng　经常 jīngcháng
往往 wǎngwǎng

时常 **(often; frequently)** 是副词。表示动作、行为多次发生。adv. indicates that an action or form of behavior takes place frequently: 开会时我们时常见面，但很少有深谈的机会。We seldom have the opportunity to discuss anything thoroughly even though we often see each other at meetings.

经常 **(day to day; everyday; daily; frequent)** 是形容词。1.表示平常的，日常的。adj. ordinary; daily: 这个工作是我们的经常工作。This is the work we normally do. 2.表示动作、行为屡次发生，时间间隔不久。describes an action which takes place repeatedly at short intervals: 他经常上图书馆去。He goes to the library regularly. / 这类问题是经常发生的。 This kind of problem frequently crops up.

往往 (**often; frequently; more often than not**) 是副词。表示根据过去的经验，在大多数情况下事情总是这样、或一般是这样的意思。adv. expresses the idea that sth. would ordinarily be the case, in the light of past experience, or would be so under most circumstances: 北京春天往往刮大风。It is very windy in Beijing in the spring. / 有些人往往只看到当前的、局部的、个人的利益。Some people are prone to see only present, partial and personal interests.

〔相同点〕: 都表示动作多次发生的意思。Syn. describing actions which take place with persistent frequency.

食品 shípǐn　食物 shíwù

食品 (**foodstuff; food; provisions**) 意义范围较窄，是食物中的一类，即经过加工制成的食物。refers specifically to processed food: 罐头食品 canned food / 食品工厂 food products factory / 食品加工 food processing

食物 (**food; comestibles**) 意义范围较广，指可以充饥的，包括加工的和未加工的。both processed and unprocessed food; it has a wide range of usage: 污染的食物 contaminated food／一位护士用汤匙把食物送到病人的嘴里。A nurse spooned the food into the patient's mouth.

〔相同点〕：都是名词。表示供人食用的东西。Syn. n. substances that can be eaten by human beings.

使命 shǐmìng　任务 rènwu

使命 (mission) 指派人办事的命令，常用来比喻重大的责任。a mission assigned to sb., often used metaphorically to mean a great responsibility: 历史使命 historical mission

任务 (assignment; mission; task; job) 表示指定担任的工作或指定担负的责任，使用范围较广。a task or responsibility entrusted to sb.; has a wide range of usage: 这个任务就交给我吧！Give this job to me!／我们保证完成任务。We guarantee to complete this task.

〔相同点〕：都是名词。表示应该完成的工作或应当担负的责任。Syn. n. a task which must be completed or a responsibility which must be shouldered.

适合 shìhé　符合 fúhé

适合 (suit; fit) 指合乎实际情况或客观的要求，彼

238

此适应协调。conforming to the actual situation or satisfying objective requirements; indicates mutual adjustment or co-ordination: 适合当地情况 to adapt to local conditions / 这类野生植物不适合用作饲料。These wild plants are not fit to be used as fodder.

符合 (accord with; tally with; conform to) 表示没有出入和差异，完合吻合。to show no divergence or difference; to be completely identical: 他完全符合入这个大学的条件。He precisely fulfills the university's entrance requirements. / 符合要求 accord with the demands

〔相同点〕：都是动词。都有相符的意思。Syn. v. to conform to; to tally with.

事情 shìqíng   事件 shìjiàn   事故 shìgù

事情 (affair; matter; thing; business) 指人生活中遇到的一切活动和一切社会现象。refers to all kinds of activities and social phenomena encountered in human life: 急待解决的事情 an urgent matter to be settled at once / 事情的真相 the truth of the matter / 大家的事情大家管。Public business is everyone's business.

事件 (incident; event) 指不平常的或比较重要的事情。an event which is out of the ordinary or very important: 流血事件 bloody incident /

239

二十世纪最重要的事件 the most important event in the 20th century

事故 (accident; mishap) 指在工作、生产或交通上发生的意外的灾祸或损失。unforeseen disaster or damage, refers chiefly to industrial and traffic accidents: 防止发生事故 try to avert accidents／这是个责任事故。This is an accident arising from negligence.

〔相同点〕：都是名词。表示遇到的或发生的社会现象。Syn. n. phenomena which occur in society; things which befall people.

收获 shōuhuò　收成 shōucheng

收获 (gather in the crops; harvest) 表示取得成熟的农作物，比喻所得的成果，还可以作动词。ripe crops which are gathered in; often used figuratively in reference to achievements or benefits; it is also used as a verb: 春天播种，秋天收获。Sow in spring and reap in autumn.／这次南方考察收获很大。Our field trip to the south was very fruitful.

收成 (harvest; crop) 指庄稼、蔬菜、果品等收获的成绩。harvest of crops, vegetables, fruits, etc.: 收成不好 poor harvest／我们夺得秋季作物的好收成。We reap a good autumn harvest.

〔相同点〕：都是名词。都有收入的意思。Syn. n.

240

what is harvested.

手法 shǒufǎ　把戏 bǎxì

手法 (skill; techniques; trick; gimmick) 原指艺术品或文学作品的技巧，现在多用来指待人接物所用的不正当的方法。originally used to indicate literary or artistic techniques, now often refers, by extension, to improper dealings with people: 国画的传统的手法 the traditional technique of Chinese painting / 贼喊捉贼的拙劣手法 the clumsy trick of thief crying "stop thief "

把戏 (acrobatics; jugglery; cheat; trick; game) 原指魔术、杂技一类的技艺，现在多用来指手段、花招、蒙蔽人的手法。originally, magic or acrobatic skill; now frequently used to denote tricks or ways to hoodwink people: 他耍鬼把戏。He plays dirty tricks.

〔相同点〕: 都是名词。都能表示不正当的手段。Syn. n. an act performed to confuse or cheat sb.

首要 shǒuyào　重要 zhòngyào
主要 zhǔyào

首要 (of first importance; first; chief) 表示头等重

241

要或重要事物中的第一个的意思。of primary importance; the foremost among various important things: 首要的事先办。First things first／首要任务 the most important task

重要 **(important; significant; major)** 指具有重大意义、作用和影响的。of great consequence; possessing great significance, effect or influence: 重要人物 important personage／这个会议很重要，你一定要参加。You must attend the meeting as it is very important.

主要 **(main; chief; principal; major)** 指一组事物中最要紧的，为主的。indicates the main, the principal element: 这次比赛的主要目的是为了增进团结和友谊。The main aim of the competition is to promote unity and friendship.／会议主要讨论两个问题。The conference dealt mainly with two issues.

〔相同点〕：都是形容词。表示事物的地位或作用十分突出，不同于一般的意思。Syn. adj. indicating that the position or effect of sth. is prominent, exceptional.

舒服 shūfu　舒适 shūshì

舒服 **(comfortable; be well)** 着重指感觉好受，跟"难受"相对，可以形容具体的感觉。refers to feelings of well-being; the opposite of 难受

242

(uncomfortable）; may be used to describe specific sensations: 她今天不大舒服。She is not well today. ／ 这把椅子坐着很舒服。This chair is very comfortable.

舒适 (comfortable; cosy; snug) 指舒服、安适。形容生活环境或东西给人的感觉。comfortable and cosy, often used to describe feelings evoked by ambience or objects in it: 房间不大，但很舒适。The room is not big but it is very cosy. ／ 孩子们都舒适地睡在小床上。All the children lay snugly in their little beds.

〔相同点〕: 都是形容词。表示心情好、感觉满意的意思。Syn. adj. being in a good mood and feeling satisfied.

熟识 shúshi 熟悉 shúxī

熟识 (be well acquainted with; know well) 指对人认识较久或对事物了解较透彻的意思，一般是具体的事物，而且往往是指人。refers to long familiarity with a person or thorough knowledge of a matter; generally used of specific things or of people: 我们交往不多，不太熟识。We don't have much to do with each other and don't know each other very well. ／ 熟识敌我双方各方面的情况 familiarize ourselves with all aspects of enemy's situation and our own

243

熟悉 **(know sth. or sb. well; be familiar with; have an intimate knowledge of)** 指知道得很详细、很清楚，对象是具体的事物和人。to know sth. minutely and clearly, used of specific things and people: 你到了那里，要先熟悉当地的情况。When you get there, you should first of all familiarize yourself with the situation. / 他对各项生产数字很熟悉。He has all the production figures at his fingertips. / 他对这个工作不熟悉。He is new and unfamiliar to the task.

〔相同点〕: 都是动词。都有不生疏、了解、知道的意思。Syn. v. to be familiar with; to understand; to know.

损害 sǔnhài   伤害 shānghài

损害 **(harm; damage; injure)** 1.着重指破坏事物的完整，使之受损失，多用于抽象的事物。to impair sth.; emphasizes the fact that its perfection or integrity is destroyed, mostly used of abstract things: 光线不好，看书容易损害视力。Reading in poor light is bad for one's eyes. 2.也能用于人，一般表示在精神或物质利益上受到损失。in reference to human beings, it generally indicates psychological harm or injury to material interests: 损害健康 harm one's health / 这封诬告信大大地损害了

他的名誉。The slanderous letter damaged his reputation.

伤害 (injure; harm; hurt) 1.着重在"伤"，可用于人或其他有生命的东西。to hurt; used in connection with people and other living things: 不要伤害益鸟。Don't harm useful birds. / 饮酒过多会伤害身体。Excessive drinking is harmful to one's health. / 伤害自尊心 hurt one's pride

〔相同点〕：都是动词。都有使受损伤、破坏的意思。Syn. v. to cause damage or injury to sth. or sb.

所有 suǒyǒu   一切 yíqiè

所有 (possessions; all; own; possess) 1.指在一定范围内所占有的一切。refers to all that is possessed or included with in a certain ambit: 把所有的劲儿都使出来。exert all one's strength 2.表示占有财物的意思，是动词。v. indicates ownership: 这些拖拉机归农场所有。These tractors are owned by the farm. 3.表示领有的东西，是名词。n. sth. that is possessed: 尽其所有 give everything one has / 他的全部所有，不过是两件衬衫和几本书而已。Two shirts and a few books form the sum of his belongings.

一切 (all; every; everything) 1.指全部的，不限于

某一定的范围，只修饰可以分类的事物。indicates totality, without any limitation of scope. It only modifies things which can be classified：抓住一切机会 seize every opportunity 2.还表示全部事物，是名词。n. everything：把一切献给祖国 give one's all to one's country / 一切为了前线的胜利。Everything is for the victory at the front.

〔相同点〕：都是形容词。表示全都包括在内。Syn. adj. indicating that all is included.

T

谈判 tánpàn   协商 xiéshāng

谈判 (negotiations; talks) 为了解决某一问题或统一某些意见、看法而进行的会谈。refers to talks carried on in order to resolve an issue or to reach unanimity of opinion：举行谈判 hold talks／贸易谈判 trade negotiations／谈判中断。The talks break down。/他们要跟我们谈判。They want to negotiate with us.

协商 (consult; talk things over) 表示在一定基础上共同商量解决问题，协商的各方一般比较接近。to confer and solve problems together on a certain basis. The parties to the consultation are usually close to each other in their views：民主协商 democratic consultation／协商会议 consultative conference／这需要和有关部门协商。It is necessary to consult with the departments concerned.

〔**相同点**〕：都是动词。表示商量解决某些重大问题。Syn. v. to consult together on major issues in order to find solutions.

247

特别 tèbié　特殊 tèshū

特别 **(special; particular; out of the ordinary;　especially; specially; particularly; going out of one's way to do sth.)** 着重指与众不同的，异乎寻常的，甚至是个别的，跟"普通"相对。to be out of the ordinary or even a special, individual case. It is the opposite of 普通 (common)：没什么特别的地方 nothing out of the ordinary／质量特别好 be of extra fine quality／他的脾气很特别。He has a peculiar temperament.／他工作特别努力。He is especially hardworking.

特殊 **(special; particular; peculiar; exceptional)** 着重指跟一般不同的，但不一定是很个别的，跟"一般"相对。to be different from the norm, though not necessarily having any marked idiosyncrasy. It is the opposite of 一般 (general)：这是特殊条件下的特殊产物。This is the special product of special conditions.／这是现代战争的特殊规律。These are the special laws of modern war.

〔相同点〕：都是形容词。都表示突出、异常、与众不同的意思。Syn. adj. conspicuous; unusual; not the run-of-the-mill.

248

特点 tèdiǎn　特色 tèsè　特性 tèxìng
特征 tèzhēng

特点 **(characteristic; distinguishing feature; peculiarity; trait)** 指事物所具有的独特之点。意义范围较广。particular feature of sth; used in a broad sense: 照顾妇女的特点 pay attention to the special needs of women／这个厂的产品有工艺精湛、经久耐用的特点。The products of this factory are noted for their fine workmanship and durability.

特色 **(characteristic; distinguishing feature)** 专指事物所表现的与众不同的色彩、风格等。unusual features of style, etc. which give sth. its characteristic flavor: 艺术特色 artistic characteristics／富有民族特色的歌舞节目 songs and dances with distinctive national features／象牙雕刻的传统特色 the traditional features of ivory carving

特性 **(specific property or characteristic)** 指事物所具有的特殊性质和性能。the particular character and function of sth.: 这种机器有什么特性？What are the special features of this machine?

特征 **(characteristic; feature; trait)** 指事物或人所特有的象征或标志。identifying features of an object or person: 面部特征 facial character-

istics / 地理特征 geographical features / 民族
特征 national traits

〔相同点〕: 都是名词。表示独特的, 不同一般。
Syn. n. special feature.

疼 téng   痛 tòng

疼　(ache; pain; sore; love dearly; be fond of; dote
on) 1.只用于肉体难受这一具体意义。physi-
cal pain: 你的牙还疼吗? Does your tooth still
hurt? / 头疼 have a headache / 胃疼 have a
stomach ache 2. 还有心爱的意思。这时是动
词。v. to love: 奶奶最疼小孙子。　Granny
dotes on her little grandson.

痛　(ache; pain; sadness; sorrow; extremely; deeply;
bitterly) 1. 可指肉体难受, 也可指精神难
受。 physical or mental suffering: 嗓子痛
have a sore throat / 这样浪费粮食叫人心痛。
It is distressing to see food being wasted like
this. 2. 可表示悲伤的意思。sad; sorrowful:
悲痛 deep sorrow 3. 还可表示尽情地、深切
地、彻底地的意思。 (to do sth.) to one's
heart's content: 痛饮 drink one's fill / 痛哭 cry
bitterly

〔相同点〕: 都是形容词。表示由于疾病、创伤等引
起的难受感觉。 Syn. adj. physical hurt or
discomfort caused by disease or injury.

250

体会 tǐhuì 体验 tiyàn

体会 (know or learn from experience; realize) 着重指透过现象领会、理解事物的精神实质。to come to know the substance, the inner reality of sth. through phenomena, experientially: 深有体会 have an intimate knowledge of something / 我谈谈我个人的体会。I'll say a few words about my personal experience. / 只有深入群众，才能真正体会群众的思想感情。Only by going among the laboring people can we have a true understanding of their thoughts and feelings.

体验 (learn through practice; learn through one's personal experience) 着重指在实践中体会、了解。对象常是生活、现实等。to learn or know sth. from practice. The object is often a word such as life or reality: 作家应该到群众中去体验生活。Writers should go to the masses to get a taste of real life.

〔**相同点**〕: 都是动词。表示通过实践，从自己的感受中认识、了解事物的意思。Syn. v. to know sth. from experience or practice.

调整 tiáozhěng　调节 tiáojié

调整 (adjust; regulate; revise) 着重指重新整顿、整理，使混乱的变为不混乱的，不合理的变为合理的，不平衡的变为平衡的等。to readjust; rearrange things so as to make them orderly or reasonable or to restore a balance: 工资调整 adjustment of wages／ 调整价格 readjust prices／ 调整生产计划 revise production plans

调节 (regulate; adjust) 表示使事物安排合理化。常指从数量上或程度上进行调配，使之适合要求。to rationalize the arrangement of things; especially, regulate the number or degree as required: 调节温度 regulate the room temperature／ 空气调节 air conditioning／ 对货币的流通不断进行调节 constantly readjust the amount of money in circulation

〔相同点〕：都是动词。表示改变原有的情况，使适合要求。Syn. v. to change the original conditions to meet the requirements.

停留 tíngliú　停止 tíngzhǐ

停留 (stay for a time; stop; remain) 着重指暂时停止而不离开某地。to stop in a certain place

252

'and stay there: 人类对自然界的认识不断发展，永远不会停留在一个水平上。Man's understanding of nature develops all the time; it never remains at the same level. / 他在西安作短暂停留。He had a brief stopover in Xi'an.

停止 (stop; cease; halt; suspend; call off) 表示暂时或永远止住不动。使用范围很广。indicates that an activity ceases temporarily or permanently. It has a wide range of usage: 停止工作 stop working / 停止营业 business suspended / 停止前进！Halt! / 停止广播 stop broadcasting

〔相同点〕：都是动词。表示事物正在进行时止住、不动。Syn. v. indicating the cessation of an action in progress.

同意 tóngyì　赞成 zànchéng

同意 (agree; consent; approve) 表示相同的意见。意义不如"赞成"积极。to share the opinion of another. Its meaning is not so strongly affirmative as that of 赞成: 我的意见你同意吗？Do you agree with me? / 他同意这项建议。He consented to the proposal. / 这一改革需要得到上级同意。The reform is subject to the approval of higher authorities. / 征求对大使提名的同意 request for agreement to the nomination of an ambassador

赞成 (approve of; favor; agree with; endorse) 表示相同的意见并积极支持，对象一般只指别人的行为、主张。to share and actively support the opinion of another. The object is normally sb. else's action or plan：咱们明天去郊游，你赞成吗？How about going on an outing tomorrow? / 赞成的请举手！Those in favor please raise their hands! / 赞成意见 assenting views

〔相同点〕：都是动词。表示对某人的作为或主张持相同的意见。Syn. v. to hold the same view as sb. or agree to a course of action.

投降 tóuxiáng　投诚 tóuchéng

投降 (surrender; capitulate) 指停止对抗、向对方屈服的意思。to stop fighting against sb. and give in：投降派 capitulationist clique / 投降敌人 capitulate to the enemy

投诚 (surrender—of enemy troops, rebels, bandits, etc.—cross over) 除具有投降的意义外，还有敌人诚心归附的意思。It refers to an enemy shifting his or her allegiance：向人民投诚 cross over to the side of the people

〔相同点〕：都是动词。都有背叛原来的立场、原有的组织而转向另一方面的意思。Syn. v. to

254

betray one's former stand, former organization and come over to another side.

推辞 tuīcí　推托 tuītuō　推卸 tuīxiè

推辞 (decline—an appointment, invitation, etc.) 泛指用言语表示拒绝。对象多指任命、邀请、馈赠。to decline an appointment, invitation or gift verbally：我请他来吃晚饭，他推辞了。I invited him to have dinner with us, but he declined.

推托 (offer as an excuse for not doing sth.; plead) 专指借故拒绝，后面常常带上拒绝的原因。多指让自己做不愿意做的事。to refuse to do sth. under a pretext, normally followed by a statement of the reason for one's refusal. The object is always sth. one is reluctant to do：她推托嗓子痛，不肯唱。Pleading a sore throat, she refused to sing.

推卸 (shirk responsibility) 着重指不肯承担。多指已经承担或应该承担的责任、义务等。to fail to assume responsibility or to do the duty which one has undertaken to perform：推卸责任，委过于人。Shirk responsibility and shift the blame onto others.

〔**相同点**〕：都是动词。表示拒绝，不肯承担的意思。Syn. v. to refuse or be unwilling to bear responsibility.

唾弃 tuòqì　抛弃 pāoqì

唾弃 **(cast aside; spurn)** 表示由于厌恶或仇恨而扔掉。是贬义词。扔掉的东西一定是坏的。pejorative; to cast from one with loathing. The object is always sth. undesirable: 逆历史潮流而动的人终将被人民所唾弃。Those who go against the trend of history will be cast aside by the people.

抛弃 **(abandon; forsake; cast aside)** 扔掉、不要的意思。是中性词。扔掉的东西可以是坏的，也可以是好的。to discard as unwanted sth. which may be either bad or good. It is a neutral term: 我们决不能抛弃真正的朋友。We shall never forsake our true friends.

〔相同点〕：都是动词。表示舍弃不要的意思。Syn. v. to discard sth.

256

W

完备 wánbèi 完美 wánměi 完善 wánshàn

完备 (complete; perfect) 着重指齐全，一样不少。常形容材料、条件、论据等。complete, with nothing lacking, often used to describe conditions, materials or arguments: 一套完备的工具 a complete set of tools / 实验室条件不够完备。The laboratory is insufficiently equipped. / 指出不完备之处 point out the imperfections

完美 (perfect; consummate) 指完整、美好、没有缺点。常形容形式、语言、结构、形象、典型等。perfect, flawless, excellent in every way; often used to describe style, language, structure, images, modes, etc.: 完美无疵 perfect or flawless / 完美的形象 a perfect image

完善 (perfect; consummate) 表示不但齐全而且良好。常形容设备、组织、制度、公式等。emphasizes the fact that sth. is not only complete but also good; often used to describe equipment, installations, organizations, systems, formulae, etc.: 设备完善 very well equipped / 新生事物难免有不够完善的地方。Anything new is bound to have teething

257

troubles. / 我们厂的规章制度日趋完善。The rules and regulations of our factory are being perfected.

〔相同点〕：都是形容词。表示应该有的全都有了。Syn. adj. possessing every essential or desirable element.

顽强 wánqiáng　顽固 wángù

顽强 (indomitable; staunch; tenacious) 有强硬和坚强两种意思。是中性词。a neutral term, strong, firm and unyielding: 同疾病进行顽强的斗争 carry on a tenacious struggle against illness

顽固 (obstinate; stubborn; headstrong) 是贬义词。表示思想保守，不愿改变，不愿接受新鲜事物。pejorative, indicates that one is bigoted and unwilling to change, or to accept new ideas and things: 顽固不化 incorrigibly obstinate / 顽固地坚持错误立场 stubbornly cling to one's wrong position

〔相同点〕：都是形容词。都有不易变化、不易动摇的意思。Syn. adj. not easily induced to change or to shift one's position.

258

忘怀 wànghuái　忘记 wàngjì

忘怀 (forget; dismiss from one's mind) 对象只能是以往的、值得怀念的人或事。比"忘记"带有较明显的感情色彩。The object can only be people or events of the past, worthy of remembrance. It has stronger emotional connotations than 忘记: 当时的情景我久久不能忘怀。For a long time afterwards I could not get the scene out of my mind.

忘记 (forget; overlook; neglect) 对象不限于以往的，还可以是将要做的事情或某种道理。The object may be an occurrence, etc. in the past or the future, or an abstract conception: 我永不会忘记我们初次见面的那一天。I shall never forget the day we first met. / 不能忘记自己的责任。One must not neglect one's duties. / 他紧张地工作，忘记了去吃晚饭。He was working so hard that he forgot to have supper.

〔**相同点**〕: 都是动词。表示不记得以往的人或事物的意思。Syn. v. to lose one's memory of people or events of the past.

伟大 wěidà　巨大 jùdà

伟大 (great; mighty) 形容人时，表示品格崇高，才识过人；形容事物时，指规模宏大，气象雄伟。表示超出一般、令人钦佩的意思。When it describes a person, it indicates lofty qualities of character combined with ability and wisdom far beyond the common run. In reference to things, it indicates magnificence, grandeur, grand scale. It refers to greatness which inspires awe and admiration：我们伟大的祖国 our great country／伟大的事业 a great undertaking／伟大的领袖 a great leader

巨大 (huge; tremendous; enormous; gigantic; immense) 是中性词。指事物规模宏大，数量很多。a neutral term, of large scale or in great quantity：巨大的胜利 a tremendous victory／巨大的力量 immense strength／巨大的工程 a gigantic project／他为取得最后胜利做出了巨大的努力。He has made gigantic efforts to win the final victory.

〔相同点〕：都是形容词。都有很大的意思。Syn. adj. great.

温和 wēnhé　温柔 wēnróu　温顺 wēnshùn

温和 **(gentle; mild; temperate; moderate) 1.** 着重指性情善良，态度和蔼。describes persons with a kind disposition and a gentle, amiable manner：性情温和 a gentle disposition / 语气温和 a mild tone **2.** 也可形容气候。describes mild climate or weather：气候温和 a temperate climate

温柔 **(gentle and soft)** 着重指态度亲切和蔼、举止轻柔的意思。多形容女性。gentle and tender, with a soft, mild manner; often used to describe women：在我的记忆中，她是一个温柔、美丽的姑娘。She remains in my memory as a gentle, beautiful girl.

温顺 **(docile; meek)** 着重指态度和蔼顺从的意思。meek and mild, having a submissive attitude：象小羊一样温顺 as meek as a lamb

〔相同点〕：都是形容词。都表示性情柔和、不粗暴、不严厉的意思，能形容性情、态度、言语等。Syn. adj. of gentle disposition; mild; not rough or severe, used to describe temperament, attitude, manner, language, etc.

261

稳重 wěnzhòng　庄重 zhuāngzhòng

稳重 **(steady; staid; sedate)** 指沉着、不轻浮，对象常是人的作风、态度。与"轻浮"相对。cool-headed; not frivolous. Often used of sb.'s attitude and modus operandi. It contrasts with 轻浮 (frivolous)：这个青年举动挺稳重。He's a very steady young man.

庄重 **(serious; grave; solemn)** 端庄持重、不轻佻的意思。常形容人的举止和品行。与"轻佻"相对。dignified and prudent; not skittish; often used to describe people's manner and conduct. It contrasts with 轻佻 (frivolous, skittish)：举止庄重 deport oneself in a dignified manner／庄重的脸色 solemn looks

〔相同点〕：都是形容词。都有郑重、严肃的意思。Syn. adj. solemn; serious.

问 wèn　打听 dǎting

问 **(ask; inquire)** 表示请人回答的除了不知道的事外，还有不明白的道理。to put questions, to seek answers or explanations about things one does not know or does not understand. It has a wide range of meaning：他在食堂问了一下开饭的时间。He inquired at the canteen about meal times. / 我问他为什么要那样做。I asked him why he did it.

打听 (ask about; inquire about, try to find out) 探问，多指跟对方无关的事情。一般是口头问一问。to inquire, normally about a third party or matters which are not the personal affair of one's interlocutor. It normally refers to verbal inquiries: 我跟你打听一件事。I would like to ask you some information. / 打听朋友的消息 inquire about one's friend / 我去打听一下公共汽车几点开。I'll go and find out when the bus is leaving.

〔相同点〕: 都是动词。都表示有不知道的事而要请人解答的意思。Syn. v. to request answers from sb. about sth.

X

稀罕 xīhan　稀奇 xīqí

稀罕 (希罕)(rare; scarce; uncommon; valued as a rarity; cherish; rare thing) 1. 着重指东西很稀少或很少见。used of sth. rare or seldom seen: 骆驼在南方是稀罕的东西。Camels are a rare sight in the south. / 这么大的人参可是个稀罕儿。Such a big ginseng root is certainly a rarity. 2. 还有动词用法，表示认为稀奇而喜爱。v. to value or cherish sth. for its rarity: 你不稀罕，我还稀罕呢。You may not value it, but I do. / 谁稀罕你的臭钱。Who cares about your lousy money?

稀奇 (rare; strange; curious) 1. 着重指新奇、奇特或很少见、很少想到的。refers to sth. novel, peculiar, seldom seen, or unexpected: 十月下雪在这儿并不是什么稀奇的事。Snow in October is nothing strange in this place. 2. 多形容人们的感觉。often refers to people's feelings: 我觉得这件事很稀奇。I thought it was very singular.

〔相同点〕：都是形容词。都表示很少有的、不平常的意思。Syn. adj. rare; uncommon.

吸取 xīqǔ   吸收 xīshōu

吸取 **(absorb; draw; assimilate)** 表示不仅收进来，而且采纳运用。指具体的东西较少，指抽象的事物较多。to absorb sth. from without, and then make use of it or apply it; mostly refers to abstract things, occasionally to concrete ones: 吸取精华 absorb the quintessence / 你应从失败中吸取教训。You should draw a lesson from your failure.

吸收 **(absorb; suck up; assimilate; imbibe; draw)** 指具体的东西居多，指抽象的事物较少。表示把外部的东西吸入内部的意思。to absorb sth. from without; mostly used of concrete things: 要吸收更多的人参加这项工作。We should recruit more people for the work. / 植物通常经过叶和根吸收养分。Plants normally imbibe nourishment through their leaves and roots.

〔相同点〕：都是动词。都有把外在的东西取进来的意思。Syn. v. to absorb sth. from outside.

希望 xīwàng   期望 qīwàng

希望 **(hope; wish; expect)** 指心里想着达到某种目的或出现某种情况。可用于对别人也可对自己。to hope to achieve a certain goal or to

265

hope that sth. will happen; used in reference to hopes entertained for oneself or for other people: 希望寄托在你们青年人身上。 Our hope is placed on you young people. / 把希望变成现实 turn hopes into reality / 那时候我们是多么希望把水引到这儿来啊! How we wished then that the water could be diverted to our area.

期望 (hope; expectation) 着重指殷切的期待，语意较重。只用于对别人。 to expect, hope ardently. It conveys great emotional intensity, and refers to one's expectations of other persons, not of oneself: 他对他的儿子寄予很大的期望。 He places high hopes on his son. / 我们决不辜负人民的期望。 We will never fall short of the people's expectations.

〔相同点〕: 都是动词，也都可作名词。都表示想要达到某种目的或者出现某种情况的意思。 Syn. v.; n. to hope to reach a certain goal or to hope that sth. will happen.

习惯 xíguàn 习气 xíqì

习惯 (habit; custom; usual practice; be used to; be inured to) 1. 是中性词。指在长时期内逐渐养成的、一时不容易改变的行为或社会风尚。使用范围广，可用于人、社会、生物。 a neutral term, refers to modes of conduct or

266

social practices which have been formed over a long period of time, and cannot easily be changed. It has a wide range of usage, and can be used of people, society and living things in general：他有每天早晨散步的习惯。He is in the habit of taking a walk every morning.／从小培养劳动习惯 cultivate from childhood the habit of doing manual labor.／这样的做法是某些外国人的习惯。It is the custom with certain foreigners to do so. 2. 还有动词意义，表示逐渐适应的意思。v. to adapt oneself to sth. gradually：这样潮湿的天气我实在不习惯。I just cannot get used to this damp weather.／他习惯于艰苦工作。He is accustomed to hard work.

习气 (bad habit; bad practice) 贬义词。指逐渐形成的坏习惯和风气。使用范围较窄，一般只用于人。pejorative, refers to bad habits and practices, which have gradually formed; has a narrow range of usage, normally limited to human beings：官僚习气 habitual practice of bureaucracy

〔相同点〕：都是名词。都表示长期形成的、一时不易改变的行为。Syn. n. behavioral patterns acquired over a long period of time, which can no longer easily be modified.

细致 xìzhì   仔细 zǐxì

细致 (careful; meticulous; painstaking) 着重指精细、周密，或指人们对细小地方都花了工夫，或指事物精细。常形容人的活动、态度、及作风等。meticulous; indicates attention to detail, used to describe actions, attitudes, style of work, etc.: 她想得很细致. She thought it over very carefully. / 这活儿做得很细致。This is a careful piece of work.

仔细 (careful; attentive; be careful; look out) 1. 着重指考虑周到、细心。一般形容人的活动，如看、听、研究等。emphasizes thorough and careful consideration; generally used to describe activities such as looking, listening or performing research: 仔细地研究文件 pore over a document / 上课仔细听讲 listen attentively in class 2. 表示小心、注意的意思。to be careful; to pay attention: 她做事很仔细。She is very careful in everything she does.

〔相同点〕：都是形容词。都表示细心周密、不放过细小的地方的意思。Syn. adj. careful; not overlooking details.

相信 xiāngxìn　信任 xìnrèn

相信 (believe in; be convinced of; have faith in) 泛指不怀疑，对象可以是自己或别人或某种事情。to consider sth. to be true, have no doubts of sth. The object can be either oneself, other people or things: 我们应当相信群众。We must have faith in the masses. / 相信自己的事业是正义的 be convinced of the justice of one's cause

信任 (trust; have confidence in) 表示不仅认为可靠、而且敢于托付的意思。对象只能是人、组织、团体。to repose one's trust and reliance in a person, organization or group: 他得到人民的信任。He enjoys the trust of the people. / 信任投票 vote of confidence

〔相同点〕：都是动词。表示对人、组织、团体等认为可靠，不怀疑。Syn. v. indicating that one believes or trusts certain persons, organizations or groups and considers them reliable.

详尽 xiángjìn　详细 xiángxì

详尽 (detailed; exhaustive; thorough) 着重在"尽"，指应有尽有，毫无遗漏，比"详细"更进一层。The key element is 尽 (to the maximum extent); thus, comprehensive containing all that it should, without the slightest omission. The meaning is deeper than that of 详细: 详尽的记载 a detailed record / 对问题进行详尽地研究 make an exhaustive study of a subject

详细 (detailed; minute) 着重指内容十分完备，具备应有的细节。跟"简略"相对。emphasizes the idea that the content is complete, in great detail. It is the opposite of 简略(simple): 请说详细点。Please explain it in greater detail. / 详细了解情况 acquire detailed knowledge of the situation / 详细占有材料 have all the available data

〔相同点〕：都是形容词。表示周密完备的意思。Syn. adj. thorough and complete.

向导 xiàngdǎo　引导 yǐndǎo

向导 (guide) 是名词。一般指人，表示带路的人的意思。n. a person acting as a guide: 没有向导爬喜玛拉雅山是很危险的。It is very dangerous to go climbing in the Himalayas without a guide.

引导 (guide; lead) 是动词。表示指引或带着人向某个目标行动。v. to show the way or lead people towards a certain objective: 主人引导

贵宾们参观了车间。The hosts showed the distinguished guests around the workshop.

〔相同点〕：都有带领、指引的意思。Syn. to lead or point the way.

向 xiàng 朝 cháo

向 **(face; turn towards)** 意义同"朝"，但在"向你学习"这类说法里，一般不用"朝"。generally interchangeable with 朝，however，朝 cannot be substituted in expressions such as 向你学习(follow your example)：葵花朵朵向太阳。Sunflowers turn towards the sun. ╱ 这间屋子向东。The room faces east.

朝 **(facing; towards)** 1.表示由一点到另一点的运动方向。indicates the direction of movement：迈开大步朝前走 march ahead with great strides ╱ 朝南走 go southward ╱ 这门朝里开还是朝外开？ Does the door open inwards or outwards? 2. 表示本身位置不动而面向某方。indicates the direction in which an object at rest faces：坐东朝西 facing west ╱ 这间屋子的窗户朝南。The windows of this room face the south.

〔相同点〕：都是介词。表示由一点到另一点的运动方向。Syn. prep. indicating direction of movement.

271

消灭 xiāomiè   幻灭 huànmiè

消灭 **(eliminate; abolish; exterminate; wipe out)** 表示施加强力，使之消失而不存在的意思。to annihilate by force: 消灭病虫害 wipe out insect pests and plant diseases / 消灭敌人一个师 wipe out an enemy division

幻灭 **(vanish into thin air)** 是指幻想或不真实的事因受到现实的打击而破灭。indicates that illusions or misconceptions cease to exist in the face of reality: 他的希望幻灭了。His hopes were dashed.

〔相同点〕：都是动词。表示事物的破灭、消灭。Syn. v. indicating that sth. is annihilated.

消息 xiāoxi   新闻 xīnwén

消息 **(news; information; tidings;)** 1. 可以指时事报道，一般是比较简短的。a report on a current event, generally a brief news item: 本地消息 local news / 头版消息 a front-page story 2. 还有音讯的意思，表示人的行踪或事物的变动情况。"新闻"不能这样用。also refers to news about sb.'s whereabouts or changes in events in this sense, it is not interchangeable with 新闻: 杳无消息 have

272

not heard from him since / 你有没有他的消息 Have you heard any news of him?

新闻 (news) 指新发生的事情，现在多用来指报刊上报道的时事。news of recent events as reported in the mass media: 新闻公报 press communique / 新闻简报 news summary / 新闻图片橱窗 exhibition of news photography

〔相同点〕：都是名词，都有最近发生的事情的意思。Syn. n. information about recent, current events.

辛苦 xīnkǔ　辛劳 xīnláo

辛苦 (hard; toilsome; laborious; work hard; go through hardships) 1. 着重指劳苦。口语和书面语均常用。expresses the idea of hard toil; often used in both spoken and written language: 犁地这活儿很辛苦。Ploughing is hard work. 2. 用来求人做事时的客气话。used when requesting sb. politely to do sth.: 这件事恐怕还得辛苦你一趟。I am afraid we will have to trouble you again.

辛劳 (pains; toil) 着重指劳累。多半用于工作。多用于书面语。emphasizes the idea of exhausting activity, especially in relation to work; most common in written language: 日夜辛劳 toil day and night / 不辞辛劳 spare no

273

pains

〔相同点〕: 都是形容词。都表示身体或精神劳苦的意思。Syn. adj. referring to toilsome labor of body and mind.

新奇 xīnqí　新鲜 xīnxiān

新奇 (strange; novel; new) 着重指奇特，特殊。indicates that sth. strikes one as strange, peculiar, special: 新奇的想法 a novel idea / 他初到矿山时，处处觉得新奇。When he first got to the mine, everything struck him as new and strange.

新鲜 (fresh; new; novel; strange) 1. 泛指刚出现的或刚知道的，不普遍的，少见的。refers to sth. which just appeared or has just become known; quite uncommon; seldom seen: 新鲜经验 a new experience / 这话真新鲜。That is a funny thing to say. 2. 还指食物不陈腐；花朵没过时；空气没污染。refers to food that has not lost its freshness; flowers that have not begun to wilt; air that is not polluted, etc.: 新鲜空气 fresh air / 鱼有点儿不新鲜了。The fish is slightly off.

〔相同点〕: 都是形容词。意思是刚出现或不普遍的或少见的。跟"陈旧"相对。Syn. adj. referring to sth. that has just appeared; uncommon;

274

rarely seen. It is the opposite of 陈旧 (outmoded, timeworn).

欣赏 xīnshǎng　观赏 guānshǎng

欣赏 (appreciate; enjoy; admire) 1.除了指视觉享受之外，还可以指听觉的、味觉的、嗅觉的或精神的享受。对象不仅限于看得见的东西，还可指思想、感情等。as well as enjoyment procured by the sense of sight, it refers to pleasure obtained through any of the other senses, and also to intellectual, aesthetic enjoyment. Used not only of objects of perception, but also of ideas and emotions: 音乐欣赏 music appreciation／欣赏风景 enjoy the scenery 2. 还表示认为好，喜欢的意思。to consider sth. to be good and enjoyable: 我很欣赏这个花园的格局。I admire the layout of this garden.

观赏 (view and admire; enjoy the sight of) 表示观看欣赏的意思，对象只能是看得见的东西。to see and enjoy. Used only of visible things: 这是观赏植物。This is an ornamental plant.

〔相同点〕：都是动词。表示通过感觉享受美好的景物的意思。对象可以是景物、美术、工艺作品等。Syn. v. to enjoy the sight of sth. The object may be scenery, arts and crafts, etc.

醒目 xǐngmù   夺目 duómù

醒目 (catch the eyes, of written words or pictures; attract attention; be striking) 一般指事物所在的部位特别显眼，或者它所表达的内容和形式特别引人注目，表示明显突出的意思。to be conspicuous and prominent, indicates that sth. is striking because of its form, content or position: 醒目的标语 eye-catching slogans / 醒目的标题 bold headlines

夺目 (dazzle the eyes) 一般指事物的光色非常耀眼。表示光彩艳丽的意思 refers to dazzling brightness and color, brilliant effulgence: 光彩夺目 with dazzling brightness

〔相同点〕：都是形容词。都有十分显眼或引人注目的意思。Syn. adj. to be conspicuous; noticeable; remarkable.

修理 xiūlǐ   修缮 xiūshàn

修理 (repair; mend; fix) 多用于具体的东西。often used of specific, concrete objects: 修理机器 fix a machine / 他正在修理鞋。He is repairing shoes.

修缮 (repair; renovate) 一般只用于建筑物。normally used only of buildings: 修缮房屋 housing maintenance

〔相同点〕：都表示使损坏的东西恢复原来的形状或
作用。都是动词。Syn. v. to restore damaged
objects to their proper form or function.

虚假 xūjiǎ　　虚伪 xūwěi

虚假 (false; sham; dishonest) "真实"的反面。多指
内容、证据、情况、情节等较抽象的事物，
有时也用于人的言行。指"情况跟事实真相不
符合"的意思。the opposite of 真实 (real, actual); refers mainly to such abstract things as
subject matter, circumstances, evidence, etc.,
but also to words and actions; means that sth.
is at odds with the facts, with the real state of
affairs: 他给我一种虚假的感觉。He gives me
an impression of spuriousness / 虚假的繁荣 false
prosperity / 虚假的安全感 a false sense of security　·

虚伪 (sham; false; hypocritical) 诚实的反面，多指
待人处事缺乏诚意，口是心非。常形容人的
品质、行为、作风等。the opposite of 诚实
(honest); often refers to duplicity, hypocrisy
in one's dealings with people; saying yes and
meaning no. It is used to describe character,
actions or style of work: 虚伪的人 hypocrite
/知识的问题是一个科学的问题，来不得半

点虚伪和骄傲。Knowlege is a scientific matter, which does not allow of the slightest dishonesty or arrogance.

〔相同点〕：都是形容词。都表示不真实、不符合实际。Syn. adj. not true; not real; at odds with the actual situation.

须要 xūyào　需要 xūyào

须要 (must; have to) 是"一定要"的意思，只能放在动词前，用来表示行为动作的必要性，不能单独作谓语。to be absolutely necessary. It is only used before a main verb; i.e., it cannot appear alone as predicate：做这种工作须要细心。This work needs to be done meticulously.

需要 (need; want; require; demand; needs) 1. 表示应该、必须的意思。should; must：这所房子需要修理。The house needs repairing. ／我告诉他需要做什么。I told him what he had to do. 2. 表示要求得到、必须有的意思。to require, need：这些幼苗需要细心照料。These seedlings need to be looked after carefully. ／我需要你的帮助。I need your help. 3. 还可作名词用，表示一种愿望或要求。n. expressing a hope or demand：保证人民吃穿的基本需要 ensure the people their basic needs in food and clothing／从民众的需要出发 make the needs of the majority of the people our starting point

〔相同点〕：都是动词。表示一定要、必须的意思。Syn. v. to be necessary; must.

寻求 xúnqiú　追求 zhuiqiú

寻求 (seek; explore; go in quest of) 着重指目标不太明确地寻找、探求。used of a quest with an indefinite goal: 寻求真理 seek truth / 寻求打开僵局的途径 explore possible paths for ending the stalemate

追求 (seek; pursue; woo; court; chase; run after) 着重指更积极更迫切地争取达到确定的目的。to strive actively and energetically for a definite aim: 追求名誉地位 be after fame and position / 单纯追求数量的倾向 the tendency to concentrate on quantity alone

〔相同点〕：都是动词。表示想方设法求得所需要的事物，如真理、思想、知识等。Syn. v. to do everything in one's power to gain the object of one's desire, e.g. truth, an idea, knowledge.

询问 xúnwèn　盘问 pánwèn

询问 (ask about; inquire) 表示征求意思或打听的意思。to ask advice or opinions, or inquire about sth.: 询问我们学习情况 ask us about our studies／询问病状 inquire about sb.'s illness／他们询问新机器的效能. They asked about the efficiency of the new machine.

盘问 (cross-examine; interrogate) 是仔细查问的意思，被盘问者多是被认为值得怀疑的人。to interrogate minutely. The object is generally a suspect: 盘问战俘 interrogate a prisoner of war

〔相同点〕：都是动词。都有问的意思。Syn. v. to ask.

迅速 xùnsù 急速 jísù

迅速 (rapid; swift; speedy; prompt) 只表示"很快"的意思。very fast: 我国石油工业发展迅速。Our oil industry is expanding by leaps and bounds.／动作迅速 swift in action／迅速作出决定 come to a prompt decision

急速 (very fast; at high speed; rapidly) 除表示快的意思外，还有急促、紧迫的意思。combines the idea of rapidity with that of hurry, urgency: 汽车急速地向前行驶。The car was travelling at high speed.／他的病情急速恶化。His condition is rapidly worsened.／情况急速变化。The situation changed quickly.

〔相同点〕：都是形容词。都表示速度很快的意思。Syn. adj. at high speed.

Y

压抑 yāyì　压制 yāzhì

压抑 (constrain; inhibit; depress; oppressive; stifling) 指对感情、力量等用较大的力量压下去，使不能充分流露或发挥。forcibly to suppress a feeling, passion, etc., so that it cannot reveal itself or develop fully: 心情压抑 feel constrained / 这部影片气氛比较压抑。The film is rather depressing. / 胸口感到压抑 feel tight in the chest

压制 (suppress; stifle; inhibit) 着重指用强力(职权等) 制止、限制、不让活动。to use force (e.g. official powers) to curb or restrict people or to deny them free movement: 压制不同意见 stifle differing opinions / 压制群众的首创精神 inhibit the initiative of the masses / 采取压制手段 adopt repressive measures

〔相同点〕: 都是动词。都表示用力量控制住，使不能随便活动。Syn. v. to control sth. with force, to deny it free rein.

281

严格 yángé　严厉 yánlì

严格 (strict; rigorous; rigid; stringent) 着重表示按照一定的格式、标准从严要求，绝不马虎的意思。常用来形容人们对法律、制度、准则等要求遵守、执行的程度。acting strictly according to a certain formal standard or requirement, not lax or approximate; used of people's adherence to laws, rules, systems, and regulations, etc.: 严格履行协定条款 strictly implement the terms of the agreement ／ 严格训练，严格要求 go in for rigorous training and set strict demands ／ 严格说来 strictly speaking

严厉 (stern; severe) 着重表示特别厉害、不温和或不相容的意思，常用来形容人对人的态度。very severe, not mild or easy-going; used of people's attitude towards others: 严厉制裁 apply stern sanctions ／ 严厉的批评 severe criticism

〔相同点〕：都是形容词。都表示很严的意思。Syn. adj. very strict.

严密 yánmì　精密 jingmì

严密 (tight; close) 着重表示严格、紧密、没有疏

282

漏的意思。多用于防范方面，如消毒、封锁等方面。emphasizes strictness, closeness, hermetic closure; often used of preventive measures such as disinfection, blockades, etc.: 严密封锁 impose a tight blockade／严密监视 put under close surveillance／严密注视国际局势的发展 closely follow the development of world events

精密 (precise; accurate) 着重表示精致、细密、不粗糙的意思。多用于机械、仪器等方面。said of sth. delicate and precise, not rough or crude; often used to describe machinery, instruments, etc.: 精密的仪器 a precision instrument

〔相同点〕：都是形容词。表示组织、结构上的紧密、完备的意思。跟"缺陷、粗糙"相对。Syn. adj. referring to compactness, completeness of structure. It is the opposite of 缺陷(defect, shortcoming) and 粗糙 (crude, rough).

严肃 yánsù　认真 rènzhēn

严肃 (serious; solemn; earnest) 指神情、气氛等使人感到敬畏。常用来形容作风、态度，也可用来修饰问题、任务等。indicates that sb.'s manner and presence are such as to inspire awe; describes a serious, scrupulous style of work; also used of problems, duties, etc.; 严肃地指出 point out in all earnestness / 严肃的态度 a serious attitude / 严肃的斗争 conduct a serious struggle

认真 **(conscientious; earnest; serious; take seriously; take to heart)** 指慎重对待、不马虎的意思。常用在动词学习、研究、解决等前边，表示慎重对待，不随便。 indicates that one takes sth. seriously. It is often used with verbs such as study, learn, solve, to indicate conscientiousness; 认真的自我批评 an earnest self-criticism / 进行认真的研究 make a serious study / 我说着玩的，他就认真了。 I was only joking, but he took it to heart. / 他对一切都特别认真。 He takes everything terribly seriously.

〔相同点〕：都是形容词。都表示郑重其事，不苟且、不马虎的意思。 Syn. adj. serious; earnest; not careless or casual.

要求 yāoqiú　请求 qǐngqiú

要求 **(ask; demand; require; claim)** 指提出具体的愿望，希望得到满足的意思。"要求"可以对自己，也可以对别人。 to express a specific desire which one hopes to have realized. It may refer to demands made of oneself or of others: 他要求发言。 He demanded to be heard./ 达到质量要求 fulfil quality requirements/ 要求赔偿 claim compensation/ 这项工作要求精神高度集中。 This job calls for intense concentration.

请求 **(ask; request)** 指说明愿望，提出申请，希望得到满足，语气较客气。只用于对别人。 to make a request or an application in the hope that it may be fulfilled; the tone is polite. It is only used of requests made of others: 请求宽恕 ask for forgiveness/ 我们应你的请求而来。 We came at your request.

〔相同点〕：都是动词和名词。都包含有给对方提出一种愿望，希望得到满足的意思。 Syn. v.; n. to express a desire to sb. in the hope that it will be fulfilled.

要紧 yàojǐn　紧急 jǐnjí

要紧 **(important; essential; be critical; be serious; matter)** 1. 是重要的意思，一般用来形容事物的性质。 important, usually describes the nature of things: 随便做什么工作，最要紧的是实事求是。 In whatever we do, the most important thing is to be realistic and down-to-earth./ 不要紧，你明天去也可以。 You can go tomorrow, it doesn't matter. 2. 还有严重的意思。 be serious: 他只受了点轻伤，不要紧。 He was only slightly injured. it's nothing serious.

紧急 (urgent; pressing; critical) 是指严重而急迫的意思，一般指必须立即采取行动，不容拖延的情况。 serious and pressing, generally referring to a situation requiring immediate action, which admits of no delay: 发出紧急呼吁 issue an urgent appeal / 情况紧急。 The situation is critical. / 紧急措施 emergency measures

〔相同点〕: 都是形容词。都有重要、不宜拖延的意思。 Syn. adj. very important; admitting of no delay.

一概 yīgài 一律 yīlǜ

一概 (one and all; without exception; totally; categorically) 相当于"全"、"都"的意思，常用于对事物的概括，一般只用于动词前面。 all; complete; often used of things. It is usually placed before a verb: 一概拒绝 reject without exception / 一概排斥 totally exclude

一律 (same; alike; uniform; all; without exception) 1. 相当于"全一样地""都一样地"。除了常用于对事物的概括，还常用于对人的概括。除用在动词前，也可用于名词或

286

名词性词组前。the same; used of things as well as persons. It may be placed before a verb, a noun or a noun phrase: 一律对待 treat in the same way／ 国家不分大小，应该一律平等。All countries, big or small, should be equal. 2. 还有形容词意义，表示一个样子的意思。adj. alike; one and the same: 不宜强求一律。No rigid uniformity should be sought.

〔相同点〕: 都是副词。都表示全体、没有例外的意思。Syn. adv. all; without exception.

一齐 yìqí 一起 yìqí

一齐 (at the same time; simultaneously; in unison) 表示同时，是行动一致的意思。at the same moment; taking concerted action: 一齐出动 go into action simultaneously／ 人和行李一齐到了。The baggage arrived at the same time as the passengers.

一起 (in the same place; together; in company) 是一同、一道的意思。together; at the same time and in the same place: 住在一起 live in the same place／ 奶奶和孙女儿一起进城。Grandmother went to town together with her granddaughter.

〔相同点〕: 都是副词。都表示共同的意思。Syn. adv. together; in common.

一瞬间 yīshùnjiān　一刹那 yīchà'nà

一瞬间 (in the twinkling of an eye) 指一眨眼之间。in the time it takes to blink: 在这一瞬间，我看见两边的庄稼在暴风雨的密网里挣扎似的摇摆着。In that instant, I saw crops on both sides struggling and swaying in the heavy storm.

一刹那 (in, for an instant) 也指极短的时间，但比"一瞬间"时间更短。indicates an extremely short time, even shorter than that implied by 一瞬间: 沉静了一刹那，他又恢复了他那经常微笑的面容。For a moment, he grew quiet, then the wonted smile returned to his face.

〔相同点〕：都是副词。表示极短时间。Syn. adv. in, for an extremely short time.

一向 yīxiàng　一直 yīzhí

一向 (earlier on; lately; consistently; all along) 着重指一定时间的全过程，过去的某一段时间或从过去到现在。refers to the whole course of a given period of time—either in the (recent) past, or extending from the past until the present: 这一向你进步不小吧。You must have made a lot of progress lately. / 前一向雨水

288

多。There was quite a lot of rain earlier on.

一直 (**straight; continuously; always; all along; all the way**) 1. 着重指动作始终不间断，或情况始终不改变。focuses on uninterrupted action or the fact that a situation has always been so, has never changed or deviated from its course: 雪一直下了两天两夜。It snowed for two days and nights on end. / 我们一直是同事。We have always been colleagues. / 我一直认为他是无罪的。I was convinced that he was innocent all along. 2. 还表示不拐弯的意思。without turning left or right: 一直走 go straight ahead

〔相同点〕：都是副词。表示动作或情况从过去到现在保持不变的意思。Syn. adv. showing that an activity or situation has continued without change up until the present.

一致 yīzhì　共同 gòngtóng

一致 (**showing no difference; identical; unanimous; consistent**) 着重指没有分歧。without divergence of opinion: 观点一致 hold identical views / 取得完全一致的意见 reach unanimity / 提案一致通过了。The resolution was adopted unanimously.

共同 (**common; together; jointly**) 着重指大家一起

（做）。in common; often refers to concerted activity: 共同关心的问题 matters of common concern / 共同行动 act in concert / 共同努力 make joint efforts / 欧洲·共同体 The European Community

〔相同点〕: 都是形容词。都表示相同的意思。Syn. adj. identical; alike.

屹立 yìlì 矗立 chùlì 耸立 sǒnglì

屹立 **(stand towering like a giant; stand erect)** 指象山峰一样高耸而稳固地立着。常用来比喻坚定不可动摇。可用于人和物。to stand towering and steadfast like a mountain; used figuratively to describe firm determination, used of people as well as of things: 他屹立在那里，象钢铁巨人。He stood there like an iron giant. / 人民英雄纪念碑屹立在天安门广场上。The Monument to the People's Heroes towers like a giant on Tiananmen Square.

矗立 **(stand tall and upright; tower over sth.)** 着重形容高而直，只用于物，不用于人。tall and straight, used only of things, not of people: 这座金色的方形大厦，矗立在天安门和正阳门之间。This square, golden edifice stands tall and upright between Tiananmen and Zhengyangmen.

290

耸立 **(tower aloft)** 着重形容向上突出。只用于物，不用于人。to project upward; used only of things, not of people: 群山耸立 a range of mountains towering to the skies

〔相同点〕：都有高耸、直立的意思，常用来形容山峰或建筑物。都是动词。Syn. v. to stand erect and tall; especially in relation to the height of the surroundings; used of mountain peaks and buildings.

义务 yìwù　责任 zérèn

义务 **(duty; obligation; volunteer; voluntary)** 指法律上、道德上应尽的职责。refers to legal and moral responsibilities: 公民的基本权利与义务 the fundamental rights and duties of citizens / 我是来尽义务的。I have come to do voluntary service.

责任 **(duty; responsibility; responsibility for a fault or wrong; blame)** 指本身职责范围内应做的事情。matters which fall within the sphere of one's responsibility and duties: 爱护公物，人人都有责任。It is everybody's duty to take good care of public property. / 我不过尽了自己的责任罢了。I have done no more than my duty. / 你不应该把责任推到别人身上。You should not shift the blame onto others. / 他没有

责任感。He has no sense of responsibility.

〔相同点〕：都是名词。表示应该做的事。Syn. n. things which one has an obligation to do.

应付 yìngfù　敷衍 fūyǎn

应付　(**deal with; cope with; handle; make do**)　是中性词。指采取与之适应的方法、措施来对待或处理。还有将就、凑合的意思。a neutral term; to use appropriate methods or measures to deal with matters. It also means to make do with sth.：准备应付可能的突然事变 be prepared against possible emergencies／应付复杂局面 deal with complicated situations／我这双凉鞋今年夏天还可以应付过去。I shall make do with these sandals for the summer.

敷衍 (**be perfunctory; go through the motions of**) 是贬义词，指做事不认真或待人不真诚，只是表面应酬。pejorative; to do things without conscientiousness or to be insincere and superficial in one's dealings with people：他工作一向敷衍了事。He always muddles through his work.／他敷衍了几句就走了。He made a few perfunctory remarks and left.

〔相同点〕：都是动词。都表示做事不认真。Syn. v. to do things without conscientiousness.

292

犹豫 yóuyù　踌躇 chóuchú

犹豫 (hesitate; be irresolute) 泛指拿不定主意，多指内心活动，也指行动。书面语和口语都常用。有重迭形式"犹犹豫豫"。indicates that one is unable to make up one's mind; generally refers to a mental state, occasionally to physical activity, used in both spoken and written language. It may be reduplicated for emphasis in the form 犹犹豫豫: 他做事总是犹犹豫豫的。He is always terribly indecisive. / 毫不犹豫 without the least hesitation

踌躇 (hesitate; shilly-shally) 着重指行动，是在具体行动上拿不定主意。多用于书面语。无重迭形式。stresses hesitation in undertaking a specific action, often used in written language. It has no reduplicated form: 踌躇不前 hesitate to move forward

〔相同点〕：表示拿不定主意的意思，常通用。Syn. be irresolute, can be interchangeable.

友情 yǒuqíng　友谊 yǒuyì

友情 (friendly sentiments; friendship) 多用于个人之间，带亲切色彩。used of friendship between individuals; indicates affection: 他对

293

老同学的友情是很深厚的。He has profound feelings of friendship for his old classmates.

友谊 (friendship) 不限于个人之间，还常用于国家、政党、民族、人民、单位。带庄重色彩。said of individuals as well as of nations, political parties, ethnic groups, work units, etc. It often has a solemn or formal tone: 深厚的友谊 profound friendship / 建立友谊 build ties of friendship / 友谊赛 friendly match

〔相同点〕：都是名词。都表示朋友间的感情。Syn. n. the affective relationship between friends.

预备 yùbèi　准备 zhǔnbèi

预备 (prepare; get ready) 强调时间性，是提前或早早安排的意思。The key element is 预 (in advance); thus, to make arrangements in advance or to make early preparations: 这男孩每天晚上熬夜准备他的功课。The boy sits up late every night to prepare his lessons. / 明年你预备去上海吗? Are you planning to go to Shanghai next year?

准备 (prepare; get ready; intend; plan) 强调针对性或目的性，常跟"充分""仔细"等词搭配。emphasizes the idea of preparation with a definite aim and purpose. It is often used

with 充分(full)、仔细(careful)、etc.: 为会议
准备文件 prepare documents for a meeting / 作
最坏的准备 prepare for the worst / 今年暑假
我准备回老家看看。I'm going to visit my native place this summer vacation. / 我们准备下
星期一开始试验。We plan to start the experiment next Monday.

〔相同点〕：都是动词。都表示1.预先安排或筹
划、做好事前应做的事的意思。2.打算。
Syn. v. 1. to plan or prepare in advance
2. to intend.

渊博 yuānbó　广博 guǎngbó

渊博 (broad and profound; erudite) 指学识深而且
广。describes profound and wide-ranging
knowledge scholarship: 他是学识渊博的
人。He is erudite.

广博 (extensive; wide; vast—person's knowledge)
指学识(见识)的范围大、方面多。不涉及深
度，常形容见识、内容等。refers to
wide-ranging, many faceted knowledge,
without, however, any particular implication
of depth; often describes knowledge, experience, subject matter, etc.: 他知识广博。He
has extensive knowledge.

〔相同点〕：都是形容词。都有见识广、知识丰富

的意思。 Syn. adj. of wide experience and rich in knowledge.

Z

遭受 zāoshòu　遭遇 zāoyù

遭受 **(suffer; be subjected to; sustain)** 着重指自身受到。emphasizes the idea of sustaining, being subjected to adversity：遭受帝国主义压迫 suffer imperialist oppression / 遭受损失 sustain losses / 遭受水灾 be hit by floods

遭遇 **(meet with; encounter; run up against; bitter experience; hard lot)** 1. 着重指在行动过程中碰上。to encounter (adversity) in the course of one's activities：遭遇不幸 meet with misfortune 2. 还表示所遇到的不幸的事情(名词)。n. misfortunes encountered：我们有着共同的历史遭遇。We share the same bitter historical experiences. / 他后来的遭遇我就不知道了。I don't know what became of him later.

〔相同点〕：都是动词。指的是遭到不幸或不利的事。宾语都是表示贬义的名词，如灾害、困难、惨事等和不及物动词如"失败"、"破产"等。Syn. v. to meet with misfortune or adversity. Its objects are all pejorative terms, such as disaster, difficulty, misery, defeat or bankruptcy.

责问 zéwèn 质问 zhìwèn

责问 (call sb. to account) 着重指责备、批判别人的过错。程度较轻。to blame or criticize sb. for his or her faults. The tone is relative light, however: 他责问我说: "你到什么地方去了? 为什么才回来?" "Where have you been? Why have you only just come back?" he reproached me.

质问 (question; interrogate; call to account) 着重指问明是非, 更强调据理追问, 常要求回答, 程度较重。to inquire into issues of right and wrong; emphasizes detailed inquiry on a logical basis; often expects an answer. The tone is more serious than that of 责问: 我质问他说: "你说他是小偷, 有什么证据?" I questioned him, "What evidence have you got for calling him a thief? " / 提出质问 bring sb. to account

〔相同点〕: 都是动词。表示据理追问的意思。Syn. v. to question sb. closely on a logical basis.

瞻仰 zhānyǎng 敬仰 jìngyǎng

瞻仰 (look at with reverence) 指恭敬地看, 侧重在往上看。对象总是指具体的事物。to look

298

upon with respect, look up to. The object is usually concrete: 瞻仰遗容 pay one's last respects / 瞻仰烈士陵园 pay a visit to the martyrs' mausoleum

敬仰 **(revere; venerate)** 指尊敬仰慕，侧重指对象的德和才，对象总是人。to respect and admire, refers mainly to persons with ability and integrity. Its object is always a human being: 她深受人民的爱戴和敬仰。She commands deep love and reverence among the people.

〔相同点〕：都是动词。都有尊敬和热爱的意思。Syn. v. to respect and love.

招呼 zhāohu 召唤 zhàohuàn

招呼 **(call; hail; greet; say hello to; notify; tell; take care of)** 1. 常用于具体意义，指用语言、手势、信号等叫人来或作其他动作。to ask sb. to come or to do sth. by language, gesture or signal: 那边有人招呼你。Someone over there is calling you. / 你如果不去，事先打个招呼。Let me know beforehand if you won't be going. 2. 还有问候、吩咐、照料等义。to greet; to look after, etc.: 昨天见到老朋友，只打了个招呼就分手了。I saw a friend of mine yesterday, but we just said hello and went our separate ways. / 招呼老人 take care of old people

召唤 (call; summon) 常用于抽象意义，比喻意义。多带庄重色彩。generally used in an abstract or metaphorical sense. It has a serious tone: 他时刻听从祖国的召唤。He is always ready to answer the call of his motherland.

〔相同点〕：都是动词。表示叫人来的意思。Syn. v. to ask sb. to come.

召集 zhàojí　召开 zhàokāi

召集 (call together; convene) 泛指把人们召唤到一起，强调聚集。to call or summon people together, with the emphasis on gathering together: 召集同学来开会 call the students to attend a meeting ／ 把他们召集在一起 call them together

召开 (convene; convoke) 只指召唤人们开会，宾语只能是表示会议的词语。to call people to a meeting. The object must be some kind of meeting: 召开一次国际会议 convene an international conference ／ 庆祝全国人民代表大会的召开 celebrate the convening of the National People's Congress

〔相同点〕：都是动词。表示把人们召唤在一起。Syn. v. to call people together.

照顾 zhàogù　照料 zhàoliào
照应 zhàoying（zhàoyìng）

照顾 (give consideration to; show consideration for; make allowance for; look after; care for; attend to) 着重特别注意，关心。多指在精神上或物质上给予优待。to pay special attention to; to concern oneself with sb. or sth.; often refers to preferential or specially favorable treatment: 照顾到两国的友好关系 out of consideration for the friendship between the two countries／照顾实际需要 take actual needs into consideration／照顾他的困难 take his difficulties into account／给予适当照顾 give appropriate preferential treatment

照料 (take care of; attend to) 着重指照看和料理。to look after and manage, tend: 她把小女儿托给一位老大娘照料。She left her baby daughter in the care of an old woman.／你放心走吧，家里的事有我们照料。Don't worry, we'll take care of things at home while you are away.

照应 (coordinate; correlate; look after; take care of) 1. 着重指照看。to look after: 火车上乘务员对顾客照应得很好。The attendants on the train take good care of the passengers. 2. 读

zhàoyìng 时，表示配合，呼应的意思。When pronounced zhàoyìng; with the final syllable in the fourth tone, it means coordinate; work in concert: 文章要前后照应 (zhàoyìng)。A composition must be well organized.

〔相同点〕：都是动词。表示关心、照看的意思。Syn. v. to care for, look after.

镇定 zhèndìng　镇静 zhènjìng

镇定 (calm; cool; composed; unruffled) 指遇到紧急情况不慌不乱的意思。偏重于"定"，语意比"镇静"重。可以作动词和形容词。The key element is 定 (stable, steady); thus, showing presence of mind and equanimity in an emergency: 神色镇定 be calm and cool / 保持镇定 keep cool / 他竭力镇定着自己焦急不安的情绪。He tried to overcome his anxiety. / 在紧急关头他表现得十分镇定。He appeared calm in the moment of crisis.

镇静 (calm; cool; composed; unruffled) 指情绪稳定或平静。偏重于"静"。只可作形容词。The key element is 静 (calm); thus, in a tranquil frame of mind; used only as adj.: 休息了一会儿，他的心情镇静多了。After having rested for a while, he calmed down. / 他遇事一向镇静自

若。He is always calm in the face of emergency.
〔相同点〕：都是形容词。表示安定不慌的意思。
Syn. adj. quiet and calm.

正规 zhèngguī　正轨 zhèngguǐ

正规 (regular; standard) 是形容词。指符合正式规
定的或一般公认的标准的意思。 adj. in
accordance with official stipulations or generally recognized standards：正规学校 regular
school／ 正规部队 regular troops

正轨 (the right or correct path) 是名词。指正常的
发展道路。 n. the path of normal develop-
ment：纳入正轨 lead onto the correct path

〔相同点〕：都有正常、不乱的意思。Syn. adj. be
normal or in order.

证明 zhèngmíng　证实 zhèngshí

**证明 (prove; testify; bear out; certificate; identifica-
tion; testimonial)** 1. 表示验证和说明的意
思，由不清楚到清楚。证明的内容是让人知
道真伪、是非等。to demonstrate, to resolve
doubts by means of evidence. Used of issues
of truth or falsehood, right or wrong, etc.：充
分证明 abundantly prove／ 无数事实已证明了
这 一 点 。 Countless facts have proved this

point. / 这个论断早已为事实证明。This thesis has long since been borne out by the facts. 1. 还指证明书、证明信等。refers to certificates, credential, testimonials, etc.: 医生证明 medical certificate / 他出示证明文件。He showed his certificate.

证实 (confirm; verify) 只说明某事或某人、某种理论等确实存在。to confirm a hypothesis, etc.: 他的身份有待证实。His identity remains to be confirmed. / 证实一个科学上的假设 verify a scientific hypothesis

〔相同点〕：都是动词。表示根据可靠的材料来表明或断定人或事物的真实性的意思。Syn. v. to establish or demonstrate the true state of affairs by means of reliable data.

正直 zhèngzhí 正派 zhèngpài

正直 (honest; upright; fair-minded) 指公正坦率的意思。just and straight-forward: 正直的人 an honest person

正派 (upright; honest; decent) 指(品行、作风)规矩、严肃的意思。indicates that sb. is well-behaved, well-disciplined and serious; refers to conduct and style of work: 作风正派 honest and upright in one's ways / 正派人 a decent person

304

〔相同点〕：都是形容词。都指人的思想、品德、作风、光明正大的意思。Syn. adj. referring to a person's moral character, mentality and style of work; open and aboveboard.

指摘 zhǐzhāi　斥责 chìzé

指摘 (pick faults and criticize; censure) 指挑出错误，再加批评的意思。强调有意地挑剔。to pick out sb.'s mistakes and criticize him or her; emphasizes deliberate nitpicking。他喜欢指摘别人。He likes to pick faults and criticize others.

斥责 (reprimand; rebuke; denounce) 指申斥、责备，强调大声地呵斥。to rebuke or reproach with emphasis on the idea of berating loudly, vociferously；厉声斥责 severely reprimand

〔相同点〕：都是动词。表示批评别人的错误的意思。Syn. v. to criticize others' mistakes.

忠诚 zhōngchéng　忠实 zhōngshí

忠诚 (loyal; faithful; staunch) 着重指诚心诚意，尽心尽力。常作褒义词。常与"老实"搭配。an approbatory term; to be earnest and sincere, to do sth. with all one's heart and all one's might. It is often used together with 老实 (honest): 忠

305

诚于教育事业 be devoted to the educational cause／ 我们对自己祖国必须忠诚老实。We must be honest and faithful to our motherland.

忠实 (true; faithful) 着重指可靠，没有二心，也指真实。是中性词，也可以用于对实际情况或原稿等。a neutral term; reliable, faithful. It can mean true to the facts or to a text: 忠实于原文 true to the original／ 忠实的信徒 faithful disciple

相同点： 都是形容词。表示对国家、人民、领导、同志、朋友、事业、理论等尽心尽力的意思。Syn. adj. exerting oneself whole-heartedly for one's country, people, leadership, comrades or friends; or for a cause or theory.

重 zhòng 沉 chén

重 (weight; heavy; important) 1. 除了指重量大之外，还用于比喻，指人所承担的事务数量多，繁重。这时可以形容抽象的事物。indicates heavy weight. It may be used figuratively, to describe abstract things which are felt to be a heavy burden: 铅是重金属。Lead is a heavy metal.／ 他的工作很重。He has a heavy work load.／ 礼轻人意重。The gift is trifling but the feeling is profound. 2. 形容分量重。还可说"味道重""颜色重""情意重"。indicates intensity,

306

weightiness; for example, strong tastes, dark colors and strong affection. 沉 is not used in this sense: 这条鱼有三斤重。The fish weighs three jin. 3. 形容厉害。如"身受重伤"、"病得很重"。这后两个意思是与"沉"的区别。badly or seriously; for example, badly wounded or seriously ill. 沉 cannot be used in this sense: 他受了重伤。He is severely injured. / 以友谊为重 set store by friendship

沉 (heavy; keep down; sink; deep; profound) 1.只指重量大，只能形容具体的东西。indicates heavy weight, used only of concrete things: 这只箱子真沉。This trunk is heavy. 2. 表示程度深，这跟"重"有区别。profoundly, to a high degree. In this sense, it cannot be replaced by 重: 他睡得很沉。He is fast asleep. 3. 往下落的意思，跟"浮"相对 v. to sink (down), opposite of 浮 (float): 船沉了。The boat has sunk.

〔相同点〕：都是形容词。表示重量大。跟"轻"相反。Syn. adj. heavy; the opposite of 轻 (light).

周密 zhōumì　周详 zhōuxiáng

周密 (careful; thorough) 指完备而细密的意思。complete and detailed: 周密思考 give thorough consideration to / 周密的分析 a detailed analysis / 周密的计划 a well-conceived

307

plan / 进行周密的调查 carry out a thorough investigation

周详 (**comprehensive; complete; careful**) 指周到而详尽的意思。thoughtful and thorough: 考虑周详 give careful consideration to

〔相同点〕：都是形容词。表示完备、周到的意思。Syn. adj. complete or carefully worked out.

主意 zhǔyi　主张 zhǔzhāng

主意 (**idea; plan; decision; definite view**) 指对事情有确定的意见，也指内心的打算。a definite idea about sth.: 打定主意 make a decision / 我一时没了主意。I was quite at a loss, then. / 拿不定主意 to be in two minds (about something).

主张 (**stand; proposition; view; position; advocate; maintain; hold.**) 1. 指对事情完整的见解和计划。an all-round view and plan about sth.: 这是我们的一贯主张。This has been our consistent stand. / 听起来两种主张都有理由。Both propositions sound reasonable. 2. 还常作动词用，表示对于怎样行动的一种看法。v. refers to one's opinion on the best course of action: 主张改革 favor reforms / 主张自力更生 advocate self-reliance

308

〔相同点〕：都是名词。表示处理事物的见解和办法的意思。Syn. n. views, schemes for dealing with matters.

注重 zhùzhòng　着重 zhuózhòng

注重 (lay stress on; pay attention to; attach importance to) 指把注意力放在某一方面、某一事情上的意思。表示对这方面特别注意，特别重视。 to concentrate one's attention on a certain point or thing; to attach special importance to sth.: 注重基本功的训练 lay stress on basic training

着重 (stress; emphasize) 指把重点放在某一方面、某一件事情上的意思。to give particular prominence to a certain aspect or certain thing: 着重指出 emphatically point out／着重说明问题的重要性 stress the importance of the matter／这里我着重讲一个问题。Here I would like to go into one question in particular.

〔相同点〕：都是动词。表示要特别重视或加强某一方面或某一部分的意思。Syn. v. to pay special attention to sth.; to give special weight to a certain aspect or certain part of sth.

自尊 zìzūn　自负 zìfù

自尊 (self-respect; self-esteem; proper pride) 是中性词。有尊重自己、不卑躬屈节、不容许别人侮辱自己的意思。a neutral term, self-respect — not bowing and scraping, not allowing others to insult one: 请不要伤了他的自尊心。Please don't hurt his self-esteem.

自负 (be responsible for one's own actions; think highly of oneself; be conceited) 1. 自以为了不起的意思。是贬义词。pejorative, having an exceedingly high opinion of oneself: 这个人很自负。This person is rather conceited. 2. 自己负责的意思。to take responsibility upon oneself: 自负盈亏 (of an enterprise.) to assume sole responsibility for its profits or losses

〔相同点〕: 都是形容词。都有相信自己的意思。Syn. adj. believing in oneself.

尊敬 zūnjìng　尊重 zūnzhòng

尊敬 (respect; honor; esteem) 着重指恭敬。程度比"尊重"深，对象常是人。多用于幼对长，下级对上级等。stresses the idea of respect, and is stronger than 尊重. The object is normally human. It is used especially of the

310

respect of young people for their elders or of juniors for seniors: 非常尊敬他 have the greatest esteem for him

尊重 (respect; value; esteem) 着重指恭敬而重视，跟"轻蔑"相对。对象较广，可以是人或抽象事物。to respect and attach importance to. It is the opposite of 轻蔑(contemptuous). It takes a wide range of objects, embracing both people and abstract things: 互相尊重 respect each other / 尊重少数民族的风俗习惯 respect the habits and customs of the minority nationalities

〔相同点〕：都是动词。表示以敬重的态度对待人。Syn. v. to treat others with respect.

索 引

A

ai	爱戴	（1）
	爱好	（2）
	爱护	（1）
	爱惜	（3）
	爱抚	（1）
an	安顿	（4）
	安定	（3）
	安放	（5）
	安静	（5）
	安居	（6）
	安排	（6）
	安全	（4）
	安适	（7）
	安慰	（8）
	安心	（9）
	安祥	（9）
	安闲	（7）
	安逸	（7）
	安葬	（10）
	安身	（6）
	安置	（7）
	暗暗	（11）
	暗含	（12）
	暗害	（11）
	暗算	（11）
	暗示	（12）
	按照	（12）
ao	懊悔	（13）
	懊妙	（14）
	懊秘	（14）
	懊恼	（13）
	傲慢	（151）

B

ba	把持	（16）
	把握	（16）
	把戏	（241）
ban	颁布	（17）
	办法	（18）
bang		
	帮助	（19）
bao	包含	（20）
	包括	（20）
	保持	（23）
	保护	（20）
	保卫	（22）

	宝贵	………	(24)		辨别	………	(39)
	饱满	………	(21)		辨认	………	(39)
	暴露	………	(25)		辩白	………	(38)
	抱歉	………	(81)		辩护	………	(38)
	抱怨	………	(26)		辩解	………	(38)
bei	背叛	………	(27)	biao			
ben	奔驰	………	(28)		标明	………	(40)
	奔跑	………	(28)		表达	………	(41)
	奔腾	………	(28)		表明	………	(41)
	本来	………	(29)		表示	………	(41)
	本领	………	(30)		表现	………	(42)
	本事	………	(30)		表扬	………	(42)
	本质	………	(31)	bu	哺育	………	(43)
bi	比赛	………	(32)		补偿	………	(82)
	鄙视	………	(32)		不单	………	(44)
	必定	………	(33)		不但	………	(44)
	必然	………	(33)		不管	………	(45)
	必须	………	(35)		不论	………	(45)
	必需	………	(36)		不免	………	(46)
	庇护	………	(21)				
	毕竟	………	(34)			**C**	
bian							
	边疆	………	(37)	cai	猜测	………	(48)
	边境	………	(37)		才干	………	(49)
	鞭策	………	(36)		才华	………	(49)
	变革	………	(40)		才能	………	(49)
	变化	………	(40)		才智	………	(50)

材料 ………… （50）

采纳 ………… （52）

采取 ………… （52）

采用 ………… （52）

can 参加 ………… （53）

参与 ………… （53）

cang

仓促 ………… （54）

ceng

曾经 ………… （55）

chan

产生 ………… （56）

忏悔 ………… （129）

chang

场所 ………… （57）

场合 ………… （57）

chao

朝 ………… （271）

嘲笑 ………… （143）

che 撤消 ………… （218）

chen

沉 ………… （307）

沉寂 ………… （59）

沉默 ………… （59）

沉思 ………… （60）

沉着 ………… （61）

陈列 ………… （58）

陈旧 ………… （59）

陈设 ………… （58）

cheng

成果 ………… （62）

成绩 ………… （64）

成就 ………… （64）

成效 ………… （64）

chi 嗤笑 ………… （143）

持续 ………… （65）

斥责 ………… （305）

chong

充分 ………… （66）

充满 ………… （68）

充足 ………… （66）

重复 ………… （66）

宠爱 ………… （190）

chou

踌躇 ………… （293）

chu 出发 ………… （203）

出生 ………… （68）

矗立 ………… （290）

chuan

传授 ………… （69）

chuang

创造 ………… （96）

chui

垂死 ………… （70）

314

　　　垂危 ········· （70）

ci　慈祥 ········· （ 9 ）

cong

　　　匆匆 ········· （55）

　　　匆忙 ········· （55）

　　　聪明 ········· （177）

　　　从来 ········· （174）

cuo　措施 ········· （18）

　　　错误 ········· （71）

D

da　答应 ········· （72）

　　　达到 ········· （73）

　　　打量 ········· （73）

　　　打算 ········· （74）

　　　打听 ········· （263）

　　　大胆 ········· （75）

dai　带 ··········· （76）

　　　戴 ··········· （76）

dan　担当 ········· （78）

　　　担任 ········· （77）

　　　担心 ········· （78）

　　　担忧 ········· （78）

　　　耽搁 ········· （76）

　　　耽误 ········· （77）

　　　诞辰 ········· （79）

　　　诞生 ········· （69）

　　　但是 ········· （79）

dao　到达 ········· （73）

　　　道歉 ········· （80）

di　抵偿 ········· （81）

　　　抵挡 ········· （82）

　　　抵抗 ········· （83）

　　　抵制 ········· （83）

　　　缔结 ········· （209）

dong

　　　动员 ········· （83）

du　督促 ········· （36）

　　　独特 ········· （203）

　　　度过 ········· （84）

　　　渡过 ········· （84）

duan

　　　端祥 ········· （74）

dun　顿时 ········· （85）

duo　多少 ········· （86）

　　　夺目 ········· （276）

　　　夺取 ········· （87）

E

e　遏止 ······ （90）

　　　遏制 ········· （90）

　　　恶果 ········· （89）

er 二 ·········· (91)

F

fa 发表 ·········· (93)
　 发布 ·········· (17)
　 发达 ·········· (94)
　 发动 ·········· (84)
　 发觉 ·········· (95)
　 发明 ·········· (96)
　 发生 ·········· (57)
　 发现 ·········· (95)
　 发展 ·········· (94)
fan 烦躁 ·········· (96)
　 反复 ·········· (67)
fang
　 妨碍 ·········· (97)
　 妨害 ·········· (97)
　 放心 ·········· (9)
fei 肥 ·········· (195)
　 废除 ·········· (155)
fen 分辨 ·········· (98)
　 分别 ·········· (99)
　 分离 ·········· (100)
　 分派 ·········· (100)
　 分配 ·········· (101)
　 愤慨 ·········· (102)

　 愤怒 ·········· (102)
feng
　 丰满 ·········· (22)
　 风景 ·········· (102)
　 风气 ·········· (104)
　 风尚 ·········· (104)
　 风俗 ·········· (104)
　 讽刺 ·········· (141)
fu 肤浅 ·········· (105)
　 敷衍 ·········· (292)
　 符合 ·········· (239)
　 浮浅 ·········· (105)
　 拂晓 ·········· (172)
　 辅导 ·········· (154)
　 抚育 ·········· (43)

G

gai 改变 ·········· (107)
　 改正 ·········· (153)
gan 干净 ·········· (107)
　 感动 ·········· (141)
　 感激 ·········· (108)
　 感谢 ·········· (108)
　 干 ·········· (109)
gao 高兴 ·········· (111)
　 搞 ·········· (109)

ge	歌唱	··········	(112)
	歌颂	··········	(112)
gen	根本	··········	(139)
	根据	··········	(113)
geng			
	更正	··········	(160)
gong			
	公布	··········	(17)
	公民	··········	(224)
	公平	··········	(116)
	公约	··········	(117)
	公正	··········	(116)
	功夫	··········	(114)
	功绩	··········	(115)
	功劳	··········	(115)
	功勋	··········	(115)
	巩固	··········	(171)
	共同	··········	(289)
gu	鼓动	··········	(230)
	鼓励	··········	(118)
	古怪	··········	(201)
	故乡	··········	(145)
guan			
	观点	··········	(163)
	观赏	··········	(275)
	关切	··········	(118)
	关注	··········	(118)
guang			
	广博	··········	(295)
	广泛	··········	(197)
gui	规划	··········	(144)
	规矩	··········	(119)
	规则	··········	(119)
	贵重	··········	(24)
guo	过程	··········	(122)
	过失	··········	(71)
	果断	··········	(120)
	果然	··········	(121)

H

hai	害怕	··········	(124)
han	含糊	··········	(124)
	捍卫	··········	(22)
hao	好象	··········	(126)
he	和蔼	··········	(127)
	和气	··········	(127)
	合作	··········	(128)
hong			
	宏大	··········	(128)
hou	后果	··········	(89)
	后悔	··········	(129)
hu	忽略	··········	(130)
hua	华丽	··········	(132)

滑稽 ………… (131)

化装 ………… (133)

化妆 ………… (133)

huai

怀念 ………… (133)

huan

幻灭 ………… (272)

豢养 ………… (134)

hui 诙谐 ………… (131)

回顾 ………… (135)

回忆 ………… (135)

会见 ………… (136)

huo 活泼 ………… (138)

活动 ………… (137)

活跃 ………… (138)

J

ji 基本 ………… (139)

激动 ………… (140)

讥讽 ………… (141)

机密 ………… (184)

讥笑 ………… (142)

急忙 ………… (143)

急躁 ………… (97)

急速 ………… (280)

几 ………… (86)

几乎 ………… (142)

计划 ………… (144)

继续 ………… (65)

jia 家属 ………… (146)

家乡 ………… (145)

家族 ………… (146)

加入 ………… (54)

jian 坚持 ………… (23)

坚定 ………… (146)

坚固 ………… (170)

坚决 ………… (147)

简便 ………… (214)

简单 ………… (148)

简略 ………… (149)

简直 ………… (142)

检查 ………… (147)

检验 ………… (148)

俭朴 ………… (150)

俭省 ………… (150)

鉴别 ………… (39)

见解 ………… (163)

jiao

骄傲 ………… (150)

交换 ………… (152)

交流 ………… (152)

矫正 ………… (152)

教导 ………… (153)

318

教室 ………… (154)

教授 ………… (69)

jie 揭露 ………… (25)

接见 ………… (136)

结果 ………… (62)

解除 ………… (155)

界限 ………… (156)

界线 ………… (156)

jin 进步 ………… (157)

进犯 ………… (158)

进攻 ………… (158)

进击 ………… (158)

紧急 ………… (286)

jing

经常 ………… (236)

精力 ………… (159)

精密 ………… (283)

精神 ………… (159)

景色 ………… (103)

景物 ………… (103)

竟然 ………… (122)

竞赛 ………… (32)

敬仰 ………… (299)

jiu 究竟 ………… (35)

纠正 ………… (160)

ju 居然 ………… (121)

巨大 ………… (260)

惧怕 ………… (124)

jue 决 ………… (161)

决定 ………… (221)

绝 ………… (161)

绝望 ………… (235)

K

kan 看 ………… (162)

看法 ………… (163)

kao 考查 ………… (164)

考察 ………… (164)

考虑 ………… (165)

ke 可是 ………… (80)

渴望 ………… (166)

课堂 ………… (154)

克制 ………… (166)

kong

空洞 ………… (167)

空虚 ………… (167)

kua 夸奖 ………… (168)

夸耀 ………… (168)

kuan

宽慰 ………… (8)

L

la 拉拢 ………… (169)

lao 牢固 ………… (170)

leng

　　冷静 ………… (61)

li 离别 ………… (100)

　　黎明 ………… (171)

　　礼拜 ………… (172)

　　历程 ………… (123)

　　立刻 ………… (85)

　　历来 ………… (173)

　　力量 ………… (174)

　　力气 ………… (174)

lian

　　连忙 ………… (144)

liang

　　两 ………… (91)

lin 临时 ………… (175)

ling

　　凌晨 ………… (172)

　　灵活 ………… (176)

　　灵巧 ………… (176)

　　伶俐 ………… (176)

liu 流畅 ………… (177)

　　流浪 ………… (178)

　　流利 ………… (177)

　　流落 ………… (178)

　　流亡 ………… (179)

long

　　笼络 ………… (169)

lü 屡次 ………… (179)

lüe 掠夺 ………… (87)

M

mao

　　毛病 ………… (181)

man

　　埋怨 ………… (26)

　　埋葬 ………… (10)

mei

　　美丽 ………… (182)

　　美满 ………… (183)

mi 弥漫 ………… (68)

　　秘密 ………… (184)

　　密切 ………… (185)

ming

　　明白 ………… (186)

　　名誉 ………… (187)

mo 模糊 ………… (125)

　　陌生 ………… (188)

N

nan 难免 ………… (46)

320

ni 溺爱 ………… (190)

ning

　凝视 ………… (191)

nong

　浓厚 ………… (192)

nuo 懦弱 ………… (227)

O

ou 偶尔 ………… (194)

　偶然 ………… (194)

P

pai 排除 ………… (229)

pan 盘算 ………… (75)

　盘问 ………… (280)

　叛变 ………… (27)

　盼望 ………… (166)

pang

　庞大 ………… (129)

　胖 ………… (195)

pao 抛弃 ………… (256)

pei 赔偿 ………… (81)

piao

　漂亮 ………… (182)

ping

　平安 ………… (4)

　平常 ………… (195)

　平凡 ………… (196)

　平静 ………… (5)

po 破除 ………… (155)

　破旧 ………… (60)

pu 普遍 ………… (196)

　朴实 ………… (197)

　朴素 ………… (197)

Q

qi 欺负 ………… (199)

　欺侮 ………… (199)

　欺压 ………… (199)

　期间 ………… (200)

　期望 ………… (266)

　奇怪 ………… (200)

　奇特 ………… (202)

　其他 ………… (202)

　其余 ………… (202)

　启程 ………… (203)

　启发 ………… (204)

　启示 ………… (204)

　企图 ………… (205)

　气愤 ………… (102)

　气概 ………… (205)

321

气派 ……… (207)

气魄 ……… (206)

气候 ……… (206)

气势 ……… (207)

契约 ……… (117)

qia 恰当 ……… (207)

恰好 ……… (208)

恰巧 ……… (208)

qian

签订 ……… (209)

前后 ……… (210)

浅薄 ……… (106)

qiang

抢救 ……… (211)

强迫 ……… (212)

强制 ……… (212)

qiao

瞧 ……… (162)

qie 切实 ……… (222)

qin 亲密 ……… (185)

勤劳 ……… (212)

勤勉 ……… (213)

qing

轻便 ……… (214)

轻视 ……… (33)

轻易 ……… (213)

清楚 ……… (186)

清洁 ……… (108)

情况 ……… (215)

情形 ……… (215)

情绪 ……… (216)

请求 ……… (285)

庆祝 ……… (216)

qu 区别 ……… (98)

屈服 ……… (217)

趣味 ……… (220)

取消 ……… (218)

去世 ……… (219)

quan

全部 ……… (220)

权力 ……… (221)

权利 ……… (221)

que 缺点 ……… (181)

缺陷 ……… (182)

确定 ……… (221)

确实 ……… (222)

R

ran 然而 …… (80)

re 热情 ……… (223)

热心 ……… (223)

ren 人民 ……… (224)

认识 ……… (225)

认为 ………… (226)
认真 ………… (284)
任务 ………… (238)

rong
荣幸 ………… (226)
荣誉 ………… (188)
容易 ………… (213)

ruan
软弱 ………… (227)

S

sao 扫除 ………… (229)
shan
煽动 ………… (230)
shang
伤害 ………… (245)
商量 ………… (230)
shen
申明 ………… (231)
深厚 ………… (192)
深思 ………… (60)
神秘 ………… (184)
慎重 ………… (232)
sheng
生活 ………… (233)
生计 ………… (234)

生命 ………… (232)
生日 ………… (79)
生疏 ………… (189)
声明 ………… (231)
shi 失望 ………… (234)
施行 ………… (235)
时常 ………… (236)
时代 ………… (200)
时间 ………… (114)
实行 ………… (235)
实质 ………… (31)
食品 ………… (237)
食物 ………… (237)
使命 ………… (238)
事故 ………… (240)
事件 ………… (239)
事情 ………… (239)
适当 ………… (208)
适合 ………… (238)
逝世 ………… (219)
嗜好 ………… (2)
shou
收成 ………… (240)
收获 ………… (240)
手法 ………… (241)
首要 ………… (241)
shu 舒适 ………… (243)

舒服 ………… (242)

疏忽 ………… (130)

熟识 ………… (243)

熟悉 ………… (244)

si 死 …………… (219)

似乎 ………… (126)

饲养 ………… (134)

song

耸立 ………… (291)

怂恿 ………… (118)

sun 损害 ………… (244)

suo 所有 ………… (245)

T

tan 谈判 ………… (247)

探测 ………… (48)

tao 逃亡 ………… (179)

讨论 ………… (231)

te 特别 ………… (248)

特点 ………… (249)

特色 ………… (249)

特殊 ………… (248)

特性 ………… (249)

特征 ………… (249)

teng

疼 ………… (250)

ti 体会 ………… (251)

体现 ………… (42)

体验 ………… (251)

tian

天气 ………… (206)

tiao

调节 ………… (252)

调整 ………… (252)

条约 ………… (117)

ting

停留 ………… (252)

停止 ………… (253)

tong

同意 ………… (253)

痛 ………… (250)

tou 偷偷 ………… (11)

投诚 ………… (254)

投降 ………… (254)

tui 推测 ………… (48)

推辞 ………… (255)

推托 ………… (255)

推卸 ………… (255)

tuo 唾弃 ………… (256)

W

wan 完备 ………… (257)

324

完美 ………… (257)

完善 ………… (257)

顽固 ………… (258)

顽强 ………… (258)

挽救 ………… (211)

wang

往往 ………… (237)

望 ………… (162)

忘记 ………… (259)

忘怀 ………… (259)

妄想 ………… (205)

wei 违背 ………… (27)

维持 ………… (24)

伟大 ………… (260)

喂养 ………… (134)

wen 温和 ………… (261)

温柔 ………… (261)

温顺 ………… (261)

稳固 ………… (170)

稳重 ………… (262)

问 ………… (262)

wu 无论 ………… (45)

武断 ………… (120)

稀罕 ………… (264)

希望 ………… (265)

吸取 ………… (265)

吸收 ………… (265)

习惯 ………… (266)

习气 ………… (267)

喜悦 ………… (111)

细致 ………… (268)

xian

先进 ………… (157)

xiang

相信 ………… (269)

降服 ………… (217)

详尽 ………… (269)

详细 ………… (270)

想念 ………… (134)

向 ………… (271)

向来 ………… (173)

向导 ………… (270)

xiao

消除 ………… (229)

消灭 ………… (272)

消息 ………… (272)

效果 ………… (63)

xie 协商 ………… (247)

协作 ………… (128)

xin 辛苦 ………… (273)

X

xi 稀奇 ……… (264)

辛劳 ………… (273)

新奇 ………… (274)

新鲜 ………… (274)

新闻 ………… (273)

欣赏 ………… (275)

心情 ………… (216)

信任 ………… (269)

xing

星期 ………… (173)

醒目 ………… (276)

性命 ………… (233)

兴趣 ………… (220)

幸运 ………… (227)

xiu 修理 ………… (276)

修缮 ………… (276)

xu 虚假 ………… (277)

虚伪 ………… (277)

须要 ………… (278)

需要 ………… (278)

xuan

宣布 ………… (93)

宣告 ………… (93)

xun 寻求 ………… (279)

寻思 ………… (61)

询问 ………… (279)

迅速 ………… (280)

Y

ya 压抑 ………… (281)

压制 ………… (281)

yan 严格 ………… (282)

严厉 ………… (282)

严密 ………… (282)

严肃 ………… (283)

掩护 ………… (21)

yao 要求 ………… (284)

要紧 ………… (285)

yi 一刹那 …… (288)

一定 ………… (34)

一概 ………… (286)

一律 ………… (286)

一齐 ………… (287)

一起 ………… (287)

一切 ………… (245)

一瞬间 …… (288)

一向 ………… (288)

一再 ………… (180)

一直 ………… (289)

一致 ………… (289)

依据 ………… (113)

已经 ………… (56)

以为 ………… (226)

屹立 ………… (290)

义务 ………… (291)

抑制 ………… (167)

yin 引导 ………… (270)

ying

应付 ………… (292)

yong

勇敢 ………… (75)

you 幽默 ………… (131)

犹豫 ………… (293)

友情 ………… (293)

友谊 ………… (294)

yu 愉快 ………… (111)

预备 ………… (294)

yuan

渊博 ………… (295)

原来 ………… (29)

圆满 ………… (183)

援助 ………… (19)

yun 允许 ………… (72)

运动 ………… (137)

Z

zan 赞成 ………… (254)

赞扬 ………… (43)

赞助 ………… (19)

暂时 ………… (175)

zao 遭受 ………… (297)

遭遇 ………… (297)

ze 责任 ………… (291)

责问 ………… (298)

zhan

瞻仰 ………… (298)

zhang

掌握 ………… (16)

zhao

招呼 ………… (299)

召唤 ………… (300)

召集 ………… (300)

召开 ………… (300)

照顾 ………… (301)

照料 ………… (301)

照应 ………… (301)

zhen

珍贵 ………… (24)

珍惜 ………… (3)

斟酌 ………… (165)

镇定 ………… (302)

镇静 ………… (302)

zheng

整个 ………… (220)

正规 ………… (303)

正轨 ………… (303)

正好 ………… (209)

正派 ………… (304)

正直 ………… (304)

证明 ………… (303)

证实 ………… (304)

郑重 ………… (232)

zhi 知道 ………… (225)

指导 ………… (154)

指摘 ………… (305)

质问 ………… (298)

制止 ………… (90)

zhong

忠诚 ………… (305)

忠实 ………… (306)

重 ………… (306)

重要 ………… (242)

zhou

周密 ………… (307)

周详 ………… (308)

zhu 主要 ………… (242)

主意 ………… (308)

主张 ………… (308)

祝贺 ………… (217)

注视 ………… (191)

注重 ………… (309)

zhuan

转变 ………… (107)

zhuang

庄重 ………… (262)

壮丽 ………… (132)

zhui

追求 ………… (279)

zhun

准备 ………… (294)

准许 ………… (72)

zhuo

着重 ………… (309)

zi 资料 ………… (51)

仔细 ………… (268)

自负 ………… (310)

自豪 ………… (151)

自尊 ………… (310)

zu 阻挡 ………… (82)

zun 尊敬 ………… (310)

尊重 ………… (311)

遵照 ………… (13)

zuo 左右 ………… (210)

做 ………… (110)

责任编辑　闫凤兰
装帧设计　武　悦

常用汉语同义词汉英双解手册

郑秀芝　王春光　编著

今日中国出版社出版

(北京市百万庄路 24 号)

中国国际图书贸易总公司发行

(中国北京车公庄西路 21 号)

北京邮政信箱第 399 号　邮政编码 100044

1991 年第一版　第一次印刷

ISBN 7-5072-0068-X／H·1

00800

9-CE-2325P